A TALE OF
THREE KINGS

A STUDY
IN BROKENNESS

BOOKS BY GENE EDWARDS

First-Century Diaries
The Silas Diary
The Titus Diary
The Timothy Diary
The Priscilla Diary
The Gaius Diary

An Introduction to the Deeper Christian Life
The Highest Life
The Secret to the Christian Life
The Inward Journey

The Chronicles of the Door
The Beginning
The Escape
The Birth
The Triumph
The Return

Healing for the Inner Man
Crucified by Christians
A Tale of Three Kings
The Prisoner in the Third Cell
Letters to a Devastated Christian

In a Class by Itself
The Divine Romance

Radical Books
Revolution: The Story of the Early Church
Overlooked Christianity
Rethinking Elders
Beyond Radical
Climb the Highest Mountain

GENE EDWARDS

A TALE OF
THREE KINGS

A STUDY
IN BROKENNESS

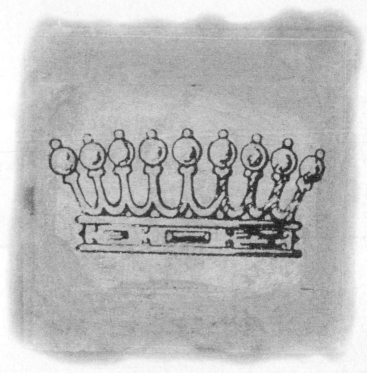

Tyndale House Publishers, Inc.
Carol Stream, Illinois

TYNDALE and Tyndale's quill logo are registered trademarks of Tyndale House Publishers, Inc.

A Tale of Three Kings

Copyright © 1980, 1992 by Gene Edwards. All rights reserved.

Designed by Justin Ahrens

This book was formerly published by SeedSowers (Christian Books Publishing House), Newnan, Georgia 30263

Scripture quotations are taken from the *Holy Bible,* King James Version.

Printed in the United States of America

ISBN-13: 978-1-4143-2175-2 (special TBN edition)
ISBN-10: 1-4143-2175-9

14   13   12   11   10   09   08   07
8   7   6   5   4   3   2   1

DEDICATION

To the brokenhearted Christians coming out of authoritarian groups, seeking solace, healing, and hope. May you somehow recover and go on with him who is liberty.

And to all brokenhearted Christians:

May you be so utterly healed that you can still answer the call of him who asks for all because he is all.

ACKNOWLEDGMENTS

To Helen, Carman, and Patty for aiding in the preparation of this manuscript.

PREFACE TO THE SECOND EDITION

When I first penned *A Tale of Three Kings,* I would have been encouraged to know it would live long enough to go through two or three printings. I utterly underestimated the number of devastated Christians out there. A far broader audience than I anticipated has taken up this book. It is an audience made up of Christians damaged by such things as church splits and individual "Christian to Christian" clashes.

I have been a little awed by the reception of this book and the fact that the reception has been worldwide. The number of Christian workers who have ordered this book in bulk, to be passed out to their people, has been only short of phenomenal. That *A Tale of Three Kings* has been turned into plays and has been read publicly from pulpits turned awe to amazement.

Obviously, there is a great deal of pain and hurt out there in Christendom that is rarely addressed or ministered to. I hope this book, as well as *Letters to a Devastated Christian*, *Crucified by Christians*, and *The Prisoner in the Third Cell*, will minister to those needs.

AUTHOR'S PREFACE

Why this book and what is its purpose? The
answer can probably be traced to my mailbox. As
one who receives correspondence from Christians
all over the world, I noted some years ago a growing number of letters from Christians devastated
by the authoritarian movement that had become so
popular with many evangelical groups. A reaction
to this totalitarian concept eventually set in. A mass
exodus was soon under way. The stories being told
by these spiritual fugitives are often terrifying and
sometimes unbelievable. I am not at all sure if it is
the doctrine itself that is causing such widespread
carnage or the inordinate practice of this doctrine.
Whatever it is, in all my long years as an evangelical Christian minister, I have never seen anything
that has damaged so many believers so deeply.
The wreckage appears to be universal, and recovery
from it is almost nil.

This book reflects my concern for this multitude of confused, brokenhearted, and often bitter Christians who now find their spiritual lives in shambles and who are groping about for even the slightest word of hope and comfort.

This book, I trust, will serve in some small way to meet this need.

There is one thing, dear reader, this book is most certainly not intended to be. It is not intended to be additional fodder in your cannon to better blast your adversaries, whatever your view. I would beg you to be done with such ancient and brutish ways. This book is intended for individual healing and for private retreat.

I trust this volume will sound a note of hope, even if that note is heard ever so distantly.

Gene Edwards

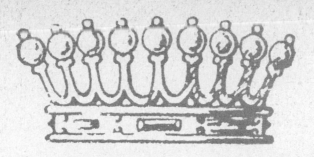

THEY HAVE SET

UP KINGS, BUT

NOT BY ME:

THEY HAVE MADE

PRINCES, AND

I KNEW IT NOT . . .

HOSEA 8:4

Well, dear reader, how nice to be with you once more. It is a privilege to spend this time with you. Thank you for meeting here, and I suggest we hasten into the playhouse, as I see that they have already dimmed the lights.

There are two seats reserved for us not too far from the stage. Quickly, let us take them.

I understand the story is a drama. I trust, though, you will not find it sad.

I believe we will find the story to be in two parts. In part 1 we shall meet an older king, Saul by name, and a young shepherd boy named David. In part 2 we shall once more meet an older king and a young man. But this time the older king is David and the young man is Absalom.

The story is a portrait (you might prefer to call it a rough charcoal sketch) of submission and authority within the kingdom of God.

Ah, they have turned off the lights, and the players have taken their places. The audience has quieted itself. The curtain is rising.

Our story has begun.

PROLOGUE

The almighty, living God turned to Gabriel and gave a command.

"Go, take these two portions of my being. There are two destinies waiting. To each unborn destiny give one portion of myself."

Carrying two glowing, pulsating lights of Life, Gabriel opened the door into the realm between two universes and disappeared. He had stepped into the Mall of Unborn Destinies.

Gabriel spoke: "I have here two portions of the nature of God. The first is the very cloth of his nature. When wrapped about you, it clothes you with the breath of God. As water surrounds a person in the sea, so will his very breath envelop you. With this, *the divine breath,* you will have his power—power to subdue armies, shame the enemies of God, and accomplish his work on the earth. Here is the power of God as a gift. Here is immersion into the Spirit."

A destiny stepped forward: "This portion of God is for me."

"True," replied the angel. "And remember, whoever receives such a great portion of power will surely be known by many. Ere your earthly pilgrimage is done, your true character will be known; yea, it will be *revealed* by means of this power. Such is the destiny of all who want and wield this portion, for it touches only the outer person, affecting the inner person not one whit. Outer power will always unveil the inner resources or the lack thereof."

The first destined one received the gift and stepped back.

Gabriel spoke again.

"I have here the second of two elements of the living God. This is not a gift but an inheritance. A gift is worn on the outer person; an inheritance is planted deep inside—like a seed. Yet, even though it is such a small planting, this planting grows and, in time, fills all the inner person."

Another destiny stepped forward. "I believe this element is to be mine for my earthly pilgrimage."

"True," responded the angel again. "I must tell you that what has been given to you is a glorious thing— the only element in the universe that can change the human heart. Yet even this element of God cannot accomplish its task nor grow and fill your entire inner being unless it is compounded well. It must be mixed lavishly with pain, sorrow, and crushing."

The second destined one received the inheritance and stepped back.

Beside Gabriel sat the angel Recorder. He dutifully entered into his ledger the record of the two destinies.

"And who shall these destinies become after they go through the door to the visible universe?" asked Recorder.

Gabriel replied softly, "Each, in his time, shall be king."

PART 1

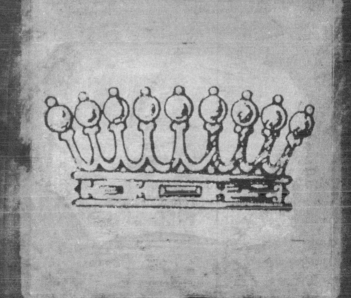

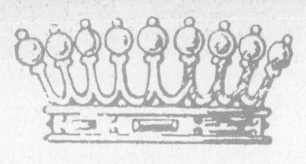

ONE

The youngest son of any family bears two distinctions: He is considered to be both spoiled and uninformed. Usually little is expected of him. Inevitably, he displays fewer characteristics of leadership than the other children in the family. As a child, he never leads. He only follows, for he has no one younger on whom to practice leadership.

So it is today. And so it was three thousand years ago in a village called Bethlehem, in a family of eight boys. The first seven sons of Jesse worked near their father's farm. The youngest was sent on treks into the mountains to graze the family's small flock of sheep.

On those pastoral jaunts, this youngest son always carried two things: a sling and a small, guitarlike instrument. Spare time for a sheepherder is abundant on rich mountain plateaus where sheep can graze for days in one sequestered meadow. But as time passed and days became weeks, the young man became very lonely. The feeling of friendlessness that always roamed inside him was magnified. He often cried. He also played his harp a great deal. He had a good voice, so he often sang. When these activities failed to comfort him, he gathered up a pile of stones and, one by one, swung them at a distant tree with something akin to fury.

When one rock pile was depleted, he would walk to the blistered tree, reassemble his rocks, and designate another leafy enemy at yet a farther distance.

He engaged in many such solitary battles.

This shepherd-singer-slinger also loved his Lord. At night, when all the sheep lay sleeping and he sat staring at the dying fire, he would strum upon his harp and break into quiet song. He sang the ancient hymns of his forefathers' faith. While he sang he wept, and while weeping he often broke out in abandoned praise—until mountains in distant places lifted up his praise and tears and passed them on to higher mountains, until they eventually reached the ears of God.

When the young shepherd did not praise and when he did not cry, he tended to each and every sheep and lamb. When not occupied with his flock, he swung his companionable sling and swung it again and again until he could tell every rock precisely where to go.

Once, while singing his lungs out to God, angels, sheep, and passing clouds, he spied a living enemy: a huge bear! He lunged forward. Both found themselves moving furiously toward the same small object, a lamb feeding at a table of rich, green grass. Youth and bear stopped halfway and whirled to face one another. Even as he instinctively reached into his pocket for a stone, the young man realized, "Why, I am not afraid."

Meanwhile, brown lightning on mighty, furry legs charged at the shepherd with foaming madness. Impelled by the strength of youth, the young man married rock to leather, and soon a brook-smooth pebble whined through the air to meet that charge.

A few moments later, the man—not quite so young as a moment before—picked up the little lamb and said, "I am your shepherd, and God is mine."

And so, long into the night, he wove the day's saga into a song. He hurled that hymn to the skies again and again until he had taught the melody and words to every angel that had ears. They, in turn, became custodians of this wondrous song and passed it on as healing balm to brokenhearted men and women in every age to come.

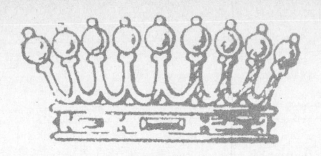

TWO

A figure in the distance was running toward him. It grew and became his brother. "Run!" cried the brother. "Run with all your strength. I'll watch the flock."

"Why?"

"An old man, a sage. He wants to meet all eight of the sons of Jesse, and he has seen all but you."

"But why?"

"Run!"

So David ran. He stopped long enough to get his breath. Then, sweat pouring down his sunburned cheeks, his red face matching his red curly hair, he walked into his father's house, his eyes recording everything in sight.

The youngest son of Jesse stood there, tall and strong, but more in the eyes of the curious old gentleman than to anyone else in the room. Kith and kin cannot always tell when a man is grown, even when looking straight at him. The elderly man saw. And something more he saw. In a way he himself did not understand, the old man knew what God knew.

God had taken a house-to-house survey of the whole kingdom in search of someone very special. As a result of this survey, the Lord God Almighty had found that this leather-lunged troubadour loved his Lord with a purer heart than anyone else on all the sacred soil of Israel.

"Kneel," said the bearded one with the long, gray hair. Almost regally, for one who had never been in that particular position, David knelt and then felt oil pouring down on his head. Somewhere, in one of the closets of his mind labeled "childhood information," he found a thought: *This is what men do to designate royalty! Samuel is making me a . . . what?*

The Hebrew words were unmistakable. Even children knew them.

"Behold the Lord's anointed!"

Quite a day for that young man, wouldn't you say? Then do you find it strange that this remarkable event led the young man not to the throne but to a decade of hellish agony and suffering? On that day,

David was enrolled, not into the lineage of royalty but into the school of brokenness.

Samuel went home. The sons of Jesse, save one, went forth to war. And the youngest, not yet ripe for war, received a promotion in his father's home . . . from sheepherder to messenger boy. His new job was to run food and messages to his brothers on the front lines. He did this regularly.

On one such visit to the battlefront, he killed another bear, in exactly the same way as he had the first. This bear, however, was nine feet tall and bore the name Goliath. As a result of this unusual feat, young David found himself a folk hero.

And eventually he found himself in the palace of a mad king. And in circumstances that were as insane as the king, the young man was to learn many indispensable lessons.

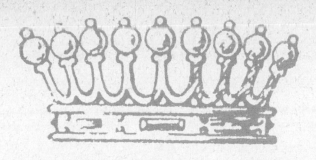

THREE

David sang to the mad king. Often. The music helped the old man a great deal, it seems. And all over the palace, when David sang, everyone stopped in the corridors, turned their ears in the direction of the king's chamber, and listened and wondered. How did such a young man come to possess such wonderful words and music?

Everyone's favorite seemed to be the song the little lamb had taught him. They loved that song as much as did the angels.

Nonetheless, the king was mad, and therefore he was jealous. Or was it the other way around? Either way, Saul felt threatened by David, as kings often do when there is a popular, promising young man beneath them. The king also knew, as did David, that this boy just might have his job some day.

But would David ascend to the throne by fair means

or foul? Saul did not know. This question is one of the things that drove the king mad.

David was caught in a very uncomfortable position; however, he seemed to grasp a deep understanding of the unfolding drama in which he had been caught. He seemed to understand something that few of even the wisest men of his day understood. Something that in our day, when men are wiser still, even fewer understand.

And what was that?

God did not have — but wanted very much to have — men and women who would live in pain.

God wanted a broken vessel.

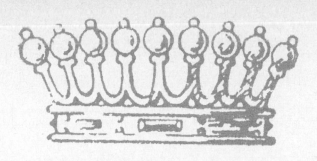

FOUR

The mad king saw David as a threat to the *king's* kingdom. Saul did not understand, it seems, that God should be left to decide what kingdoms survive which threats. Not knowing this, Saul did what all mad kings do. He threw spears at David. He could. He was *king.* Kings can do things like that. They almost always do. Kings claim the right to throw spears. Everyone knows that kings have that right. Everyone knows very, very well. How do they know? Because the king has told them so—many, many times.

Is it possible that this mad king was the *true* king, even the Lord's anointed?

And what about your king? Is he the Lord's anointed? Maybe he is. Maybe he isn't. No one can ever really know for sure. Men say they are sure. Even *certain.* But they are not. They do not know. God knows. But he will not tell.

If your king is truly the Lord's anointed, and if he also *throws spears*, then there are some things you *can* know, and know for sure:

Your king is quite mad.

And he is a king after the order of King Saul.

FIVE

God has a university. It's a small school. Few enroll; even fewer graduate. Very, very few indeed.

God has this school because he does not have broken men and women. Instead, he has several other types of people. He has people who claim to have God's authority . . . and don't—people who claim to be broken . . . and aren't. And people who *do have* God's authority, but who are mad *and* unbroken. And he has, regretfully, a great mixture of everything in between. All of these he has in abundance, but broken men and women, hardly at all.

In God's sacred school of submission and broken-ness, why are there so few students? Because all students in this school must suffer much pain. And as you might guess, it is often the unbroken ruler (whom God sovereignly picks) who metes out the pain. David was once a student in this school, and Saul was God's chosen way to crush David.

As the king grew in madness, David grew in understanding. He knew that God had placed him in the king's palace under true authority.

The authority of King Saul was *true?* Yes, God's chosen authority. *Chosen for David.* Unbroken authority, yes. But divine in ordination, nonetheless.

Yes, that is possible.

David drew in his breath, placed himself under his mad king, and moved farther down the path of his earthly hell.

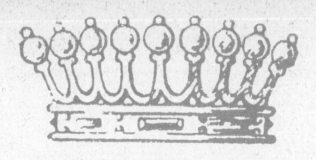

SIX

David had a question: What do you do when someone throws a spear at you?

Does it seem odd to you that David did not know the
answer to this question? After all, everyone else in
the world knows what to do when a spear is thrown
at you. Why, you pick up the spear and throw it
right back!

"When someone throws a spear at you, David, just
wrench it out of the wall and throw it back. Everyone else does, you can be sure."

And in performing this small feat of returning
thrown spears, you will prove many things: You
are courageous. You stand for the right. You boldly
stand against the wrong. You are tough and can't be
pushed around. You will not stand for injustice or
unfair treatment. You are the defender of the faith,
keeper of the flame, detector of all heresy. You will

not be wronged. All of these attributes then combine to prove that you are also a candidate for kingship. Yes, perhaps *you* are the Lord's anointed.

After the order of King Saul.

There is also a possibility that some twenty years after your coronation, you will be the most incredibly skilled spear thrower in all the realm. And also by then . . .

Quite mad.

SEVEN

Unlike anyone else in spear-throwing history, David did *not* know what to do when a spear was thrown at him. He did not throw Saul's spears back at him. Nor did he make any spears of his own and throw them. Something was different about David. All he did was dodge the spears.

What can a man, especially a young man, do when the king decides to use him for target practice? What if the young man decides not to return the compliment?

First of all, he must pretend he cannot see spears. Even when they are coming straight at him. Second, he must learn to duck very quickly. Last, he must pretend nothing happened.

You can easily tell when someone has been hit by a spear. He turns a deep shade of bitter. David never got hit. Gradually, he learned a very well-kept secret. He discovered three things that prevented him from ever being hit.

One, never learn anything about the fashionable, easily mastered art of spear throwing. Two, stay out of the company of all spear throwers. And three, keep your mouth tightly closed.

In this way, spears will never touch you, even when they pierce your heart.

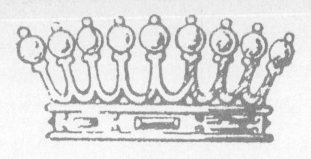

EIGHT

"My king is mad. At least, I so perceive him. What can I do?"

First, recognize this immutable fact: You cannot tell (none of us can) who is the Lord's anointed and who is not. Some kings, whom all agree are after the order of King Saul, are really after the order of David. And others, whom all agree are after the order of David, really belong to the order of King Saul. Who is correct? Who can know? To whose voice do you listen? *No man* is wise enough ever to break that riddle. All we can do is walk around asking ourselves this question:

"Is this man the Lord's anointed? And if he is, is he after the order of King Saul?"

Memorize that question very well. You may have to ask it of yourself ten thousand times. Especially if you are a citizen of a realm whose king just might be mad.

Asking this question may not seem difficult, but it is. Especially when you are crying very hard . . . and dodging spears . . . and being tempted to throw one back . . . and being encouraged by others to do just that. And all your rationality and sanity and logic and intelligence and common sense agree. But in the midst of your tears and your frustration, remember that you know only the question, not the answer.

No one knows the answer.

Except God.

And he *never* tells.

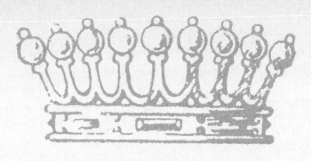

NINE

"I did not like that last chapter. It skirted the problem. I'm in David's situation, and I am in agony. What do I do when the kingdom I'm in is ruled by a spear-wielding king? Should I leave? If so, how? Just what does a person *do* in the middle of a spear-throwing contest?"

Well, if you didn't like the *question* found in the last chapter, you won't like the *answer* found in this one.

The answer is "You get stabbed to death."

"But what is the good in being speared?"

You have your eyes on the wrong King Saul. As long as you look at your king, you will blame him, and him alone, for your present hell. But be careful, for God has *his* eyes fastened sharply on another King Saul. Not the visible one standing up there throwing spears at you. No, God is looking at *another* King Saul. One just as bad—or worse.

God is looking at the King Saul in *you.*

"In *me?!*"

Saul is in your bloodstream, in the marrow of your bones. He makes up the very flesh and muscle of your heart. He is mixed into your soul. He inhabits the nuclei of your atoms.

King Saul is one with you.

You are King Saul!

He breathes in the lungs and beats in the breast of all of us. There is only one way to get rid of him. He must be annihilated.

You may not find this to be a compliment, but at least now you know why God put you under someone who just might be King Saul.

David the sheepherder would have grown up to become King Saul II, except that God cut away the Saul inside David's heart. That operation, by the way, took years and was a brutalizing experience that almost killed the patient.

And what were the scalpel and tongs God used to remove this inner Saul? God used the outer Saul.

King Saul sought to destroy David, but his only

success was that he became the instrument of God to put to death the Saul who roamed about in the caverns of David's own soul. Yes, David was virtually destroyed in the process, but this had to be. Otherwise the Saul in him would have survived.

David accepted this fate. He embraced the cruel circumstances. He lifted no hand nor offered resistance. Nor did he grandstand his piety. Silently, privately, he bore the crucible of humiliation. Because of this he was deeply wounded. His whole inner being was mutilated. His personality was altered. When the gore was over, David was barely recognizable.

You weren't satisfied with the question in the last chapter? Then you probably didn't like the answer in this one.

None of us do.

Except God.

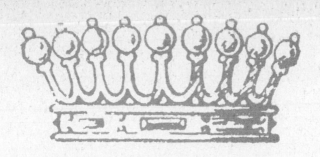

TEN

How does a person know when it is finally time to leave the Lord's anointed—especially if the Lord's anointed is after the order of King Saul?

David never made that decision. The Lord's anointed made it for him. The king's own decree settled the matter!

"Hunt him down; kill him like a dog."

Only then did David leave. No, he fled. Even then, he never spoke a word or lifted a hand against Saul. And please note this: David did not split the kingdom when he made his departure. He did not take part of the population with him. He left *alone*.

Alone. *All* alone. King Saul II never does that. He always takes those who "insist on coming along."

Yes, people do insist on going with you, don't they?

They are willing to help you found the kingdom of King Saul II.

Such men *never* dare leave alone.

But David left alone. You see, the Lord's true anointed can leave alone.

There's only *one* way to leave a kingdom:

Alone.

All alone.

ELEVEN

Caves are not the ideal place for morale building. There is a certain sameness to them all, no matter how many you have lived in. Dark. Wet. Cold. Stale. A cave becomes even worse when you are its sole inhabitant . . . and in the distance you can hear the dogs baying.

But sometimes, when the dogs and hunters were not near, the hunted sang. He started low, then lifted his voice and sang the song the little lamb had taught him. The cavern walls echoed each note just as the mountains had once done. The music rolled down into deep cavern darkness that soon became an echo-ing choir singing back to him.

He had less now than when he was a shepherd, for now he had no lyre, no sun, not even the company of sheep. The memories of the court had faded. David's greatest ambition now reached no higher than a shepherd's staff. *Everything* was being crushed out of him.

He sang a great deal.

And matched each note with a tear.

How strange, is it not, what suffering begets?

There in those caves, drowned in the sorrow of his song and in the song of his sorrow, David became the greatest hymn writer and the greatest comforter of broken hearts this world shall ever know.

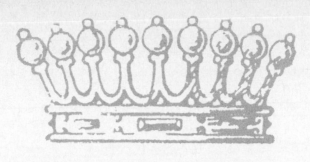

TWELVE

He ran—through soggy fields and down slimy
riverbeds. Sometimes the dogs came close; sometimes they even *found* him. But swift feet, rivers,
and watery pits hid him. He took his food from the
fields, dug roots from the roadside, slept in trees,
hid in ditches, crawled through briars and mud. For
days he ran—not daring to stop or eat. He drank the
rain. Half naked, all filthy, on he walked, stumbled,
crawled, and clawed.

Caves were castles now. Pits were home.

In times past, mothers had always told their children
that if they did not behave they would end up like
the town drunk. No longer. They had a better, more
frightening story. "Be good, or you'll end up like the
giant killer."

In Jerusalem, when teachers taught students to
be submissive to the king and to honor the Lord's

anointed, David was the parable. "See, this is what God does to rebellious men." The young listeners shuddered at the thought and somberly resolved never to have anything to do with rebellion.

So it was then, so it is now, and so it shall ever be.

Much later, David would reach a foreign land and a small—very small—measure of safety. Here, too, he was feared, hated, lied about, and plotted against. He shook hands with murder on several occasions.

These were David's darkest hours. We know them as his pre-king days, but he didn't. He may have assumed this was his lot forever.

Suffering was giving birth. Humility was being born.

By earthly measures he was a shattered man; by heaven's measure, a broken one.

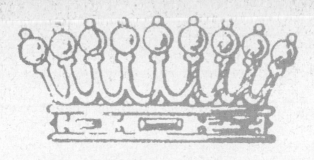

THIRTEEN

Others had to flee as the king's madness grew. First one, then three, then ten, and eventually hundreds. After long searching, some of these fugitives made contact with David. They had not seen him for a long time.

The truth was that when they did see him, they didn't recognize him. He had changed. His personality, his disposition, his total being had been altered. He talked less. He loved God more. He sang differently. They had never heard these songs before. Some were lovely beyond words, but some could freeze the blood in your veins.

Those who found him and decided to be his fellow fugitives were a sorry, worthless lot: thieves, liars, complainers, fault-finders, rebellious men with rebellious hearts. They were blind with hate for the king and, therefore, for all authority figures. They would have been troublemakers in paradise, if ever they could have gotten in.

David did not lead them. He did not share their attitudes. Yet, unsolicited, they began to follow him.

He never spoke to them of authority. He never spoke of submission. But every one of them submitted. He laid down no rules. *Legalism* is not a word found in the vocabulary of fugitives. Nonetheless, they cleaned up their outward lives. Gradually, their inward lives began to change, too.

They didn't fear submission or authority. They didn't even think about the topic, much less discuss it. Then why did they follow him? They didn't, exactly. It was just that he was . . . well . . . David. That didn't need explanation.

And so, for the first time, true kingship had its nativity.

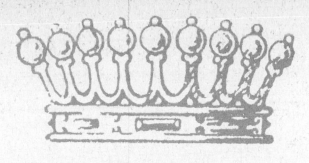

FOURTEEN

"Why, David, why?"

The place was another nameless cave.

The men stirred about restlessly. Gradually, and very uneasily, they began to settle in. All were as confused as Joab, who had finally voiced their questions.

Joab wanted some answers. Now!

David should have seemed embarrassed or at least defensive. He was neither. He was looking past Joab like a man viewing another realm that only he could see.

Joab walked directly in front of David, looked down on him, and began roaring his frustrations.

"Many times he almost speared you to death in his

palace. I saw that with my own eyes. Finally, you ran away. Now for years you have been nothing but a rabbit for him to chase. Furthermore, the whole world believes the lies he tells about you. He has come—the king himself—hunting every cave, pit, and hole on earth to find you and kill you like a dog. But tonight *you* had *him* at the end of his own spear and you did nothing!

"Look at us. We're animals again. Less than an hour ago you could have freed us all. Yes, we could all be free, right now! Free! And Israel, too. She would be free. Why, David? Why did you not end these years of misery?"

There was a long silence. Men shifted again, uneasily. They were not accustomed to seeing David rebuked.

"Because," said David very slowly (and with a gentleness that seemed to say, I heard what you asked, but not the way you asked it), "because once, long ago, he was not mad. He was young. He was great. Great in the eyes of God and men. And it was God who made him king—God—not men."

Joab blazed back, "But now he is *mad!* And God is no longer with him. And David, he will yet kill you!"

This time it was David's answer that blazed with fire.

"Better he kill me than I learn his ways. Better he kill me than I become as he is. I shall not practice the ways that cause kings to go mad. I will not throw spears, nor will I allow hatred to grow in my heart. I will not avenge. I will not destroy the Lord's anointed. Not now. Not ever!"

Joab could not handle such a senseless answer. He stormed out into the dark.

That night men went to bed on cold, wet stone and muttered about their leader's distorted, masochistic views of relationships to kings—especially mad ones.

Angels went to bed that night, too, and dreamed, in the afterglow of that rare, rare day, that God might yet be able to give his authority to a trustworthy vessel.

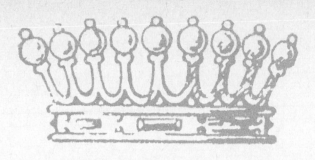

FIFTEEN

What kind of man was Saul? Who was this one who
made himself David's enemy? Anointed of God.
Deliverer of Israel. And yet remembered mostly for
his madness.

Forget the bad press. Forget the stinging reviews.
Forget his reputation. Look at the facts. Saul was
one of the greatest figures of human history. He was
a farm boy, a country kid who made good. He was
tall, good-looking, and well-liked.

He was baptized into the Spirit of God.

He also came from a good family. In his lineage were
some of the greatest historical figures of all humanity.
Abraham, Jacob, Moses—these were his ancestors.

Do you remember the background? Abraham had
founded a nation. Moses had set that nation free
from slavery. Joshua gave those people a toehold in

the land that God had promised them. The judges kept the whole thing from disintegrating into total chaos. That's when Saul came along. It was Saul who took these people and welded them into a united kingdom.

Saul united a people and founded a kingdom. Few men have ever done that. He created an army out of thin air. He won battles in the power of God, defeated the enemy again and again, as few men have ever done. Remember that, and remember that this man was immersed in the Spirit. Furthermore, he was a prophet. The Spirit came on him in power and authority. He did and said unprecedented things, and it was all by the power of the Spirit resting on him.

He was everything people today are seeking to be . . . empowered with the Holy Spirit . . . able to do the impossible . . . for God. A leader, chosen by God with power from God.

Saul was given authority that is God's alone. He was God's anointed, and God treated him that way.

He was also eaten with jealousy, filled with self-importance, and willing to live in spiritual darkness.

Is there a moral in these contradictions? Yes, and it will splinter a lot of your concepts about power, about great men and women under God's anointing, and about God himself.

Many pray for the power of God. More every year. Those prayers sound powerful, sincere, godly, and without ulterior motive. Hidden under such prayer and fervor, however, are ambition, a craving for fame, the desire to be considered a spiritual giant. The person who prays such a prayer may not even know it, but dark motives and desires are in his heart . . . in *your* heart.

Even as people pray these prayers, they are hollow inside. There is little internal spiritual growth. Prayer for power is the quick and the short way, circumnavigating internal growth.

There is a vast difference between the outward clothing of the Spirit's power and the inward filling of the Spirit's life. In the first, despite the power, the hidden man of the heart may remain unchanged. In the latter, that monster is dealt with.

Interesting about God. He hears all those requests for power, which fervent young men and women pray (in every generation), and he answers them! Very often he grants these requests for power, for authority. Sometimes, in answering them, he says yes to some very unworthy vessels.

He gives unworthy people his power? Even though they are a pile of dead men's bones inside?

Why does God do such a thing? The answer is both simple and shocking. He sometimes gives unworthy vessels a greater portion of power so that others will eventually see the *true* state of internal nakedness within that individual.

So think again when you hear the power merchant. Remember, God sometimes gives power to people for unseen reasons. A person can be living in the grossest of sin, and the outer gift will still be working perfectly. The gifts of God, once given, cannot be recalled. Even in the presence of sin. Furthermore, some people, living just such lives, *are* the Lord's anointed . . . in the Lord's eyes. Saul was living proof of this fact.

The gifts cannot be revoked. Terrifying, isn't it?

If you are young and have never seen such things, you may be certain that sometime in the next forty years you will see. Highly gifted and very powerful men and women . . . reputed to be leaders in the kingdom of God, do some very dark and ugly deeds.

What does this world need: gifted men and women, outwardly empowered? Or individuals who are broken, inwardly transformed?

Keep in mind that some who have been given the very power of God have raised armies, defeated the enemy, brought forth mighty works of God, preached and prophesied with unparalleled power and eloquence . . .

And thrown spears,

And hated other people,

And attacked others,

And plotted to kill,

And prophesied naked,

And even consulted witches.

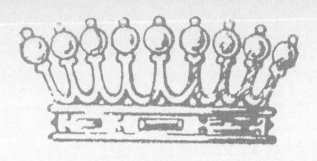

SIXTEEN

"You still haven't answered my question. The man I sit under: I think he is a King Saul. How can I know with certainty?"

It is not given to us to know. And remember, even Sauls are often the Lord's anointed.

You see, there are always people—everywhere, in every age, and in every group—who will stand and tell you: "That man is after the order of King Saul." While another, just as sure, will rise to declare, "No, he is the Lord's anointed after the order of David." No one can *really* know which of the two is correct. And if you happen to be in the balcony looking down at those men screaming at one another, you may wonder to which order *they* belong.

Remember, your leader may be a David.

"That's impossible!"

Is it? Most of us know at least two men in the lineage of David who have been damned and crucified by other men. By men who were absolutely certain the ones they were crucifying were *not* Davids.

And if you don't know of two such cases, for sure you know of one.

Men who go after the Sauls among us often crucify the Davids among us.

Who, then, can know who is a David and who is a Saul?

God knows. But he won't tell.

Are you so certain your king is a Saul and not a David that you are willing to take the position of God and go to war against your Saul? If so, then thank God you did not live in the days of crucifixion.

What, then, can you do? Very little. Perhaps nothing.

However, the passing of time (and the behavior of your leader while that time passes) reveals a great deal about your leader.

And the passing of time, and the way you react to that leader—be he David or Saul—reveals a great deal about *you*.

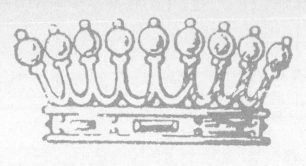

SEVENTEEN

Two generations after the reign of Saul, a young
man enthusiastically enrolled himself into the ranks
of Israel's army under a new king, the grandson
of David. He soon began hearing tales of David's
mighty men of valor. He set out to discover if one of
those mighty men might still be alive and, if so, to
find him and talk to him, though he calculated that
such a man would be over a hundred years in age.

At last he discovered that, sure enough, one such
man still lived. Having learned of his whereabouts,
the youth hastened to his dwelling. Anxiously, if not
hesitantly, he knocked on the door. Slowly it opened.
There stood a giant of a man, gray . . . no, white
haired . . . and wrinkled beyond expectation.

"Are you, sir, one of David's mighty men of long
ago—one of those men of whom we have heard so
much?"

For a long moment the old man surveyed the young man's face, his features, his uniform. Then, in an ancient but firm voice, he replied, never taking his steady gaze off the young man's face.

"If you are asking if I am a former thief and cave dweller and one who followed a sobbing, hysterical fugitive, then yes, I was one of the 'mighty men of David.'"

He straightened his shoulders with those last words. Nonetheless, his sentence ended in a chuckle.

"But, sir, you make the great king sound like a weakling. Was he not the greatest of all rulers?"

"He was no weakling," said the old man. Then sizing up the motivation for the eager young man's presence at his door, he replied wisely and softly, "Nor was he a great leader."

"Then what, good sir? For I have come to learn the ways of the great king and his . . . uh . . . mighty men. What *was* the greatness of David?"

"I see you have the ambitions typical of youth," said the old warrior. "I have the distinct notion you dream of leading men yourself one day." He paused, then continued reflectively. "Yes, I'll tell you of the greatness of my king, but my words may surprise you."

The old man's eyes filled with tears as he thought

first of David and then of the foolish new king only recently crowned.

"I will tell you of my king and his greatness: My king never threatened me as yours does. Your new king has begun his reign with laws, rules, regulations, and fear. The clearest memory I have of my king, when we lived in the caves, is that his was a life of *submission*. Yes, David showed me submission, not authority. He taught me not the quick cure of rules and laws, but the art of patience. *That* is what changed my life. Legalism is nothing but a leader's way of avoiding suffering.

"Rules were invented by elders so they could get to bed early! Men who speak endlessly on authority only prove they have none. And kings who make speeches about submission only betray twin fears in their hearts: They are not certain they are really true leaders, sent of God. And they live in mortal fear of a rebellion.

"My king spoke not of submitting to him. He feared no rebellion . . . because he did not mind if he was dethroned!

"David taught me losing, not winning. Giving, not taking. He showed me that the leader, not the follower, is inconvenienced. David shielded us from suffering; he did not mete it out.

"He taught me that authority yields to rebellion, especially when that rebellion is nothing more

dangerous than immaturity, or perhaps stupidity."
The old man was obviously remembering some very
tense and perhaps humorous episodes in the caves.

"No," he said, now in a voice with a touch of
eloquence, "authority from God is not afraid of chal-
lengers, makes no defense, and cares not one whit if
it must be dethroned.

"That was the greatness of the great . . . of the *true*
king."

The old man began to walk away. Both anger and
regal patience were evident in his bearing as he
turned. Then he faced the youth once more, thunder-
ing one last salvo: "As far as David's having authority: Men who don't have it talk about it all the time.
Submit, submit! That's all you hear. David had
authority, but I don't think that fact ever occurred
to him. We were six hundred no-goods with a leader
who cried a lot. That's all we were!"

Those were the last words the young soldier heard
from the old warrior. Slipping back into the street,
he wondered if he would ever again be happy serv-
ing under Rehoboam.

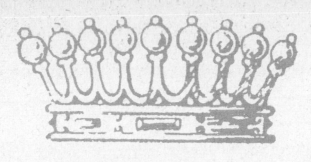

EIGHTEEN

So, having come to the end of our study of Saul and David, do you feel greatly assisted? What's that? You are now certain the man you are under is not truly from God . . . or if he is, he is at best only a Saul? My, how certain we mortals can be . . . of things even angels do not know.

May I ask you then, what you plan to do with this newly acquired knowledge? Yes, I am aware that you yourself are neither a Saul nor a David . . . but only a peasant of the realm. You do plan, though, to share your new discoveries with a few friends? I see. Then perhaps I should warn you that there is great danger with this heady new knowledge of yours. A strange mutation can take place within your own heart. You see, it is possible . . . but wait!

What is it I see over there? There . . . in that distant mist behind you. Turn. Do you see? Who is that

figure making his way through the fog? It seems
I have surely seen him before.

Look closely. Is it not possible for us to make out
what he is doing?

He appears to be bending over some ancient chest.
Yes, he has opened it.

Who is he? And what is he doing?

He has taken something out of the chest. A cloak? It
is some kind of cape. Why, he is putting it on! The
thing fits him perfectly, falling about his shoulders
like a mantle.

Now what? He reaches again into that chest. I know
I have seen that person somewhere before. What is
it he pulls forth this time? A shield? No, a coat of
arms. Yes, a coat of arms from some ancient, long-
forgotten order. He holds it up as one who would
make that order his own! Who is that man? The
bearing. The stance. The carriage. I've seen it before.
I'm sure.

Ah! He has moved out of the mist into the light. We
will see him clearly now.

That face. Is it not you?!

Yes. It is. It is *you!* You who can so wisely discern the
presence of an unworthy Saul!

Go! Look in yon mirror. That man is *you!* Look, too, at the name upon that coat of arms.

Behold: Absalom the Second!

PART 2

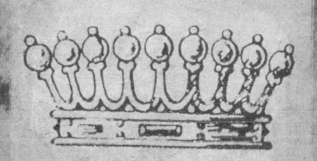

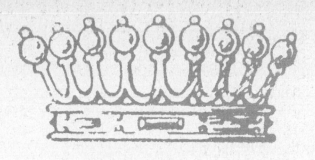

NINETEEN

"Look! Here comes David!"

Bright smiles, a few giggles, some light laughter.

"See! It's David, no less."

Again, wide grins, a wave, and quiet amusement.

"That isn't King David," exclaimed a youth to his guardian as the two walked along the side of the street. "Why do they speak that way? That man is not David!"

"True, child, it is not David. It's only Absalom coming from the gate."

"Why do they call him David?" the boy asked, looking back over his shoulder at the handsome man in the chariot with the fifty men running before him.

"Because he reminds us all of David when he was young. And because we are all so glad that such a fine young man will take David's place someday. And perhaps, too, because Absalom is even better looking than David. He may be the most handsome man alive."

"Will Absalom be king soon? How old is King David, anyway? Is he about to die?"

"Of course not, my boy. Let's see . . . how old is David? Probably about the same age as King Saul when his reign came to an end."

"How old is Absalom?"

"About the same age as David when Saul was trying so hard to kill him."

"David is Saul's age. Absalom is the age of David when he first became king," mused the boy. They walked on silently for a while. The boy, obviously deep in thought, spoke again.

"Saul was very hard on David, was he not?"

"Yes, very."

"Is King David going to treat Absalom the same way Saul treated David? Will David be hard on Absalom?"

The guardian paused to consider the question, but the child went on: "If David treats Absalom badly, will Absalom behave with as much grace as David did?"

"Child, the future will surely tell us. My, you ask such questions! If, when you are grown, you can give answers as well as you now ask questions, you will surely be known as the wisest man on earth."

The two turned in at the palace gate.

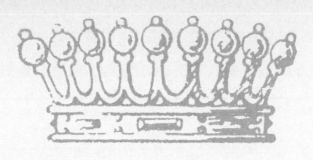

TWENTY

It warmed your heart to know a man who saw things so clearly. Discerning. Yes, that was the word that best described Absalom—*discerning*. He could penetrate to the heart of any problem.

Men felt secure just being with him. They even longed to have time with him. Talking with him, they realized that they themselves were wiser than they realized. Such a revelation made them feel good. As he discussed problem after problem and solution after solution, men began to long for the day when this one would be their leader. He could right so many wrongs. He gave them a sense of hope.

But this imposing, insightful man would never deliberately hasten the day of his own rule. They were confident of that. He was far too humble, too respectful of his father. And those around him began to feel a little frustrated that they would have to keep waiting for the better days of this man's rule.

The more they sat in his living room and talked, the more they realized that things were amiss in the kingdom. Yes, things amiss that they had never thought of before. And problems. Problems were coming to light of which they had never dreamed. Yes, they really were growing in wisdom and insight.

As the days passed, more and more of them came to listen. Word spread quietly. "Here is one who understands and has the answers." The frustrated came. They listened. They asked questions. They received excellent answers and began to hope.

Heads nodded. Dreams were born. As time passed, there were more such gatherings. Ideas turned into stories, stories of injustice that others might have deemed trivial. But not this listener! He was compassionate. And as those around him talked, the discovered injustices seemed to grow in number and severity. With each new story, men were more shocked at unfairness that was now, it seemed, rampant.

But the wise young man sat quietly and added not a word to these murmurings. He was too noble, you see. He always closed the evening conversations with a humble word of deference toward those in positions of responsibility. . . .

But it was too much to expect that any man could sit quietly by forever. This endless parade of injustice was bound to stir even the most respectful man. Even the purest in heart would be smitten with anger. (And this man was certainly the very purest in heart!)

Such a compassionate man could not forever turn his face from these sufferings nor forever remain silent. Such a noble character as this had to speak out someday.

Finally, his followers, which he vowed he did not have, were almost livid. Their insights into the wrongdoings of the kingdom not only grew but abounded. They all wanted to do something about these endless injustices.

At last, it seemed, the magnificent young man might concede. At the outset it was only a word. Later, a sentence. Men's hearts leaped. Joy, if not glee, reigned. Nobility was at last being aroused to action. But no! He cautioned them not to misunderstand. He was grieved, yes, but he could not speak against those in seats of responsibility. No, absolutely not. No matter how great the grievances, no matter how justified the frustration. He would not.

Yet he grieved more and more. It was obvious that some reports drove him to agony. Finally, his righteous anger broke out in cool, controlled words of strength. "These things ought not to be." He stood, eyes blazing. "If I were in responsibility, this is what I would do. . . ."

And with these words, the rebellion was ignited.

Ignited in all but one, that is. In the man who seemed noblest and purest, this was not the case.

Rebellion had been in his heart for years.

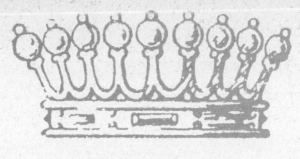

TWENTY-ONE

"Sage!"

"Yes?"

"Sage, may I have a moment of your time?"

"Why, of course. I have a great deal of time."

"You have just come from a gathering of friends at Absalom's home?"

"Yes, that is correct."

"Would you mind sharing some of the impressions you had while there?"

"You mean a general impression of Absalom and his friends?"

"Yes, that would be good enough."

"Well, I have met many men like Absalom. Many."

"Then what is he like?"

"He is both sincere and ambitious. A contradiction, perhaps, but true, nonetheless. He probably means some of what he says. But his ambition will continue long after he discovers his inability to do the things he promises. Righting the wrongs always becomes secondary to ascent to power."

"I'm sorry, Sage, I do not understand."

"Two things stand out in my mind. At one gathering, when Absalom was answering questions, he was very emphatic that there should be more freedom in the kingdom. Everyone liked that. 'A people should be led only by God and not by men,' he said. 'Men should do only what they feel led of God to do. We should follow God, not a man.' I believe those were his words.

"At another meeting he spoke of the great visions he had for God's kingdom—of the great achievements the people were capable of. On the other hand, he spoke of many changes he would make in the way the kingdom is run. Although he did not seem to notice it, he had stated two irreconcilable propositions: many changes, more freedom.

"Yes, indeed, he does remind me of many other men I have encountered over the passing years."

"Sage, I think I understand what you've said, but I'm not sure what your point is."

"Absalom dreams. Dreams of what should be, of what *will* be: 'This is what *I* will do,' he says. But to fulfill those dreams, he must have the people's coop-eration. Ah, this is the point often overlooked. Such dreams rest totally on the premise that the people of God will follow the new leader, that *all* will see as he sees. Such men as Absalom can envision no problems in their own future kingdom. Possibly the people *will* follow, but possibly they will not.

"At most, the Lord's people will follow a leader for a few years. They never support anyone very long. Generally, people do what they please. They can be stopped to do someone else's pleasure for a time, but not for long. People will not work too hard, even if they are following *God*.

"What will Absalom do when people stop following *him* willingly? Ah, now there is a question.

"You see, there is no kingdom without discord. Even God had his critics in heaven, you know. All king-doms follow a bumpy course. And people, especially God's people, never follow any dream in unison. No, to accomplish all he spoke of tonight will take time. Not all will be willing to go along. Will he still be determined to put all his dreams into being? If so, then Absalom has but one recourse: *dictatorship*. Either that, or he will see few, if any, of his grand dreams accomplished. And if he does become a dictator, I can assure you that soon there will be discontent with *him,* just as there is now with the present king. Yes, if Absalom becomes king, soon thereafter you will see new meetings like the one we have just come from tonight . . . only with new faces, new dreams, and plans for a new rebellion. And that gathering will be against Absalom! Then, when *Absalom* hears of such a meeting and of discussion about a rebellion, he will have but one recourse."

"What do you feel he will do, Sage?"

"Rebels who ascend to the throne by rebellion have no patience with other rebels and their rebellions. When Absalom is faced with rebellion, he will become a tyrant. He will bring ten times the evil he sees in your present king. He will squelch rebellion and rule with an iron hand . . . and by fear. He will eliminate all opposition. This is always the final stage of high-sounding rebellions. Such will be Absalom's way if he takes the throne from David."

"But, Sage, have not some rebellions been of benefit, throwing out brutes and despots?"

"Oh, yes, a few. But I remind you: This particular kingdom is different from all others. This kingdom is composed of God's people. It is a spiritual kingdom. I tell you emphatically, no rebellion in the kingdom of God is proper, nor can it ever be fully blessed."

"Why do you say this, Sage?"

"For many reasons. One is obvious. In the spiritual

realm, those who lead rebellions have already proven, no matter how grandiose their words or angelic their ways, that they have a critical nature, an unprincipled character, and hidden motives in their hearts. Frankly, they are thieves. They create dissatisfaction and tension within the realm and then either seize power or siphon off followers. They use their followers to found their own dominions. Such a sorry beginning, built on the foundation of insurrection. . . . No, God never honors division in his realm.

"I find it curious that those who feel qualified to split God's kingdom do not feel capable of going somewhere else—to another land—to raise up a completely new kingdom. No, they must steal from another leader. I have never seen the exception. They seem always to need at least a few prepackaged followers.

"Beginning empty-handed and alone frightens the best of men. It also speaks volumes of just how sure they are that God is with them. Their every word, if truly understood, tells of their insecurity.

"There are many lands unspoiled and unpossessed. There are many people in other places waiting to follow a true king, a true man of God. Why don't 'would-be kings and prophets' simply walk quietly away, alone, then find another people in another place, and there raise up the kingdom they envision?

"Those who lead rebellions in the spiritual world are

unworthy. There are no exceptions. And now I must go. I must join the passing parade."

"Tell me, Sage, what is your name?"

"My name? I am History."

TWENTY-TWO

David stood on the balcony overlooking the gardened terrace of his palace. The lights from the houses in the Holy City twinkled below him. From behind, a man approached. David sighed and, without turning, spoke. "Yes, Joab, what is it?"

"Have you heard?"

"Yes, I've heard," he replied quietly.

"How long have you known?" asked Joab with anxious surprise.

"For months, years, perhaps a decade. Perhaps I have known for thirty years."

Joab was not sure, after this answer, if they were speaking of the same subject. Absalom, after all, was not much past thirty. "Sir, I speak of Absalom," he said a little hesitantly.

"As do I," said the king.

"If you have known so long, why did you not stop him?"

"I was just asking myself that same question."

"Shall I stop him for you?"

David whirled round! In one instant, Joab's query had resolved his dilemma.

"No! Nor shall you speak one word to him. Nor shall you criticize him. Nor shall you allow anyone else to speak critically of him or what he is doing. Certainly you shall not stop him."

"But will he not then take the kingdom?"

David sighed again, softly, slowly. For a moment he balanced between tears and a smile. Then he smiled lightly and said, "Yes, perhaps he will."

"What will you do? Do you have plans?"

"No. None. Quite frankly, I have no idea what to do. I have fought many battles and faced many sieges. I have usually known what to do. But for this occasion, I have only the experience of my youth to draw on. The course I followed at that time seems to be the best I can follow now."

"And what course was that?"

"To do absolutely nothing."

TWENTY-THREE

David was alone again. Slowly, quietly, he walked the length of his rooftop garden. Finally he paused and spoke aloud to himself.

"I have waited, Absalom. I have waited and watched for years. I have asked again and again, 'What is in the heart of this young man?' And now I know. You will do the unthinkable. You will divide the very kingdom of God. All else was talk."

David was quiet for a moment. Then, almost in awe, he spoke, his voice hushed. "Absalom does not hesitate to divide the *kingdom of God*.

"Now I know. He seeks followers. Or at least he does not turn them away. Though he seems magnificently pure and noble, still he divides. His followers grow, even though he states convincingly that he has none."

For a long time David said nothing. Finally, with a trace of humor in his words, he began to address himself. "All right, good King David, you have one issue resolved. You are in the middle of a division, and you may very well be dethroned. Now, to the second issue." He paused, lifted his hand and, almost fatally, asked, "What will you *do?*

"The kingdom hangs in the balance. It seems I have two choices: to lose everything or to be a Saul. I can stop Absalom. I need only to be a Saul. In my old age, shall I now become a Saul? I feel the Lord himself awaits my decision.

"Shall I now be a Saul?" he asked himself again, this time loudly.

A voice from behind answered, "Good King, he has been no David to you."

David turned. It was Abishai who had approached unannounced.

"A crowded place, this terrace," quipped David.

"Sir?" said Abishai.

"Nothing. Suffice it to say I have not been without visitors today—a day when I would have chosen solitude. What did you say to me? In fact, what did I say?"

"You said, 'Shall I be a Saul to Absalom?' and I replied, 'He has been no young David to you.' "

"I never challenged Saul; I never attempted to divide the kingdom during his reign. Is that what you are saying?"

"More," replied Abishai strongly. "Saul was evil toward you and made your life torture. You responded only with respect and private agony. The bad things that happened in those days came only from one side. All fell on you. Yet you could have divided the kingdom and probably could have overthrown Saul. But rather than do that, you left the kingdom. You fled rather than cause division. You risked your life for unity and sealed your lips and eyes to all his injustices. You had more cause to rebel than any man in the history of this—or of any kingdom that has ever been. Absalom has to twist hard to conjure up his list of injustices . . . few of them significant, I might add.

"Has Absalom behaved as you did? Has Absalom respected you? Does Absalom seek to preserve the kingdom? Does he refuse to speak against you? Does Absalom turn aside followers? Has Absalom left the land to prevent its being sundered? Is Absalom respectful? Does he bear suffering in silent agony? Have bad things fallen on Absalom?

"No, he is only pure and noble!"

Abishai's last words came out almost in bites. Then he continued, more gravely this time.

"His grievances are minor compared to your rightful

grievances toward Saul. You never mistreated Saul. And you have never, in any way, been unfair to Absalom."

David interrupted with a grin. "I seem to have a gift for making old men and young men hate me without a cause. In my youth, the old attacked me; when I am old, the young attack me. What a marvelous achievement."

"My point," continued Abishai, "is that Absalom is no David. Therefore I ask you: Why don't you stop his rebellion? Stop him, the miserable . . ."

"Careful, Abishai. Remember he is also a son of the king. We should never speak ill of the son of a king."

"Good King, I remind you that you refused to raise your sword or your spear even once against Saul. But Absalom speaks against you night and day. He will one day—soon—raise an army against you. Nay, a nation. *This* nation! Young Absalom is no young David. I counsel you to stop him!"

"You are asking me, Abishai, to become a Saul," David replied heavily.

"No, I'm simply saying he is no David. Stop him!"

"And if I stop him, will I still be a David? If I stop him, will I not be a Saul?" asked the king, his eyes piercing Abishai. "To stop him, I must become either a Saul or an Absalom."

"My king and my friend, I speak to you fondly: I sometimes think you are a bit insane."

"Yes, I can see why," chuckled David.

"Dear King, Saul was a bad king. Absalom is, in some ways, a youthful incarnation of Saul. You alone are constant. You are forever the brokenhearted shepherd boy. Tell me truthfully, what do you plan?"

"Until now, I have not been sure. But of this I am certain: In my youth I was no Absalom. And in my old age I shall not be a Saul. In my youth, by your own words, I was David. In my old age I intend to be David still. Even if it costs me a throne, a kingdom, and perhaps my head."

Abishai said nothing for a while. Then, slowly, he spoke, making sure he grasped the significance of David's decision.

"You were not an Absalom, and you refuse to be a Saul. Sir, if you are not willing to put Absalom down, then I suggest we prepare to evacuate the kingdom. For Absalom will surely take the throne."

"Only as surely as King Saul killed the shepherd boy," replied the wise old king.

"What?" asked Abishai, startled.

"Think on it, Abishai. God once delivered a defenseless shepherd boy from the powerful, mad king. He can yet deliver an old ruler from an ambitious young rebel."

"You underestimate your adversary," retorted Abishai.

"You underestimate my God," replied David serenely.

"But why, David? Why not fight?"

"I will give you the answer. And you will recall—for you were there—that I once gave this same answer to Joab in a cave long ago!

"It is better that I be defeated, even killed, than to learn the ways of . . . of a Saul or the ways of an Absalom. The kingdom is not that valuable. Let him have it, if that be the Lord's will. I repeat: I *shall not* learn the ways of either Saul or Absalom.

"And now, being an old man, I will add a word I might not have known then. Abishai, no man knows his own heart. I certainly do not know mine. Only God does. Shall I defend my little realm in the name of God? Shall I throw spears, and plot and divide . . . and kill men's spirits if not their bodies . . . to protect *my* empire? I did not lift a finger to be *made* king. Nor shall I do so to preserve a kingdom. Even the kingdom of God! God put me here. It is not my responsibility to take, or *keep*, authority. Do you not realize, it may be *his* will for these things to take place? If he chooses, God can protect and keep the kingdom even now. After all, it is *his* kingdom.

"As I said, no man knows his own heart. I do not know mine. Who knows what is really in my heart? Perhaps in God's eyes I am no longer worthy to rule. Perhaps he *is* through with me. Perhaps it is his will for Absalom to rule. I honestly don't know. And if this is his will, I want it. God may be finished with me!

"Any young rebel who raises his hand against a Saul, or any old king who raises his hand against an Absalom, may—in truth—be raising his hand against the will of God.

"In either case, I shall raise no hand! Wouldn't I look a little strange trying to stay in control if God desires that I fall?"

"But you know that Absalom should not be king!" replied Abishai in frustration.

"Do I? No man knows. Only God knows, and he has not spoken. I did not fight to be king, and I will not fight to remain king. May God come tonight and take the throne, the kingship, and . . ." David's voice faltered. "And his *anointing* from me. I seek his will, not his power. I repeat, I desire his will more than I desire a position of leadership. He may be through with me."

"King David?" A voice came from behind the two men.

"Yes? Oh, a messenger. What is it?"

"Absalom. He wishes to see you a moment. He wants to ask permission to go to Hebron to make a sacrifice."

"David," said Abishai hoarsely, "you know what that really means, don't you?"

"Yes, I do."

David turned to the messenger. "Tell Absalom I will be there in a moment."

David looked one last time at the quiet city below, then turned and walked toward the door.

"*Will* you let him go to Hebron?" Abishai demanded.

"I will," said the great king. "Yes, I will."

Then he turned to the messenger. "This is a dark hour for me. When I have finished speaking to Absalom, I shall retire. Tomorrow have one of the prophets come to me for consultation. Or a scribe. On second thought, send me Zadok, the high priest. Ask him to join me here after the evening sacrifice."

Abishai called out once more, softly this time. Admiration flashed across his face. "Good King, thank you."

"For what?" the puzzled king asked as he turned back in the doorway.

"Not for what you have done, but for what you have

not done. Thank you for not throwing spears, for not rebelling against kings, for not exposing a man in authority when he was so very vulnerable, for not dividing a kingdom, for not attacking young Absaloms who look like young Davids but are not."

He paused. "And thank you for suffering, for being willing to lose everything. Thank you for giving God a free hand to end, and even destroy, your kingdom — if it pleases him. Thank you for being an example to us all.

"And most of all," he chuckled, "thank you for not consulting witches."

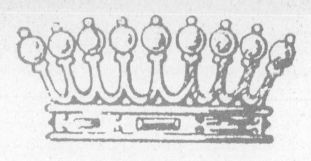

TWENTY-FOUR

"Nathan!"

"Yes? Oh, it's you, Zadok."

"You will pardon my intrusion, Nathan, but I have been observing you for several moments now. You were about to enter the throne room, I believe, to see King David?"

"Yes, Zadok. That was my intent, but I have thought better of it. The king has no need of me."

"I am disappointed, Nathan. In my judgment the king has great need of you. He is facing the gravest test of his life. I am not sure he can pass a test as demanding as this one."

"He has *already* passed this test, Zadok," countered Nathan with a sureness in his voice that showed him to be a prophet of God.

"David has already passed this test? Forgive me, Nathan, but I have no idea what you mean. This crisis, as you well know, has just begun."

"Zadok, your king passed *this* test long ago, when he was a young man."

"You speak of Saul? But that, my friend, was a wholly different matter."

"Not at all. It is *exactly* the same. There is really no difference at all. As David related to his God and to the man over him at that time long ago . . . so now David will also relate to his God and to the man under him. There can be no difference. Not ever.

"True, circumstances may be altered . . . slightly. Ever so slightly, I might add. But the heart! Ah, the heart is always the same.

"Zadok, I have always been grateful Saul was our *first* king. I shudder to think of the trouble he might have caused if, as a young man, he had found himself under some other king. There is no real difference between the man who discovers a Saul in his life and the man who finds an Absalom in his life. In either situation, the corrupt heart will find its 'justification.' The Sauls of this world can never see a David; they see only Absalom. The Absaloms of this world can never see a David; they see only Saul."

"And the pure heart?" asked Zadok.

"Ah, now there is a rare thing indeed. How does a

man with a broken heart handle an Absalom? The way he handled a Saul? We will soon know, Zadok!"

"You and I were not privileged to be there when David came to his hour with Saul. But we are privileged to be present in his hour with Absalom. I for one intend to watch this unfolding drama very closely. And in so doing, I have the good expectation of learning a lesson or two. Mark my words, David will work his way through this thing—and he will pass this test with the same grace he displayed in his youth."

"And Absalom?"

"What of Absalom?"

"In a few hours he may be our king. Is that not your point?"

"There is that possibility," replied Zadok, almost with humor.

Nathan laughed. "If Absalom gains the throne, may heaven have mercy on all the Sauls, Davids, *and* Absaloms of the realm!

"In my judgment our young Absalom will make a splendid Saul," continued Nathan as he turned and strolled down the long corridor.

"Yes. A splendid Saul. For in every way but age and position, Absalom is already a Saul."

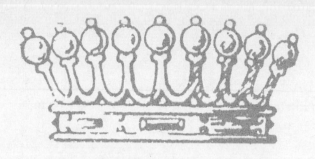

TWENTY-FIVE

"I thank you for coming, Zadok."

"My king."

"You are a priest of God. Could you tell me a story of long ago?"

"What story, my king?"

"Do you know the story of Moses?"

"I do."

"Tell it to me."

"It is long; shall I tell it all?"

"No, not all."

"Then what part?"

"Tell me about Korah's rebellion."

The high priest stared at David with eyes burning. David stared back, his also ablaze. The two men understood.

"I shall tell you the story of Korah's rebellion and of Moses' behavior in the midst of that rebellion.

"Many have heard the story of Moses. He is the supreme example of the Lord's anointed. God's true government rests upon a man—no, upon the contrite heart of a man. There is no form or order to God's government; there is only a man or woman with a contrite heart. Moses was such a man.

"Korah was not such a man, although he was the first cousin of Moses. Korah wanted the authority Moses had. One peaceful morning, Korah awoke. There was no discord among God's people that morning, but before the day was over he had found 252 men to agree with his charges against Moses."

"Then there were problems in the nation when Moses ruled?" asked David.

"There are always problems in any kingdom," replied Zadok. "Always. Furthermore, the ability to be able to see those problems is a cheap gift, indeed."

David smiled and asked, "But, Zadok, you know there have been unjust kingdoms and unjust rulers and pretenders and liars who have ruled and governed. How can a simple people know which is a kingdom with faults but led by men of God, and which is a kingdom unworthy of men's submission? How can a people know?"

David stopped; he realized that he had hit upon what he wished most of all to know. Heavily, he spoke again. "And the king—how can he know? Can he know if he is just? Can he know if the charges are of great worth? Are there signs?" David's final words were anxious.

"Are you looking for some list let down from heaven, David? Even if there were such a list, even if there were a way to know, wicked men would arrange their kingdoms to fit the list! And if such a list existed and a good man filled it to perfection, there would be rebels claiming he had not fulfilled one qualification listed therein. You underestimate the human heart, David."

"Then how shall the people know?"

"They cannot know."

"You mean that in the midst of a hundred voices making a thousand claims, the simple people of God have no assurance of who is truly anointed to bear God's authority and who is not?"

"They can never be certain."

"Who, then, can know?"

"God always knows—but he does not tell."

"Is there no hope, then, for those who must follow unworthy men?"

"Their grandchildren will be able to see the matter clearly. *They* will know. But those caught up in the drama? They can never be certain. Nonetheless, a good thing will come from it all."

"What is that?"

"As surely as the sun rises, people's hearts will be tested. Despite the many claims—and counter-claims—the hidden motives within the hearts of all who are involved will be revealed. This might not seem important in the eyes of men, but in the eyes of God such things are central. The motives of the heart will eventually be revealed. God will see to it."

"I despise such tests," replied David wearily. "I hate such nights as this one. Yet God seems to send many, many things into my life to test this heart of mine. Once more, this night, I find my heart on trial.

"Zadok, there is something that bothers me above all else. Perhaps God *is* finished with me. Is there not some way for me to know?"

"I know of no other ruler in all history who would even ask the question, Good King. Most other men would have ripped their opponent—or even their imagined opponent—to shreds by now. But to answer your questions, I know of no way for you to be certain that God is—or is not—finished with you."

David sighed and choked back a sob. "Then continue with the story. Korah had 252 followers, did he? What happened next?"

"Korah approached Moses and Aaron with his followers. He informed Moses that he had no right to all the authority he exercised."

"Well, we Hebrews are consistent, aren't we?" laughed David.

"No, the heart of man is consistent, David," replied Zadok.

"Tell me, what was Moses' response to Korah?"

"At the age of forty, Moses had been an arrogant, self-willed man, not unlike Korah. What he might have done at forty, I cannot say. At eighty, he was a broken man. He was . . ."

"The meekest man who ever lived," interrupted David.

"The man who carries the rod of God's authority should be. Otherwise God's people will live in terror. Yes, a broken man faced Korah. And I believe you already know what Moses did, David. He did . . . nothing."

"Nothing. Ah, what a man."

"He fell on his face before God. That is all he did."

"Why did he do that, Zadok?"

"David, you of all men must know. Moses knew that God alone had put him in charge of Israel. There was nothing that needed to be done. Korah and his 252 followers would seize the kingdom—or God would vindicate Moses. Moses knew that."

"Men would find it hard to imitate such a life, would they not? An imposter surely could not fake such surrender, could he? But tell me, how did God vindicate Moses?"

"Moses told the men to return the next day with censers and incense . . . and God would decide the issue."

"So!" cried David. "So!" he exclaimed again even louder. "Sometimes God *does* tell," he said excitedly. "Please continue."

"Korah and two of his friends were swallowed by the earth. The other 250 died by . . ."

"Never mind," said David. "Suffice it to say that Moses was proven to be in authority . . . by God! God *did* tell! The people knew who really had authority from God, and at last Moses had rest."

"No, David. He did not find rest, and the people were not satisfied with God's answer! The very next day the whole congregation murmured against Moses, and they would all have died except for the prayers of Moses."

"And men fight to become kings!" David shook his head in perplexity.

Zadok paused, then continued: "David, I perceive that you are torn by the question of what is true authority and what is not. You want to know what to do with a rebellion, if indeed it is a rebellion and not the hand of God. I trust you will find the only pure thing to do — and do it. And thereby you will teach us all."

The door opened, and Abishai rushed in. "Good King! Your son, your own flesh and blood, has proclaimed himself *king* in Hebron. At first impression, it seems all Israel has gone over to him. He plans to take the throne. He marches toward Jerusalem. Some of the men closest to you have gone over to him."

David walked away. He spoke quietly to himself. "Israel's third king? Do true leaders of the kingdom of God gain authority in this way?"

Zadok, not certain if he should be hearing David's words or not, spoke out. "My king?"

David turned, his eyes moist.

"At last," David said quietly. "At last this matter will be resolved. Perhaps tomorrow someone besides God will know."

"Perhaps," said Zadok, "but perhaps not. Such questions may be debated even after we are all dead."

"That might also be tomorrow," laughed David. "Go, Abishai, tell Joab. You will find him in the turret of the east wall."

Abishai departed as he had entered, in haste and in fury.

"I wonder, Zadok," mused David, "if a man can force God into a position where he *must* tell."

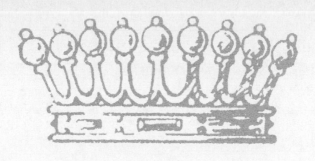

TWENTY-SIX

Abishai rushed across the courtyard and into the eastern rampart, where he charged up the spiral staircase. At the top of the stairs, Joab stared down at Abishai. In the flickering light of torches, each man studied the face of the other.

Abishai spoke. "Have you heard, Joab?"

"Have I heard! 'Tis midnight, yet half the city is awake with the word. How can it be, Abishai—a son against his own father!"

"When kingdoms are vulnerable, men see queer sights," responded Abishai with a distant stare.

"And they'll sacrifice anything to satisfy ambition," added Joab angrily. "What think you of these things, Abishai?"

"What think I?" responded Abishai, matching Joab's

anger with his own rage. "This! Absalom has no authority in the kingdom. He holds no power, no office, yet he has risen up to divide the kingdom. He has raised his hand against the very anointed of God—against David! David—who has never done or spoken one evil word against him.

"What think I?" Abishai's voice rose toward a crescendo. "If Absalom, who has no authority, will commit this deed; if Absalom, who is nothing, will divide the very kingdom of God—" His voice now rolled like thunder. "If Absalom will do these evil things *now*, what in the name of sanity might that man do if he be *king?*"

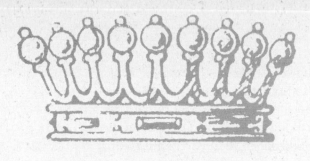

TWENTY-SEVEN

David and Zadok were alone once more.

"And now, what will you do, David? In your youth, you spoke no word against an unworthy king. What will you do now with an equally unworthy youth?"

"As I said," replied David, "these are the times I hate the most, Zadok. Nonetheless, against all reason, I judge my own heart first and rule against its interests. I will do what I did under Saul. I will leave the destiny of the kingdom in God's hands alone. Perhaps he is finished with me. Perhaps I have sinned too greatly and am no longer worthy to lead. Only God knows if that is true, and it seems he will not tell."

Then, clenching his fist, yet with a touch of wry humor in his voice, David added emphatically, "But today I shall give ample space for this untelling God of ours to show us his will. I know of no other way to bring about such an extraordinary event except by doing *nothing!* The throne is not mine. Not to have, not to take, not to protect, and not to keep.

"I will leave the city. The throne is the Lord's. So is the kingdom. I will not hinder God. No obstacle, no activity on my part lies between me and God's will. Nothing will prevent him from accomplishing his will. If I am not to be king, God will find no difficulty in making Absalom to be Israel's king. Now it is possible. God shall be God!"

The true king turned and walked quietly out of the throne room, out of the palace, out of the city. He walked and he walked . . .

Into the bosoms of all men whose hearts are pure.

Well, dear reader, the time has come for us to say good-bye once more. I will leave you to your thoughts and to reflect on the hidden motives of your own heart.

Oh, by the way, the players are working on a love story. Perhaps we can see it together when it is performed. I believe it shall be called . . . The Divine Romance.

I trust, then, by the mercy of God, we shall meet again.

ABOUT THE AUTHOR

Gene Edwards was born and raised in east Texas, the son of an oil-field roughneck. He was converted to Christ in his junior year in college. He graduated from East Texas State University in Commerce, Texas, at the age of eighteen, with majors in English literature and history. His first year of postgraduate work was taken at the Baptist Seminary in Ruschlikon, Switzerland. He received his master's degree in theology from Southwestern Baptist Theological Seminary in Ft. Worth, Texas, at the age of twenty-two. He served as a Southern Baptist pastor and then as an evangelist for ten years.

Gene and his wife, Helen, now make their home in Jacksonville, Florida. His ministry includes conferences on the deeper Christian life and on living that life in the context of a practical experience of church life.

The author can be reached at the following address:

Gene Edwards
P.O. Box 3450
Jacksonville, FL 32206
www.geneedwards.com

If you have enjoyed *A Tale of Three Kings,* you will want to read *The Divine Romance.* It is a magnificent saga that will take your breath away. Here is an incomparable love story—told in almost childlike simplicity yet revealing some of the deepest truths of the Christian faith. Readers everywhere have acclaimed *The Divine Romance* as one of the finest pieces of Christian literature of our time.

The sequel to *A Tale of Three Kings* is *The Prisoner in the Third Cell.*

Also, in the same genre, is the spellbinding story of the history of God's people . . . as seen by the angels—The Chronicles of the Door series *(The Beginning, The Escape, The Birth, The Triumph, The Return)*. In addition, The First-Century Diaries series presents the sweeping panorama of the entire saga of the first-century church.

Gene Edwards has written three books that serve as an introduction to the deeper Christian life: *The Highest Life, The Secret to the Christian Life,* and *The Inward Journey*. For a list of books by Gene Edwards, see the page opposite the title page.

Table Of Contents

Unless otherwise indicated, all Scripture quotations are taken from the King James Version of the Bible.

The Wisdom Commentary, Volume 1
Wisdom Book # B-136
ISBN 1-56394-132-5
Copyright © 2002 by *MIKE MURDOCK*
All publishing rights belong exclusively to Wisdom International

Published by The Wisdom Center · P. O. Box 99 · Denton, Texas 76202
1-888-WISDOM-1 (1-888-947-3661) · Website: www.thewisdomcenter.cc

≈ 1 ≈

ABILITIES

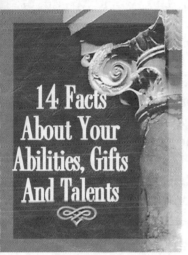

14 Facts About Your Abilities, Gifts And Talents

Everyone Possesses Special Abilities. Few recognize their *dominant* gift.

David recognized his dominant gift. He was more than a singer. He was more than a shepherd boy. He was a warrior and he knew it. That is why he recognized an opportunity for his gift to flourish when Goliath cursed his God.

Joseph knew his dominant gift. He was more than an interpreter of dreams. In fact, the Scriptures only document two or three occasions of it. His gift was uncommon compassion. That gift caused him to recognize the countenances of the butler and the baker in the prison. Their unhappiness was the Golden Door to his ascent to the throne.

I love what my dear friend Sherman Owens always teaches: "Listen to *happy* voices for *encouragement;* listen to *unhappy* voices for *ideas.*"

The Apostle Paul knew his dominant gift. "I am called an apostle...." He was more than a thinker. He was more than a talker. His gift was to reveal the revelation of God.

1. *Jesus Wanted Us To Recognize That God Gives Wonderful Gifts To Us.* "If ye then, being evil, know how to give good gifts unto your children, how much more shall your Father which is in Heaven give good things to them that ask Him?" (Matt. 7:11).

2. *The Holy Spirit Gives You All The Gifts, Talents And Abilities You Possess.* "Now there are diversities of gifts, but the same Spirit" (1 Cor. 12:4).

3. *The Holy Spirit Gives Different Gifts To Us, Relative To Our Assignment On Earth.* "But all these worketh that one and the selfsame Spirit, dividing to every man severally as He will. For as the body is one, and hath many members, and all the members of that one body, being many, are one body: so also is Christ" (1 Cor. 12:11,12).

4. *Your Gifts Were Given To Help Men Of God Fulfill Their Instructions And Visions From God.* "Then wrought Bezaleel and Aholiab, and every wise-hearted man, in whom the Lord put Wisdom and understanding to know how to work all manner of work for the service of the sanctuary, according to all that the Lord had commanded. And Moses called Bezaleel and Aholiab, and every wise-hearted man, in whose heart the Lord had put Wisdom, even every one whose heart stirred him up to come unto the work to do it:" (Ex. 36:1,2).

5. *Your Gift Was Imparted To You To Solve Problems For Those Closest To You.* "Withhold not good from them to whom it is due, when it is in the power of thine hand to do it" (Prov. 3:27).

6. *When Your Dominant Gift Becomes Your Seed In The Lives Of Others, God Guarantees To Generously Compensate You.* "Knowing that whatsoever good thing any man doeth, the same shall he receive of the Lord, whether he be bond or free" (Eph. 6:8).

7. *Few Ever Recognize Their Dominant Gift.* This explains why millions live life unrewarded for the gift they contain. Nothing is more tormenting than living life uncelebrated for the difference within you.

8. *Obsession With Your Flaws Will Often Blind You To Your Dominant Gift.* We study ourselves. As we stand before a mirror each morning, we rehearse the qualities that discourage us the most. It is a costly exercise.

Marilyn Hickey, my longtime friend, shared an interesting experience. She had just returned from China. When I finished speaking at their church in Denver, Colorado, she leaned over and told me this story. China has the greatest ping-pong players on earth. So, she asked the master Mentors of their champions how they handled the weaknesses of their protégés. They explained that they *ignore* them, choosing rather to spend all of their teaching time on developing their *dominant* trait or gift to its highest level possible. They explained that if the dominant strength of a player received total focus, it would compensate for any weakness elsewhere in their form.

9. *Your Dominant Gift Will Operate Well In A Hostile Environment.* A brilliant young boxer said the other day, "The greater the challenge, the more energy arises within me." A house painter may receive $15 an hour, but if you bring him 50 floors high on a skyscraper, his income will multiply. An adversarial atmosphere will always magnify the rewards possible through your gift. Stop thinking your gift cannot be used because of a climate of hostility around you.

It will magnify the reward of it like David was rewarded for killing Goliath.

10. *The Focus Of Others Often Distorts Our Personal Awareness Of Our Dominant Gift.* Our families and relatives may study our flaws from childbirth. Our weakness becomes their focus. Unfortunately, we adapt to it. We start looking at the thing they despise.

11. *Admiration Of Others With Different Gifts Often Blinds Us Toward Our Own Dominant Gift.* It happened with me as a young boy. Everyone honored my father. My mother continuously expressed her respect and admiration. Daddy was quiet while I was growing up. Seven of us kids remember a very quiet, non-talkative father at the table. So, since he was the idol of those I loved, he became my idol. I wanted to be like Daddy. Well, my personality was quite different. I talked a lot. In fact, I made very low grades in conduct in school throughout my 12 years!

But, it appeared that quietness was magnetic. Everyone loved a quiet person, it seemed. So, I wrote scriptures out on 3 x 5 index cards, emphasizing the importance of silence. "Set a watch before my mouth...." "Study to be quiet...." Every time I felt the urge to talk in a group of people, I pulled my cards out. I read them feverishly and intensely. I wanted to be a "quiet person" more than anything else I knew.

It became more than I could bear.

Finally, I screamed out to my mother, "Mother, I have got to talk!"

She suggested something nobody else had ever thought about. "Son, maybe there is a gift involved. Now, we have got to pray and ask the Lord to give you something to say that folks would not mind listening to." That birthed my obsession for substance and essence in every conversation.

12. *Your Gift Will Be Removed From You Unless You Use It.* "Take therefore the talent from him, and give it unto him which hath ten talents...cast ye the unprofitable servant into outer darkness: there shall be weeping and gnashing of teeth" (Matt. 25:28,30).

13. *What You Would Love To Do Most Every Day Of Your Life Is A Clue To Your Dominant Gift.* If money were not involved, if convenience were not the consideration, what would you attempt to do with your life?

Here is a little test: If every human on earth were only permitted to receive $10 per hour for working (taxicab driver or the President of the United States), what would you want to do every day for the rest of your life?

14. *Your Significance Is Not In Your Similarity To Another But In Your Point Of Difference From Another.* You did not marry your husband because he reminded you of a previous boyfriend. He was *unlike* your old boyfriend. You don't attend your local church because it reminds you of one across town. It is *unlike* the one across town.

Celebrate Your Difference. It is wonderful to learn from others. Implement their knowledge and skills.

Uncommon Men Are Simply Common Men Who Have Recognized Their Uncommon Gift.

Recognition Of Your Dominant Gift Can Move You From Obscurity To Significance In A Day.

RECOMMENDED BOOKS AND TAPES ON THIS TOPIC

B-05   Finding Your Purpose in Life (Book/$3)
B-09   Four Forces That Guarantee Career Success (Book/$3)
B-73   The Mentors Manna on Abilities (Book/$3)
B-74   The Assignment (The Dream & The Destiny) Vol. 1 (Book/$10)
B-75   The Assignment (The Anointing & The Adversity) Vol. 2 (Book/$10)
B-100   The Holy Spirit Handbook (Book/$10)
TS-22   The Assignment (Six tapes/$30)
TS-23   31 Secrets of the Uncommon Problem Solver (Six tapes/$30)
TS-29   Double Diamond and Gifts, Goals and Guts (Six tapes/$30)
TS-68   The Holy Spirit Handbook (Six tapes/$30)

❧ 2 ❧

ACHIEVEMENT

Design The Life You Want.

The day you do, your world will change.

Once you determine it's God's will for you to succeed, then it is only a matter of you learning the principles that govern the God-kind of success. By carefully reading the Word of God, we *learn* to use the Golden Key of Wisdom to unlock the doors of success.

You can change the course of your life. A newcomer to town may fail to notice a traffic light and a collision results. Knowing the STOP and GO lights of life determines your tears or triumphs.

Here Are 10 Steps To Uncommon Achievement

1. *Discern The True Definition Of Success.* It is *not* necessarily popularity, possessions or prestige. Success is the *progressive achievement of a God-given goal.* It results in an inner awareness that you are a worthy person. Success results in happiness, really feeling good about yourself (read Mk. 3:35, Josh. 1:7,8).

2. *Set Definite Goals For Yourself.* God is a Goal-Setter. He scheduled the birth of a Savior and the Return of Christ hundreds of years in advance. It is not wrong to set goals. Jesus cautioned in Matthew 6 against *worrying* over them. James warned against *excluding God from them.* You do not merely set *your* goals, but set them under *divine guidance* (see Eph. 5:17). *Deadlines* help you to redeem the time for the days are evil (see Eph. 5:16). "We should make plans counting on God to direct us" (see Prov. 16:9 TLB).

3. *Make Your Goals Balanced And Reasonable.* Many fear the setting of goals because they think, "I might not make it." Don't make unreasonable expectations of yourself and others.

There are six basic areas of success: 1) Spiritual, 2) Financial, 3) Physical, 4) Mental, 5) Social and 6) Family. Overemphasis in one area often causes another area to deteriorate. You should be growing in all areas. Learn to break down big goals into smaller ones. "The wise man looks ahead..." (Prov. 14:8 TLB).

4. *Meditate On Scripture*. The mentality of God is absorbed through simply *reading the Word of God*. *Just read it*. Find an easy book like John. Read it, again and again. *Something will come to life inside you*. The Bible helps you to *think* as God thinks. It sharpens your response to the Holy Spirit. *It keeps you from falling*. Psalm 37:31 says, "The law of his God is in his heart; none of his steps shall slide." It gives you *discerning ability* for what is false, and what is true (see Ps. 119:130). I suggest that you read Psalm 1:1-3; Joshua 1:7,8; Psalm 119, for more encouragement in this area.

5. *Discern The Spiritual Mentor That Most Increases Your Love For God*. Do not attend a church just because of convenience, or because the preacher is a "nice guy." Listen to God. *Where does He want you?* It may take you 30 minutes of driving instead of ten, but it can make the difference for the entire week! Invest a little time and research in finding the right church. Then, *be loyal*. Stand one hundred percent behind that church, its activities, and your pastor (see Heb. 10:25).

6. *Pursue Quality People In Your Life*. Spend time with uncommon people. Be a learner. "He that walketh with wise men shall be wise..." (Prov. 13:20). Pray and expect God to send uncommon people across your path.

7. *Invest In Yourself*. Spend time, effort and dollars in developing your *mind*, your *spirit*, and your *inner* man. If a $20 meal makes your stomach feel good for four hours, think what it could do to your mentality and power-life to invest $20 in tapes or books that soak your mind and spirit in the anointing of God and give guidance in your life! Buy music tapes that fill your home and car with the presence of God! Hunters invest in guns. Nations buy tanks and weapons. The *successful person* is one who invests in equipping himself (see 2 Tim. 2:15).

8. *Make Your Time Count*. Time-wasters grieve God. People who sit around for hours joking and talking about nothing will guarantee your failure. Certainly, there is need for relaxation, recreation and fellowship, but America's obsession for fun is causing a deterioration of purpose. Idleness results in frustration, boredom and possibly even depression. Productive people rarely find time for depression (see Eph. 5:16; Ecc. 3:1-8).

9. *Find What You Are Good At, Whether It's Mechanical Work, Public Speaking, Or Artwork.* Take a good look at yourself. Spend time finding out how to be the best at what you do. Most humans are born with abilities of some sort. You are accountable to God for developing your skills (read Matt. 25:14-30).

10. *Cultivate A Teachable Spirit.* Willingness to change is not necessarily a compromise of principles. Flexibility and openness to truth are evidence you are uncommon. "A wise man will hear..." (Prov. 1:5). "As an earring of gold, and an ornament of fine gold, so is a wise reprover upon an obedient ear" (Prov. 25:12).

Sometimes it takes courage to listen. Time and knowledge should *enlarge* you. Let it. *Listen.* Don't be a "know-it-all."

Champions Make Decisions That Will Create The Future They Desire.

So, design the life you want. Nobody else can.

The Anointing
You Respect
Is The Anointing
That Increases
In Your Life.

-MIKE MURDOCK

❧ 3 ❧

ANOINTING

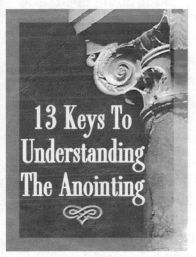

The Anointing Is The Power Of God.

The Anointing is provided to us to remove a burden or destroy a yoke of bondage existing on another. "And it shall come to pass in that day, that his burden shall be taken away from off thy shoulder, and his yoke from off thy neck, and the yoke shall be destroyed because of the anointing" (Isa. 10:27; see also Isa. 61:1-4 and Isa. 14).

An Assignment requires an anointing.

Specific Assignments require specific anointings.

A *leadership* anointing enables you to *love.*

An *administrative* anointing produces *order.*

A *healing* anointing releases *health.*

A *Psalmist* anointing unlocks *worship.*

A *Wisdom* anointing *illuminates.* "For the Word of God is quick, and powerful, and sharper than any two-edged sword, piercing even to the dividing asunder of soul and spirit, and of the joints and marrow, and is a discerner of the thoughts and intents of the heart" (Heb. 4:12).

A *prophetic* anointing *reveals the will of God.*

2 Tragedies In The Body Of Christ

▶ Many Never Walk In Joy And Do Not Sense The Pleasure Of Achievement Because They Have Not Recognized The Anointing God Has Placed On Their Own Life. They do not recognize how God has chosen to use them in the lives of others.

▶ Many Never Receive Miracles Or Blessings Because They Do Not Respect And Celebrate The Difference Of The Anointings God Has Placed On Those Near Them. They do not discern how God desires to use others to bless them.

13 Keys To Understanding The Anointing

1. *The Anointing Is The Power Of God.* "And it shall come to pass in that day, that his burden shall be taken away from off thy shoulder, and his yoke from off thy neck, and the yoke shall be destroyed because of the anointing" (Isa. 10:27).

2. *The Anointing Is The Power Of God To Conquer Any Enemy That Emerges In Your Life.* "How God anointed Jesus of Nazareth with the Holy Ghost and with power: Who went about doing good, and healing all that were oppressed of the devil; for God was with Him" (Acts 10:38).

3. *You Always Possess Something God Desires To Anoint.* Moses had a rod. David had a slingshot. Surrender increases your *dependence on God.*

4. *Your Success In Life Or Ministry Will Depend On The Anointing You Choose To Respect.* Zacchaeus recognized the difference in Jesus. Jesus bonded with him because of it.

5. *The Anointing Increases In Your Life Proportionate To Your Dependence On God.* Your prayer life reveals your humility or pride. Any attempt to accomplish anything apart from God eventually paralyzes the flow of that anointing through you. "But the manifestation of the Spirit is given to every man to profit withal" (1 Cor. 12:7).

6. *An Increase Of The Anointing Will Increase Order In Your Life.* "Let all things be done decently and in order" (1 Cor. 14:40). "For God is not the author of confusion, but of peace, as in all churches of the saints" (1 Cor. 14:33).

7. *The Anointing Turns Common Things Into Uncommon Weapons.* The simple rod of Moses became a snake. Stretched over the Red Sea, it divided the waters. The simple slingshot of David destroyed Goliath, and ushered David into kingship.

8. *The Anointing That Attracts Some Often Alienates Others.* "Think not that I am come to send peace on earth: I came not to send peace, but a sword. For I am come to set a man at variance against his father, and the daughter against her mother, and the daughter in law against her mother in law. And a man's foes shall be they of his own household" (Matt. 10:34-36). When you obey the Holy Spirit, some will withdraw from you.

9. *The Anointing Is Determined By The Will Of God, Not Your Perfection.* "For I know that in me (that is, in my flesh,) dwelleth no good thing:" (Rom. 7:18).

10. *Any Destructive Act Against The Anointed Is Forbidden In Scripture.* "Touch not Mine anointed, and do My prophets no harm" (Ps. 105:15). It is dangerous to speak slanderously of men God is using greatly.

11. *Your Respect For The Anointing Will Create Access To It.* During the famine, Elijah was sent only to the widow, *who respected his counsel.* Jesus went home with Zacchaeus, because of *the respect* he had toward Jesus. "And when Jesus came to the place, He looked up, and saw him, and said unto him, Zacchaeus, make haste, and come down; for to-day I must abide at thy house" (Lk. 19:5).

12. *Your Respect For The Anointing On Others Increases The Blessing Of God Upon Your Life.* The widow respected Elijah and experienced abundant provision through a famine (see 1 Kings 17). David respected the anointing on Saul and received the kingship. Joshua respected the anointing on Moses and received his inheritance.

13. *The Anointing You Respect Is The Anointing That Will Grow In Your Life.* The respect of Joshua for Moses moved Joshua into leadership. When you respect the anointing for healing, miracles of healing will flow. When you respect an anointing for *financial break-through*, debt can be eliminated. When you respect an anointing for *Wisdom*, ideas and favor will flow like unstoppable currents.

In my book, "The Holy Spirit Handbook," chapter 11 contains 18 facts you should know about The Anointing. I urge you to read this powerful and revealing book.

A Special Note:

One of the tragedies in our present generation is the disrespect toward the financial anointing resting on a few leaders. Few Financial Deliverers exist in the body of Christ. Those who walk in the *center* of that focus and abandon themselves completely to that calling often become the focus of ridicule, contempt and even anger.

"But, Mike, that preacher on television only talks about finances the entire program! He never talks about anything else! He should be balanced!" someone complained to me.

"Are you angry at the dentist because he refuses to mow your grass?" I asked. "Are you mad at your lawyer because he will not pull your teeth when they hurt? Are you angry at the evangelist who preaches salvation but does not have a healing line for the sick? Are you angry about the veterinarian who will not become a contractor and build an extra room on your house? Is your eye angry because the ear refuses to see?"

Function is determined by God. Not us. One lady was very upset with her pastor because he spoke on financial keys for 15 minutes before the offering was received in her church. "I cannot believe my own pastor talked about money for 15 minutes on Sunday morning!" she said.

I asked her how many hours it took for her to get dressed each morning, the drive to her job, the hours she worked each day and the time it took to drive back home in the evening traffic. The total hours she spent involved in her work was 55 hours each week.

"Explain something to me," I requested. "Why are you angry with a pastor who encourages you for 15 minutes a week to *expect* financial blessing when you have invested 55 hours of your life that week in pursuit of money?"

The criticism toward Financial Deliverers is demonic.

Patients rarely hate their Healers.

If you are critical toward healing ministries, do not expect the wave of healing to flow into your house.

If you are critical toward financial ministries, do not expect ideas for financial blessing to explode within you.

If you defy the anointing of those in authority over you, do not expect the rewards of protection, provision and promotion.

What You Respect Will Move Toward You.

What You Disrespect Will Move Away From You.

Recognition Of The Unique Anointing Of God On Others Could Increase Your Own Anointing One Thousand Times More (see Deut. 1:11).

❧ 4 ❧

ASSIGNMENT

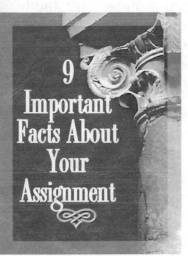

9 Important Facts About Your Assignment

You Are Here For A Reason.

1.   *Everything Created Contains An Instruction, An Assignment, To Solve A Specific Problem.*

2.   *Your Assignment Is Not Decided By You, But Discovered by You.*

Within you is an invisible calling, purpose and destiny (see Jer. 1:4-8).

Instructions may be unknown, ignored, or distorted, but they do exist. These instructions are invisible, yet cannot be doubted. Examine a watermelon seed carefully. It is impossible, even with the microscope, to see a written and clearly defined instruction to that seed to produce more watermelons. Yet the command cannot be doubted. Plant a million watermelon seeds and none of them will produce a tomato. The instruction is already defined. It cannot be refuted. *The product is the proof.*

Look inside the tomato seed. Analyze it. If you try for a lifetime to locate the instruction to produce tomatoes, you will never find it. *Those instructions are not visible.* Yet tomatoes are produced from the seed.

Within everything created is a desire and command to *increase,* *produce* and *multiply.* Something within you wants to solve a problem for someone, somewhere, sometime. That is your Assignment.

Especially mankind. "So God created man in His own image, in the image of God created He him; male and female created He them. And God blessed them, and God said unto them, Be fruitful, and multiply, and replenish the earth, and subdue it: and have dominion over the fish of the sea, and over the fowl of the air, and over every living thing that moveth upon the earth" (Gen. 1:27,28).

3.   *Your Assignment Is Something You Alone Must Discern And Discover While You Are On Earth* (see Rom. 14:12). That is why your

relationship with God is an absolute *necessity*.

4. *Nobody Else Knows Your Assignment.* You cannot even prove it to another person. It is invisible, and yet it is clearly defined *within you. It cannot be doubted when you are in the presence of the One Who made you, the Holy Spirit.*

"The Spirit of God hath made me, and the breath of the Almighty hath given me life" (Job 33:4).

"I will praise Thee; for I am fearfully and wonderfully made: marvelous are Thy works; and that my soul knoweth right well. My substance was not hid from Thee, when I was made in secret, and curiously wrought in the lowest parts of the earth. Thine eyes did see my substance, yet being unperfect; and in Thy book all my members were written, which in continuance were fashioned, when as yet there was none of them" (Ps. 139:14-16).

5. *Your Assignment Is God's Total Focus.* "Thou compassest my path and my lying down, and art acquainted with all my ways" (Ps. 139:3). *God Carefully Examines Every Word You Speak Daily.* "For there is not a word in my tongue, but, lo, O Lord, Thou knowest it altogether" (Ps. 139:4).

6. *The Holy Spirit, Who Created You, Decides Your Assignment.* He keeps His hand upon your life. "Thou hast beset me behind and before, and laid Thine hand upon me" (Ps. 139:5).

"I have set the Lord always before me: because He is at my right hand, I shall not be moved...Thou wilt shew me the path of life: in Thy presence is fulness of joy; at Thy right hand there are pleasures for evermore" (Ps. 16:8,11; see Acts 8:26 and Acts 13:1-6).

7. *The Holy Spirit Is Your Constant Advisor For Your Assignment.* "Whither shall I go from Thy Spirit? or whither shall I flee from Thy presence? If I ascend up into Heaven, Thou art there: if I make my bed in hell, behold, Thou art there. If I take the wings of the morning, and dwell in the uttermost parts of the sea; even there shall Thy hand lead me, and Thy right hand shall hold me" (Ps. 139:7-10).

8. *It Is Your Own Responsibility To Identify Your Assignment.* So, do not expect others to define your Assignment for you. It is not their responsibility to do so. *They have a personal responsibility to discover their own Assignment.* It will take their entire life and mental focus to complete it. You must discover your own Assignment for yourself. God intended it to be so. This will require your personal reaching, pursuing and moving *toward His presence.* "So then every

one of us shall give account of himself to God" (Rom. 14:12).

9. *The Word Of God Is The Blueprint For Your Assignment, And Must Become Your Daily Focus.* Hearing from Him will make your Assignment clear, irrefutable and immovable. "Thou hast dealt well with Thy servant, O Lord, according unto Thy Word" (Ps. 119:65).

You Are On The Earth To Solve A Problem.

That is why it is called...The Assignment.

RECOMMENDED BOOKS AND TAPES ON THIS TOPIC

B-74   The Assignment (The Dream & The Destiny) Vol. 1
         (Book/$10)
B-75   The Assignment (The Anointing & The Adversity) Vol. 2
         (Book/$10)
B-97   The Assignment (The Trials & The Triumphs) Vol. 3
         (Book/$10)
B-98   The Assignment (The Pain & The Passion) Vol. 4 (Book/$10)
TS-22   The Assignment (Six tapes/$30)

What You Fail
To Master
In Your Life
Will Eventually
Master You.

-MIKE MURDOCK

❧ 5 ❧

BITTERNESS

11 Steps In Overcoming Bitterness

One Of The Most Effective Tools Against Sincere Christians Is The Tool Of Bitterness.

I do not recall my very first experience with a satanic attack of bitterness, but I have had enough throughout the years that I feel very qualified to speak about it.

Some years ago I knelt beside a man who was an ex-preacher. When I started talking to him about his soul, he looked up at me with an attitude of condescension: "Son, don't hand me those cliches. I've preached three times more than you have and to three times more people. I know all those scriptures that you are quoting to me. I simply can't get right with God. I'm *past feeling*."

I felt crushed. I looked at him with compassion. I did not recognize it at the time, but he was dying with a broken heart and a *spirit of bitterness*.

He explained. Some preachers had failed to stand by him during an attack upon his character. His wife had deserted him for another man. His children never telephoned him. He felt even church members were too busy gossiping to spend time helping an "ex-preacher" who *willingly* became a servant to bitterness.

Bitterness will make you a slave.

Bitterness will kill your spirit.

Bitterness will wipe the smile off your face and will sap and drain the river of blessing to your soul.

Bitterness will *paralyze your effectiveness for God.*

You must master bitterness or it will master you. It happens to teenagers who trust someone and are betrayed. It happens to parents who do all they know to do and still their children quit going to church. It happens to wives who try to follow the Scriptural pattern to lead their husbands to the Lord while they refuse to acknowledge the truth.

Why I Almost Left The Ministry

I was almost destroyed some years back through bitterness. I was preaching for several ministers I had idolized for years since my youth. Large offerings were given to my ministry by the congregation. But, when church leaders would often withhold half of my offerings for themselves, my heart literally broke. I was hardly given enough to pay my trailer note and car note, much less my house note and living expenses. To my amazement, the coming weeks did not improve. The pattern continued to repeat itself during two months of meetings.

After eight weeks, I went into my trailer and began to cry. For two solid hours I wept; not mad at God, but wounded toward people and preachers. I felt shoved to the side. *Mistreated*. Nobody cared about me. "Nobody cares," I spoke to a friend through heavy crying. "This is it. I am leaving the ministry. I don't have to put up with preachers and churches who don't care about my needs and family. I'm going into business. I will support the men I believe in, but God can have the rest of them!"

At that moment, satan and God were in combat. *My eyes were on people. I had made preachers, churches and people the source of my supply instead of God.* God was wanting to teach me a lesson.

I almost did not learn it.

To be honest with you, I did not see a vision. I saw no stars nor received any singing telegrams sung by angels at the foot of my bed. No man seven feet tall touched my shoulder, but in a matter of weeks, as the anointing of God oozed out of my spirit, I suddenly lost confidence and faith in people.

I lost my desire for the Word.

I did not want to pray. I literally lost my desire to live. Yet, I was still attempting to minister each night in the crusades, but harboring bitterness in my spirit.

I woke up one morning at 5:00 a.m. and the Spirit impressed me to pray. I stumbled into the sanctuary (I was staying in evangelist's quarters) and knelt down. Suddenly, my very soul erupted like a volcano. I gushed with tears (and I don't cry easily). God showed me I had let friends *encourage* my bitterness. I had not yet looked at the *lesson* God wanted me to learn through the experience. God showed me my *disappointment and hurt* was because of my pride and doubt in His promises and provision.

God heard my cry for help.

Needless to say, the *spirit of joy* returned to my life and my ministry. (On several occasions, I had to return to that "Bethel" for a second touch.)

You can win over your experience with bitterness. The bitterness may come through a divorce that occurs. A sickness. The loss of a friend. The death of a child. A financial setback. Regardless of what happens to you, make up your mind to overcome it!

1.   Admit That You Are Living With The Root Of Bitterness In Your Heart.

2.   Admit That It Is Wrong And Damaging To You.

3.   Admit Your Own Mistakes.

4.   Look For The Lessons The Spirit Wants To Teach You.

5.   Do Not Talk Your Bitterness To Others.

6.   Stay In Harmony With Godly Friends.

7.   Soak Your Soul In The Scripture, Preferably The Psalms Of David As He Cried Unto The Lord.

8.   Plan New Projects In Your Future.

9.   Think Ahead And Not Backward.

10.   Discuss Everything With The Holy Spirit—Bitterness Will Literally Be "Choked Out" And Displaced.

11.   Study Winners In The Bible, Those Who Won Over Bitterness (like Joseph toward his brothers).

Never allow the root of bitterness to rob you of the success and joy you can experience!

The Person Of Jesus
Creates Your *Peace;*
The Principles Of Jesus
Create Your *Prosperity.*

-MIKE MURDOCK

≈ 6 ≈

BLESSING

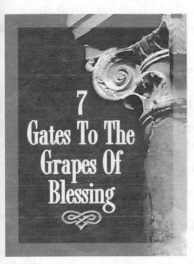

7 Gates To The Grapes Of Blessing

You Were Born To Taste The Grapes, Born To Enjoy Royalty And The Blessings And Benefits Of God.

You have the instinct for improvement. You have a motivation for increase. *Something inside you gravitates toward growth.* You were created for expansion. God created you that way, and you will never be happy any other way.

Now, I could discuss forever these Grapes and how luscious and tasty they are. Grapes of *Wealth, Health, Peace, Power, Success*—but unless you know how to obtain the Grapes, it will not help you.

1. *The Gate Of Obedience.*

Deuteronomy 28:1 says, "...if thou shalt hearken diligently unto the voice of the Lord thy God..."

This simply means doing what God has told you to do. It means living up to the knowledge you have received. If you are a *gallon*, live up to gallon knowledge. If you are a *pint*, live up to pint knowledge. You can move into states of perfection and maturity as God reveals Himself to you. Abraham was called a *friend* of God *because he obeyed God.*

God said, "Abraham, I want you to move from your comfortable situation and go to a new country." Abraham *obeyed* God. If God has been talking to you about something, *do it.*

Don't negotiate. *Only Fools Negotiate With Givers.*

That raises a question: How can we know the voice of God? It is impossible to describe the voice of God. Oh, I could give you some guidelines, but when it comes to *knowing* when God is speaking, you have to become addicted to Him. I don't have to ask, "I wonder if this man is my brother." I know His voice. If you have spent time in the presence of God, you will know His voice.

If God is drawing you, speaking to you and dealing with you, *obey Him*. It may even appear to be a step backward. It may be something you do not really want to do. But if you will say, "Father, I will do what You ask me" and will step through the Gate of Obedience, all of Heaven will open for you. God is standing by the Windows of Heaven ready to pull them open and unload an Avalanche of Blessings if you will just obey Him (see Mal. 3:10). He said, "If ye abide in Me, and My Words abide in you, ye shall ask what ye will, and it shall be done unto you" (Jn. 15:7). Oh, unleash the powerful benefits of obedience!

2. *The Gate Of Knowledge.*

God says, "My people are destroyed for lack of knowledge..." (Hos. 4:6). What you do not know can destroy you. God wants you knowledgeable. Information is God's business. All of Heaven is involved in distributing information. Angels bring information. The Bible is an information manual. It is literally the *"Winner's Digest,"* informing us about God—His power, nature and thoughts about us—and about satan, angels and demon spirits.

You have a right to the blessings of God. You are a child of the Most High God, an heir of God, a joint-heir with Jesus; He is your *elder brother*. You have a right to enter into the Holy of Holies. You have on your behalf a *High Priest,* an *Intercessor* beside the right hand of the throne of God. But you cannot take hold of the grace and blessings of God unless you have *knowledge* of what He has provided for you. I am saying that *you have to know what belongs to you.* You must open and walk through the *Gate of Knowledge.* "But without faith it is impossible to please Him: for he that cometh to God must believe that He is, and that He is a rewarder of them that diligently seek Him" (Heb. 11:6).

A woman came forward for prayer one night, and I asked her, "Do you want God to heal you?"

"Well," she responded, "I think He is trying to show me something." Imagine such ignorance!! Have you ever heard of *"Disease University?"*

Many people have accepted disease and sickness as teachers. The Bible says that the *Holy Spirit will lead you into all truth.* Not, "Yea, I will send disease and it will teach you and lead you into all truth."

Know what the Word of God says, and believe it. Pray, "God, Your Word says that You were wounded for my transgressions, bruised for my iniquities and by Your stripes I am healed" (Isa. 53:5). Embrace the Word and stand upon it. You can spend your energy *explaining your sickness*, or you can spend your energy *reaching for a miracle*.

Do you have a thorough knowledge of the Grapes God has provided? Find out what the Scriptures teach; know about the Grapes you are reaching for. A lot of people have not because they do not even know the Grapes exist. You were born to taste the Grapes and you need to have the knowledge that God made them available and accessible to you.

3. *The Gate Of Visualization.*

Visualize the Grapes. If you cannot see the Grapes in your *mind*, you will not see them in your future. Your mind is a force that affects everything else in your life. *The renewing of your mind is the secret of transformation* (see Rom. 12:1,2). Your mind is a powerful force.

The woman with the issue of blood said to herself, "If I may touch but His clothes, I shall be whole" (Mk. 5:28). She visualized. *It happened in her mind before it happened in her body*. Visualize the Grapes. See yourself tasting the Grapes. See yourself with victory. Some of you have never seen yourself victorious like God means for you to see yourself. Visualize where God wants you to be. Then, act as if you are *already* there.

Jesus visualized Himself in victory: "...for the joy that was set before Him [He] endured the cross" (Heb. 12:2). He endured the present suffering for the joy that was set before Him; His mind was picturing victory. When Jesus walked to Calvary, He was not looking at the cross; He was looking at the *resurrection*.

If you have always longed to be victorious in an area, *get your mind on the Grapes* until you can visualize them and see them in your grasp. Is there a habit in your life you want to conquer? *Do not* concentrate on the habit; *concentrate on victory*. This is called the *Law of Displacement*. It means you *displace* evil by the *entrance* of good. We do not go into a building and suggest to darkness, "Would you mind leaving, because if you leave we can have light?" We bring in light, and the *entrance of light forces the exit of darkness*.

Some people spend their lives saying, "Oh, I wish I could quit thinking bad thoughts."

You'll never stop thinking bad thoughts, you'll never stop thinking doubt, until you start thinking faith and you start seeing yourself victorious. That picture drives out evil. Visualize it right now.

Whatever it is, see yourself with it.

4. *The Gate Of Forgiveness.*

The Fourth Gate to the Grapes is Forgiveness, which simply

means the transferal of the right to judge and penalize. It means that you give up your position on God's vengeance team. *Forgiveness does not flow to you until it can flow through you.* You can ask for forgiveness, beg God for forgiveness, offer Him "double tithe," but nothing will happen inside you until you permit God alone to penalize others for doing you wrong.

"Well, Mike, I want to teach him a lesson."

That's understandable, but it is wrong. God is the One in charge of payment; He is the Judge. Exercise the ability to *withhold* judgment and let God perform His program of restoration and forgiveness.

Forgiveness is not the removal of information. It is the removal of the pain of it. There is no entry into Heaven until you walk through the Gate of Forgiveness. There are no Grapes of Blessing, no Grapes of Reward, until you "remember...not the former things" (Isa. 43:18).

Forgive not only other people, but forgive yourself. That is just as important. There are people who have never forgiven themselves. *Never advertise your mistakes.* Lay the memory of them at the cross and *leave them there.*

   5. *The Gate Of Persistence.*

What is the Gate of Persistence? Simply make up your mind, regardless of how far away the Grapes appear, to push on for The Blessing. Sometimes it will seem like they are a thousand miles away. Friends may try to discourage and disillusion you. They may not understand your dream, your goal. It will not fall into your lap automatically. It will not be easy. But every man or woman who has ever achieved anything had to *persist.* They made up their minds to go after what they believed in.

I met a young man the other day—sharp, nice. He could be a great preacher. Will he ever be? I doubt it. Why? No persistence: "I tried and it didn't work. I think I will quit. I don't know if I am called."

The Rewards Belong To The Persistent. For ten days the disciples waited in the Upper Room. Can you imagine the first day? Someone says, "Well, He said for us to just wait; here we are."

Second day, third, fourth, fifth, sixth. Another says, "You know, if God *really* wanted us to have power, He wouldn't make us just sit here and wait for it." Seventh day. Eighth. Ninth. Tenth—suddenly, a sound from Heaven as a rushing mighty wind fills the room (see Acts 2:2). Cloven tongues of fire sat upon their heads, and they began to speak in tongues as the Spirit of God gave them utterance. Why?

Persistence.

Say it: *"Persistence."* Say it until your whole body feels it. There will be times you will not feel like you can make it. At times you will feel like asking, "Why am I doing this anyway?" Or, you will feel like "It's no use, nothing is going to work out." Stay there! The diseased woman did not feel like pushing her way through the crowd, *but she had a goal.* I am certain Peter did not always feel like an overcomer, but God gave him such a victory that when he, the man who had denied the Lord, began to preach he said, "You folk need to repent; you denied the Holy One of Israel" (see Acts 2:23). *He persisted until the power of God came into his life, and he walked in that power.*

6.   *The Gate Of Sowing.*

You cannot reap Grapes until you sow Grapes. The Blessing *follows* the Blesser. *Whatever Good Thing You Do For Another, God Is Going To Do For You* (see Eph. 6:8). If you want to taste Grapes, you have to distribute Grapes. You have to bless *other* people if you want God to bless *you.*

If you want something good to happen in your life, you must make something good happen for your sister or brother. You must first perform for *others* what God wants to perform for you.

Jesus did not say that if you treat your brother or sister right he or she will love you. He said that if you do right to others *God* will do right by you. Everything reproduces after its own kind. If you want healing, start praying for *others* to experience healing. If you want blessings, start concentrating on *others' receiving* their blessing. Jesus concentrated on other people's needs. He went around doing good, healing all that were sick and oppressed of the devil (see Acts 10:38). What You Make Happen For Others, God Will Make Happen For You.

7.   *The Gate Of Praise.*

Judah, which means praise, was the first tribe into battle. Praise is the sound that makes hell sick; it unnerves demons. Satan used to be the song leader in Heaven, but God kicked him out. Anytime you start praising God, all of Heaven notices it. Let the redeemed of the Lord say so! Make a joyful noise! Clap your hands.

▶ *Praise is an act of the will.* It is not something you have to *feel* in order for it to be real. It is *not* meditation; it is something that is *heard.* Praise is articulated sound and opinion. It is your *recognition* of Jesus as Lord of everything, that Jehovah is still on the throne.

▶ *When you begin praising God, something miraculous happens.*

I don't care how you feel; if you start saying, "God, I love you," something *loosens*. Talk about smashing the locks of your prison; praise does that! Now, praise has nothing to do with feelings. You don't have to say, "God, I feel great," or, "I feel lousy." Praise has to do with *Him* and *it takes your mind off yourself.*

▶ *Praise lifts you to where God is.*

▶ *God is very comfortable with praise.* In fact, that is where He chooses to *dwell* (see Ps. 22:3). God likes praise, and He *responds* to it. Not only does God respond to praise, demons repulse at it.

▶ Praise is something you deliberately *choose to do*, to acknowledge the power of God.

▶ The purpose of praise is not just to make you feel good, but it is also to stir others.

God values recognition. He does things in a big way. You never see God "sneaking" around saying, "You be quiet now and have a good time." He is a *celebration* God, an *expressive* God.

You were born to taste the Grapes of God's blessing. The silver and gold are His. He gives us the power to get wealth. Everything that God has, everything that He is, He is willing to pour *into* us and *through* us. The Grapes are not for the holy, they are for the *hungry*. They are not placed within your mouth; they are placed within your *reach*. So, enter the gates and reach for the Grapes.

They are *accessible...today*.

RECOMMENDED BOOKS AND TAPES ON THIS TOPIC

B-28   The Blessing Bible (Book/$10)

B-82   31 Reasons People Do Not Receive Their Financial Harvest (Book/$12)

B-104   7 Keys to 1000 Times More (Book/$10)

TS-1   Born to Taste the Grapes (Six tapes/$30)

TS-82   31 Reasons People Do Not Receive Their Financial Harvest (Six tapes/$30)

VI-16   7 Keys to 1000 Times More (Video/$30)

VI-17   31 Reasons People Do Not Receive Their Financial Harvest (Video/$30)

7

CAREER

Your Career Matters.

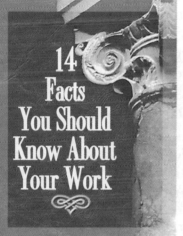

There Are 14 Facts Achievers Should Understand About Their Work

1. *Work Began In The Garden Of Eden.* Adam was to dress the garden and keep it (see Gen. 2:15). This work was an activity blessed of the Lord to provide Adam with a sense of achievement and self-worth.

Then Adam sinned. His disobedience turned work into a curse: "In the sweat of thy face shalt thou eat bread, till thou return unto the ground; for out of it wast thou taken: for dust thou art, and unto dust shalt thou return" (Gen. 3:19).

2. *Obedience To The Laws Of God Can Activate The Blessings Of Work.* Deuteronomy 28:8 states: "The Lord shall command the blessing upon thee in thy storehouses, and in all that thou settest thine hand unto." Many despise their jobs. Husbands lash out at their wives in frustration. Many wives arrive home work-weary and angered at the expectations of the family to "keep on working" after they get home.

3. *If You Are Unhappy At Work, It Will Affect Your Family Life, Even Your Health.* Take time to plan your career and life's work. It deserves your attention. Do not accept a job based simply on convenient location or financial sufficiency or even friendship.

4. *You Must Find What You Are Good At And Do It With All Your Heart.* Be proud of what you are involved in. Never "put down" your occupation. See and cultivate an awareness of its important place in the lives of people. Strive to be the best you can be: "For which of you, intending to build a tower, sitteth not down first, and counteth the cost, whether he have sufficient to finish it?" (Lk. 14:28).

5. *You Must Learn To Conquer Conflict On The Job.* One of the

frustrations people face on their jobs is *people-conflict*. Anger, hostility and open resentment have caused some to leave their jobs prematurely. God has really touched my spirit in this area. As a minister, many times I am in a "controlled" climate. Since I am with fellow Christians and many other top quality people most of the time, it is sometimes easy to forget the intense pressure many husbands and wives face on the everyday job.

6. *Conflict With Your Boss May Be Caused By Different Reasons*. He may be having personal problems at home and is trying to compensate through job productivity. He may be experiencing the pressure of a power struggle from within the organization. He may be suppressing hostility stemming from an attitude he has discerned in you. *Talk travels!* Have you shown a rebellious attitude or expressed it to another? Do you follow his instructions? Does he continually find it necessary to repeat his instructions to you?

7. *Misunderstandings Occur When The Details Of A Job Are Not Clearly Defined*. Take the time to grasp clearly what your boss or employees expect. Take nothing for granted. Aim for quality in your work production.

8. *You Must Remind Yourself That God Is Your True Employer*: "With good will doing service, as to the Lord, and not to men" (Eph. 6:7).

9. *Those Who Are Faithful In The Little Things, Advance To Greater*. "Servants, be obedient to them that are your masters... Knowing that whatsoever good thing any man doeth, the same shall he receive of the Lord..." (Eph. 6:5,8).

10. *You May Be On The Wrong Job*. Are you happy with what you are doing? Is God happy with your present work? Do you work as if God is your "boss?" Are you really giving your *best*? Be honest with yourself and do something about it! (You may want to order a copy of my powerful booklet, "Four Forces That Guarantee Career Success." It is only $3.00. It could change your life.)

11. *You May Be On The Right Job Presently But En Route To Something More Suitable*. Your present job could be a "temporary training ground." So, stay steady. Don't ruin friendships and your reputation through an outburst of anger or frustration. *Wait. Do your best "as unto the Lord."*

12. *Your Business Is Very Important*. It provides a sense of accomplishment that is essential for self-esteem. It releases your God-given *talents*. It *provides* for your family. That's why one of satan's

goals is to destroy your self-confidence and your sense of worth. A feeling of inadequacy can be the "cancer" that eats away your vitality and enthusiasm.

13. *Your Work Should Be A Source Of Joy!* "To rejoice in his labour; this is the gift of God" (Ecc. 5:19). "Mine elect shall long enjoy the work of their hands" (Isa. 65:22). "The Lord shall command the blessing upon thee...and in all that thou settest thine hand unto..." (Deut. 28:8).

14. *Being On The Proper Job And In The Right Career Is An Important Key For Total Happiness.* Some blame families, their mate, their children for their frustrations, when the truth would reveal that job unhappiness is "eating them up" inside.

Your work is a master Key to unlocking your significance, security and success.

Discern where you belong.

RECOMMENDED BOOKS AND TAPES ON THIS TOPIC

B-44   31 Secrets for Career Success (Book/$10)

B-91   The Leadership Secrets of Jesus (Book/$10)

TS-23   31 Secrets of the Uncommon Problem Solver (Six tapes/$30)

Anything That Does Not Change You Is Unnecessary In Your Life.

-MIKE MURDOCK

～ 8 ～

CHANGE

You Can Change Your Life.

There are six things you must eliminate to create dramatic positive change to your life.

1. *Wrong Relationships.* Ask yourself: "Will this friendship bring me closer to Jesus? Or, will it soil the beauty of what God has begun?" Get rid of anything that clouds your mind or spirit.

2. *Moral Impurity.* Nothing can destroy your testimony and inner joy faster than immorality.

When satan plants the "Seed" of a bad thought in your mind, immediately resist it. Exercise your authority! Say: "Satan, I bind you and resist your ungodly suggestions. I am a child of God walking in the power of the Holy Spirit. I cast your thought back to you. I am a new creation in Jesus!" Immediately, thank God aloud for good, wholesome thoughts.

3. *Ungodly Mind-Manipulators.* We are influenced greatly by what we see and hear: "Mine eye affecteth mine heart..." (Lam. 3:51). Depressing television shows, sensual music and suggestive books guarantee spiritual suicide. Replace these by saturating your life and home with wholesome books, tapes and Christian materials.

4. *Negative Conversation.* Words minister life or death (see Prov. 18:21). Put off the former conversation. Ephesians 4:29 instructs: "Let no corrupt communication proceed out of your mouth, but that which is good to the use of edifying, that it may minister grace unto the hearers." Psalm 50:23 says: "...to him that ordereth his conversation aright will I shew the salvation of God." Insist on positive and uplifting conversation.

5. *Bitterness And All Other Sin.* In Ephesians 4:31 Paul tells us: "Let all bitterness, and wrath, and anger, and clamour, and evil speaking, be put away from you..." Bitterness is like a cancerous sore that deteriorates the inward soul of man. Sin is the deceptive snare

that poisons the possibilities of a would-be winner. It promises roses, but delivers *thorns*. Repent and ask God to pour out His love through you to others.

6. *Time Wasters*. God is a Planner. From the creation of a world in seven days, including a rest zone, to a scheduled rapture, even a marriage supper of the Lamb projected thousands of years in advance, it is easy to conclude that our Father is a Master in details, goal setting, priorities, and order. Learn to avoid non-essentials, and energy wasters. *Make your time count:* "See then that ye walk circumspectly, not as fools, but as wise, Redeeming the time, because the days are evil" (Eph. 5:15,16).

Chart your course hourly. Daily. Monthly. Stay on target. Schedule every small success literally. Time spent with *God*, time spent with *others* and time for *yourself*.

Nobody else can change your life for you.

You must do it.

So, do it today.

RECOMMENDED BOOKS AND TAPES ON THIS TOPIC

TS-1   Born to Taste the Grapes (Six tapes/$30)

TS-83   School of Wisdom, Vol. 3 - What I'd Do Differently If I Could Begin My Life Over Again (Six tapes/$30)

TS-90   School of Wisdom, Vol. 2 - 101 Wisdom Keys That Have Most Changed My Life (Six tapes/$30)

B-17   Seeds of Wisdom on Overcoming (Book/$3)

B-48   31 Keys to a New Beginning (Book/$5)

B-80   The Greatest Success Habit on Earth (Book/$3)

⇌ 9 ⇌

CHILDREN

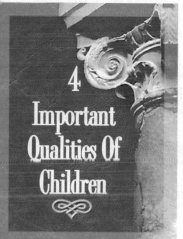

4 Important Qualities Of Children

A Child Is A Gift From God.

"Lo, children are an heritage of the Lord: and the fruit of the womb is his reward. As arrows are in the hand of a mighty man; so are children of the youth" (Ps. 127:3,4).

1. *Children Listen.*

Children *observe*. They *absorb*. They are like "containers." In their ears we deposit faith or fear, victory or defeat, motivation or depression. Unfortunately, in their early years they are unable to push the "reject" button when error is introduced.

When the disciples rebuked children, Jesus said, "Suffer little children, and forbid them not, to come unto Me: for of such is the kingdom of Heaven" (Matt. 19:14).

At eight years of age, after my father finished preaching, I walked to an altar in Waco, Texas, and publicly committed my life to Jesus Christ. *I still remember the experience.* I felt something stir inside me and it still exists today.

What are your children hearing? My father has never allowed a television in his home...nor cursing...nor screaming. Strict? Perhaps, but he knew the *influence* of what we heard. Instead, we heard him and my mother weeping and praying daily for our salvation and understanding of truth.

The difference has been permanently engraved upon my heart.

2. *Children Learn.*

Through you, your children learn to laugh or criticize, rebel or cooperate, take or give. *You stand at their crossroads.* You are their signpost. *You* are their *source of education* in spiritual things.

The mentality of the unbelieving dad still stuns me. How can a man hug his child and say "I love you" then never help that child serve Christ, but *watch him go to hell?*

Tragic ignorance. "But whoso shall offend one of these little ones which believe in Me, it were better for him that a millstone were hanged about his neck, and that he were drowned in the depth of the sea" (Matt. 18:6).

3. *Children Lean.*

Youth *long* for a sign of *strength*. They will test every emotional fiber of a parent. In the midst of an inner roller coaster, they are searching for a *rock*. Sometimes they even panic in their search.

Mom and Dad, your children need you. They may not say it. They may not *know* it. But stand strong. They want to see you *win* in adversity. *You may be the only visible source of faith they have.* Please don't destroy that.

They lean on *your* Wisdom, *your* experience with God. They lean on you for affection and love. *Give it.* Resist those awkward feelings and dare to *reach* out to your family. "He that troubleth his own house shall inherit the wind..." (Prov. 11:29).

Your home and family are irreplaceable.

4. *Children Love.*

They are not burdened with memories of injustices. They are not people-users to climb the "corporate ladder." They are "channels of love." Let's learn from them. Jesus said that unless we are as little children we will not enter the Kingdom of God.

Be *thankful* for the gift of your children.

Don't wait until they are gone to celebrate their invaluable presence.

Loss Is The Quickest Cure For Ingratitude.

RECOMMENDED BOOKS AND TAPES ON THIS TOPIC

B-30	The Teens Topical Bible (Book/$10)
B-35	The Fathers Topical Bible (Book/$10)
B-36	The Mothers Topical Bible (Book/$10)
B-49	The Proverbs 31 Woman (Book/$7)
B-51	The One-Minute Pocket Bible for Fathers (Book/$5)
B-52	The One-Minute Pocket Bible for Mothers (Book/$5)
B-57	Thirty-One Secrets of an Unforgettable Woman (Book/$10)
B-70	The Gift of Wisdom for Mothers (Book/$10)
B-77	The Gift of Wisdom for Fathers (Book/$10)
TS-57	Thirty-One Secrets of an Unforgettable Woman (Six tapes/$30))

❧ 10 ❧

DATING

You Are Designed For Connection.

Eyes require a view. Ears require sound. The mind requires thoughts.

Aloneness creates vulnerability. God knew it. "And the Lord God said, It is not good that the man should be alone," (Gen. 2:18).

God loves marriage. He hates divorce. Marriage is not a mere reproduction center for human babies. Marriage is sowing ground where you sow your patience, love and enthusiasm and then watch it multiply in those around you who celebrate your presence.

God Will Never Give You A Gift That Will Replace His Presence. That is why a mate is not designed to produce your joy. The presence of God creates your joy. "In Thy presence is fulness of joy" (Ps. 16:11). Fullness implies "requiring nothing in addition."

Your mate is a gift from God to you. That gift is intended to:

1) protect your focus,

2) reduce distractions, and

3) create a climate of protection.

Focus often creates blindness. When you are looking north, you cannot see south. Someone else is needed for your protection. So, God provides the gift of a Mate. Unfortunately, some who qualify for your attention may not be qualified to receive your heart.

Having been single for over 20 years, I have often analyzed the failures and successes of relationships.

Here Are Some Suggestions

1.   *Think Twice If You Do Not Possess A Passionate Desire To Give To Them. The Proof Of Love Is The Desire To Give.* Jesus explained it. "For God so loved the world, that He *gave* His only begotten Son..." (Jn. 3:16).

Too often, marriage becomes an exchange. Exchange is the evidence of business, not love.

You should desire to *give* Time, the greatest gift God gave you.

The Proof Of Uncommon Love Is The Investment Of Time.

2. *Think Twice If They Do Not Possess A Passionate Desire To Give Back To You.* I am not referring to expensive gifts, huge amounts of money or clothes. A listening ear, flexibility, patience and the willingness to be corrected are also gifts.

3. *Think Twice If Your Personal Achievements Have Not Created Excitement In Them.* When good things happen, who is the first person you desire to telephone? Pay attention to that. *Celebration Is A Compass.* Those you love to celebrate with are clues to the puzzle of your life. When Uncommon Love exists, Uncommon Celebration is normal. Uncommon Love does not compete with the success of another. It savors and enjoys the pleasure of another.

4. *Think Twice If They Have Not Been Captivated By What Has Captivated You.* Several years ago, a lady excited me. Yet, the relationship struggled. Something simply could not seem to "catch fire." She did not enjoy sitting with me when I wrote my books. She enjoyed play far more than the presence of the Holy Spirit in the Secret Place. A minister friend explained gently to me, "Mike, she simply has not been captivated by what has captivated you." It is not enough for your mate to be captivated by you; *they must be stirred by the same thing that stirs you.*

When I address women's conferences, I stress this.

You cannot know a man by studying *him*.

You know a man by *studying his obsession*.

5. *Think Twice If You Have Lost Your Desire To Impress Them.* I watched a wife wave good-bye to her husband one morning. She was at the front door waving. Missing buttons on her gown, a torn pocket, breakfast stains and hair up in rollers—she was everything a man wants to *forget*. I understood easily why he was so excited about driving off to work...where someone would greet him at the door with a bright smile, pressed clothes and perfume to *impress* him.

You are a walking message system to those you love. Would *you* fly on a plane with seats broken, egg on the tie of the pilot, missing buttons and torn seats? Of course not. You would think, "That's *visible* damage. What else has not been corrected in the engine?"

Something is wrong when you no longer desire to present your best to your Mate.

I was so impressed one day when I saw a friend's wife set the table with the most expensive silverware and fine china for her husband. She explained to me, "The most special person in my life is my husband. I would never save my beautiful silverware for an occasional visitor when my husband is The King in this house."

6.   *Think Twice If They Never Ask Quality Questions Concerning Your Greatest Dreams And Goals.* Questions reveal desire. Questions reveal humility.

7.   *Think Twice If They Ignore Worthy Counsel From Qualified Mentors In Their Life.* Who are their heroes? You become like those you admire. You adapt their habits. Who is their dominant *Mentor?* At whose feet do they sit consistently? A Mentor is a prophecy of a Protégé. If they rebel against the counsel of their pastor, they are living undisciplined, uncovered and unadvised. Tragedy is scheduled.

8.   *Think Twice If They Have Not Yet Impressed Their Pastor.* I was attracted to a lady and inquired about her to the pastor and his wife. They exchanged glances and said quietly, "She has come a long way." I understand *preacher talk.* That simply said, she is a long way from where she should really be.

9.   *Think Twice If You Do Not See Continuous Improvement In The Relationship.* Improvement is revealed by the *decrease of conflict.* Conflict occurs through opposite goals, philosophies or beliefs. Bonding should increase unity and bring a decrease in contention and strife.

Strife Is The Evidence Of Opposite Belief Systems.

10.   *Think Twice If They Show Little Pain Or Remorse Concerning Their Past.* Repentant people are not arrogant. Repentant people do not blame others for their decisions.

Memories of mistakes *should* produce sorrow and heartache. When regret is not expressed, the offense usually occurs again. Some people never repent for past mistakes. Why? They have not tasted the painful consequences of their rebellion.

They do not possess a true fear of God. They believe they are beyond judgment. It is futile to pursue a relationship with someone who does not possess an obvious fear of God.

Uncorrected Conduct Becomes Repeated Conduct. The *fear of God* keeps a mate faithful. Beauty will not. One lady explained to me, "I will keep myself so beautiful, he will not even look at another woman." How foolish! *Your* beauty does not make *another* woman ugly.

Beauty cannot guarantee faithfulness. The fear of God keeps us faithful.

Some of the best articles written are in women's magazines. However, it saddens me deeply to watch some Mentors of women teach the art of manipulation, intimidation and deception to deceive the men they are pursuing. *You will never respect anyone you are capable of deceiving.*

11. *Think Twice If They Enjoy The Climate And Atmosphere Of Rebels.* I met a very striking lady who was a brilliant conversationalist. Quite impressive. Class. Elegance. Knowledgeable.

Something did not seem quite right, but I ignored it. One day she exclaimed excitedly, "Oh, I just love working with homosexuals. They are just so enjoyable. I would rather work around homosexuals than anyone." She was unoffended by the sin of homosexuality.

Obviously, God loves every one of us regardless of our sin. However, anything that *grieves* the heart of God *should* grieve us.

Anything that angers *God* should anger you. Anything that saddens *God* should sadden *you*.

If you insist on dating someone comfortable with rebellious, stubborn, arrogant, God-despising people...you will be heartbroken.

An actress became a personal friend. Excellent conversationalist. Appeared to love God with all of her heart. Continuously I heard, "My best friend this...my best friend that...we have been best friends for a million years." Then, I found out that her best friend has been living with a man for fourteen years. Her best friend sneers at the law of God, belittles preachers and thinks that holy living is a joke. Yet, this was her *best* friend! This was her *confidante*! Yet, she was completely comfortable in the presence of someone living in defiance of God. A godly relationship for us was impossible.

12. *Think Twice If The Atmosphere Of Unbelievers Excites Them.* I once heard the wife of a preacher say, "I just love to go to the shows in Las Vegas. I enjoy Tom Jones and the atmosphere so much! He excites me!" Was I shocked over their divorce later? Of course not. The atmosphere of the ungodly excited her flesh and she *fed* it.

I love the presence of God. I crave His Voice. I am ecstatic over His Word. My favorite atmosphere is not a smoke-filled, curse-saturated, filthy-joking, beer-drinking crowd. My favorite atmosphere is the House of God with hands uplifted, loving, praising and worshipping the One Who created me.

You have no future with someone who insists on fueling their passion in the atmosphere of the ungodly.

13. *Think Twice If They Have An Obsession To Attract The Attention Of The Opposite Sex.* Some women are unhappy unless every man in the room gravitates around her as the "center of attention." I have known men who cannot pass by a mirror without sitting down for a while and staring, mesmerized by their imagined grandeur.

14. *Think Twice If Breaking The Law Is Humorous And Exciting To Them.* When I see a radar detector on the dash of a car, I recognize that I am in the presence of someone who despises restraint, sneers at the law and wants the world to know it.

15. *Think Twice If They Show Little Respect For The Agenda And Schedule Of Others.* I dated a lady for a long time. One night, I waited 45 minutes in the restaurant for her. She finally showed up and explained, "Well, I met some friends that I have not seen in a long time and I just simply forgot the time. Sorry!"

I replied, "I understand. I have been waiting 45 minutes. I regret that the presence of others made you forget me. I am sure God has someone else exciting for your future." It was over. Your respect for the schedule of others reveals much about you.

16. *Think Twice When It Is Obvious That You Will Never Become Their Focus And Assignment.* They may enjoy you, laugh with you and even like you. They may even be truly trustworthy as a confidante, but a Mate is a different matter. When God brings you a Mate, that person becomes your Assignment. The wife of a young preacher was obviously agitated and frustrated. As we drove home from a crusade late one night, she looked at me with great exasperation and said, "I must find out what my Assignment is!"

I replied gently, "He is there *beside* you. God calls him your husband. He is your Assignment. You are his Assignment." She was incensed.

Many marriages of ministers are fragmented today. Good men and women of God are often in miserable marriages. Publicly, their life looks glamorous and exciting. Many are even famous and well known, but they despise their marriage because they have ceased to view *the other* as their true Assignment.

17. *Think Twice When They Embrace An Accusation Against You Before They Have Heard Your Side Of The Matter.* Loyalties will be identified and exposed eventually. The weakness of a very important relationship was exposed to me. Late one night, my telephone rang. The young lady tore into me like a hurricane. Not once did she ask me

if the details of a situation were accurate. She never assumed that those around her might be lying or misinformed. It was absurd. What did I realize? *Truth* was not her focus. My opinion was unimportant. It was a heartbreaking revelation, but I realized that others could lie about me and my explanation would never be valued nor believed.

18.   *Think Twice If They Have Not Exited Previous Relationships Peaceably.*   Many thrive on strife. They will destroy anything they cannot own or control. Peace bores them. Silence nauseates them. Warfare is their fuel. They will speak any words necessary to find the boundary lines and limitations around them. It will be impossible to have an enjoyable marriage with them.

19.   *Think Twice If Their Parents Have Contempt For You Or Your Assignment In Life.* The bloodline is more powerful than anyone can imagine. It is a spiritual thing. It is a spirit connection. God arranged it Himself.   So, you may marry a rebel who even despises his parents...but when crisis comes, he will reach back to the bloodline for affirmation. If you marry someone whose parents look condescendingly upon you because of your lack of education, social class or finances, remember that they will be the *third party* always speaking into the heart of your mate.

20.   *Think Twice If They Refuse To Sit Consistently Under The Mentorship Of A Spiritual Leader*. Changes will not occur without worthy Mentors or uncommon pain. Unwillingness to sit under the Mentorship of a proven man of God is a devastating revelation of potential failure.

21.   *Think Twice If Pebble Problems Unleash Mountains Of Anger In Them*. I will never forget it as long as I live. While sitting with several in a beautiful restaurant, the waiter forgot to bring lime for the water glass of the lady I was dating. She was furious. In fact, not only did she look angry at the waiter, but she decided that his incompetence would become *the focus* of the evening conversation. She could not differentiate between things that were important and things that were trivial.

22.   *Think Twice If They Refuse To Find A Job*. It is a *sin* not to work. I would never allow my daughter to marry a man unwilling to *earn* his living. Money is a reward for solving problems. If you never have any money, you are probably refusing to solve the problems nearest you, or for someone you should.   You often hear of a multimillionaire marrying a waitress he met in a small cafe. Why? He observed her work habits. At three o'clock a.m., she was there bringing pancakes and eggs to truck drivers...with a smile on her face.

It was one of the secrets of Solomon. He only hired happy people. It is important to marry someone happy *before* you enter their life.

Paul warned, "This we commanded you, that if any would not work, neither should he eat. For we hear that there are some which walk among you disorderly, working not at all, but are busybodies...And if any man obey not our word by this epistle, note that man, and *have no company with him*, that he may be ashamed" (2 Thess. 3:10-14).

Productive women excite productive men. It attracted Boaz to Ruth.

23. *Think Twice If Their Own Dreams Are Not Big Enough To Motivate Them.* If they can sleep in all day, watch television all night and refuse to produce anything significant with their life...you better think twice before pouring your life into them. Every person should have a dream big enough to get him out of bed every morning or keep him up at night!

24. *Think Twice If They Are Uncomfortable In The Presence Of God.* As I told one of my sisters, you can date a man who is handsome, has developed muscles and throws you a rose to watch you dive—but if he hates the presence of God, there is little hope of greatness ever being birthed within him. The man you see will never be more than what he is today. Every preacher will become his rival. He will become intimidated by your church attendance. When you come home late after a Wednesday night service, he will accuse you of meeting somebody "on the side." Unsaved men are often intimidated by believing men because they know in their heart that a man who walks with God has something they lack.

25. *Think Twice If They Feel Inferior To You.* True, everyone is superior to others in some way, but it is important that those who walk beside you feel confident, qualified and called of God to be your Mate.

26. *Think Twice If They Do Not Long To Understand And Pleasure You.* Uncommon love longs to pleasure another. Uncommon love seeks every opportunity to communicate itself. What do you enjoy? What books do you love to read? Where do you want to go for vacation? What is your favorite flower? Your Mate should long to know.

27. *Think Twice If Continuous Strife Exists Between Them And Their Parents.* Honoring our parents was the first commandment with a promise. Those who celebrate the authority over their life ultimately succeed.

28. *Think Twice If They Treat The Favor Of Others With Ingratitude.* Countless times, I have paid for meals at restaurants and

never received a single thanks for it. I dated a lady for many months without receiving a thank you for anything I purchased or did for her during that year.

Her explanation, "I simply wasn't taught to say the word 'Thanks.' I will show it in other ways."

Unthankful People Are Always Unhappy People.

29. *Think Twice If They Do Not Have A Hunger To Know The Voice Of God*. Obedience is the secret of every successful person. The Bible is His Voice. If a man or woman disdains the Voice of Truth and Wisdom—they will birth a parade of tragedies and catastrophes.

Their *decisions* will create losses.

Their *weaknesses* will flourish.

Unlawful desires will rage like an inferno.

Such a marriage is an invitation to spiritual suicide.

30. *Think Twice If You Are Not Excited About Introducing Them To Those You Love.* When you are truly in love, that's all you want to talk about. Are you ashamed? Why? Be truthful with yourself.

31. *Think Twice If They Show Little Respect For The Battles You Have Won Throughout Your Lifetime.* Have you mastered prejudice, fears or poverty? When someone loves you, they admire your victories.

32. *Think Twice If Conversation With Them Has Become Burdensome.* I have been with some who left me frazzled and exhausted and I did not know why.

Right people *energize* you.

Wrong people *exhaust* you.

True love will *energize*.

33. *Think Twice If They Make Major Decisions Of Their Life Without Pursuing Your Views Or Counsel.* I was stunned one night when a lady I had dated for some time suddenly said, "I quit my job last week. I'm going to Bible School tomorrow." She had been considering leaving her career for nine months and going to a Bible School. She never told me. It was obvious—my feedback was unimportant.

34. *Think Twice If Your Time Spent With Them Always Ends With Personal Guilt Or Disappointment.* Withdrawal from any relationship occurs if guilt, fear or a sense of entrapment emerges.

35. *Think Twice If People Of Excellence Do Not Surround Them.* Study the kinds of people that your potential mate finds enjoyable. That is a clue to their life and your future with them.

36. *Think Twice If They Are Unwilling To Follow Your Personal*

Advice And Counsel. A godly wife is The Prophetess in the bosom of her husband. A husband should be a Well of Wisdom for his wife.

37. *Think Twice If You Do Not Admire And Respect The Mentor At Whose Feet They Sit.* Their Mentor is feeding either a strength or a weakness. If you oppose their Mentor, a happy marriage is impossible.

38. *Think Twice If You Only Enjoy Them During Your Moments Of Weakness Instead Of Your Moments Of Strength.* One woman explained to me, "I don't really want to be with him. I feel very vulnerable around him. But, I am often lonely. So, when I get so lonely I can't stand it—I accept his invitation for a date." Some relationships exist because of mutual *weakness,* rather than mutual goals.

39. *Think Twice If They Continuously Give You Counsel Contrary To The Word Of God.* The Word of God is Truth. It will withstand any test. It destroys wrong desires within you. It unleashes your faith. It produces hope. It purifies your mind. It is the Master Key to all success on earth. Your reaction to the Word of God determines God's reaction to your own children (see Hos. 4:6). God will become their enemy if they continue to defy His Word. It would be tragic to bond with someone God may ultimately destroy.

40. *Think Twice If Their Presence Does Not Motivate You To A Higher Level Of Excellence.* You already possess weaknesses. You do not require anyone to feed them. Anyone can pull you down. That is why God gives you a Mate to lift you up.

41. *Think Twice If You Cannot Trust Them With The Knowledge Of Your Greatest Weakness.* Each of us contain weaknesses that embarrass us. We despise them. It may be anger, fear or lust. Your Mate is there to strengthen you, not weaken you. If you believe it is necessary to hide your weakness instead of share it, you may have the wrong Mate.

42. *Think Twice If You Cannot Trust Them With Your Finances.* This narrows down the field considerably, doesn't it? Do not bond your life with someone too immature to handle the importance of financial responsibility. One young man explained to me, "I do not want my fiance to know anything about my money or she will spend it. As soon as she discovers I have some extra money, she persuades me to run up my credit cards."

43. *Think Twice If You Cannot Trust Them With Your Most Painful Memories.* Every person is running from a painful memory. Multimillionaires often share that their days of poverty have

motivated them. Their painful memories have driven them to Uncommon Achievement. Some explain a father who beat them mercilessly. It left them marked forever. Memories are keys to understanding another.

44. *Think Twice If You Cannot Trust Them With Your Greatest Fears Or Secrets.* Fear often limits us. It should motivate us...to change. It may be the fear of flying, or the dark. It may be a fear of dying with disease. Whatever it is—think twice if the love is not strong enough to destroy fear. "Perfect love casteth out fear:" (1 Jn. 4:18).

45. *Think Twice If You Cannot Trust Them Around Your Closest Friends.* Flirtation is deadly. The death of many marriages begins with flirtation. It is not harmless. Ever.

46. *Think Twice If You Cannot Trust Them In Your Absence.* Jealously is a cruel dictator and tyrant. It is often unfounded and produced by a painful memory of disloyalty or betrayal. Yet, I have seen many marriages unravel because of a deep sense of distrust. Note the signals.

47. *Think Twice If You Cannot Trust Them To Pursue God Without Your Constant Encouragement.* Several years ago, I met an exciting woman. She was one of the most articulate, vibrant and lovable humans I had ever known. I tried hard to push the relationship through, to engagement and marriage, but it was this key that opened my understanding. She only attended church because of my persistence, nagging and begging. She really did not know God at all. Nor did she truly desire God. Without the authority of God in her life, any hope of a happy marriage with her was a mere fantasy. Bring your potential Mate into God's presence with you. Talk to God together. Truth will emerge in His presence that cannot emerge anywhere else. Interrogation will never produce what His presence will.

Invest the Seed of time...and watch it grow. Time will expose what a thousand investigators could never produce.

Define your present relationships honestly and clearly. If you persist in an unwholesome relationship, painful consequences will teach you. Never lean to your own understanding. Lean to the heart of God. Ask the Holy Spirit what He sees in those near you. He always will reveal truth to the seeker.

Recognition Of The Mate God Approves For You Will Bring Years Of Joy, Enthusiasm And Fulfillment.

≈ 11 ≈

DEPRESSION

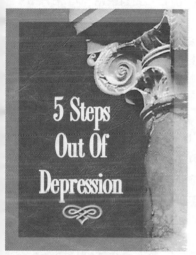

5 Steps
Out Of
Depression

It Was Past Midnight.

The crusade was over and I sat in an expensive home of the fine pastor of a very successful church. Two Cadillacs were parked in the drive. From *outward* appearance, life couldn't be better.

Yet, he was weeping.

"I have been in the ministry more than 20 years. God has blessed me more than I ever dreamed. Yet, I have been living with a depression that has brought me to the very brink of leaving the ministry. It is like a wave about to drown me and my entire family. What in the world is going wrong?"

Frankly, I had no pat answers. All I knew was that this scene was being repeated all too often in the ministry. *And if this was happening to clergymen, the leadership, what must be happening to our people?*

Certainly there are normal setbacks that motivate us to action. Temporary knocks that deflate our arrogance. But the depression in my minister friend was not the Godly sorrow of 2 Corinthians 7:8-10 that "worketh repentance..." It was the sorrow of disobedience that *worketh death.*

Your *motivation* is drained.

Your desire to *pursue* God is gone.

Your *conversations* become sour.

You are *blinded* to current blessings.

Your enthusiasm is *forced.*

You are *in a daze* regarding future plans.

You see *thorns* instead of *roses.*

There are *five steps* you can take out of such a state of mind. *There is a way out!* And it is a condition of the mind! *"...for as he thinketh in his heart, so is he..."* (Prov. 23:7). So, Paul encourages *thought-control.* "...whatsoever things are true...honest...just...pure...

lovely...of good report...think *on these things"* (Phil. 4:8).

My father calls it "The Whatsoever-Formula." Your depression can be *temporary*. Our Heavenly Father will *"give thee rest from thy sorrow"* (Isa. 14:3). Read on in faith! Regardless of how dark your circumstances, God's Word *"giveth light"* (Ps. 119:130).

1. *Understand That Depression Can Come To Every One Of Us.* Your feelings are not unique or unusual. Biographies of notables Abraham Lincoln and Winston Churchill record periods of great depression of these gifted personalities.

According to one survey by the National Institute of Mental Health, at any one time, perhaps one-third of the population is *experiencing* depression!

The Bible fascinates us with such details about the feelings of *highs* and *lows* of Spirit-filled men!

DAVID, a musician and king, sobbed: "Why art thou cast down, O my soul? and why art thou disquieted within me?" (Ps. 42:11).

One preacher thought the motel business would be better than the ministry! *JEREMIAH* cried, "Oh that I had in the wilderness a lodging place of wayfaring men; that I might leave my people, and go from them" (Jer. 9:2).

Even a *prophet* lost confidence in people: *MICAH* cried, "The best of them is as a brier: the most upright is sharper than a thorn hedge...Trust ye not in a friend..." (Micah 7:4,5).

That *man of power, ELIJAH*, who outran horses for 30 miles, was fed miracle-meals by birds and called down fire on water-soaked sacrifices, once became so despondent he asked God to KILL him! (see 1 Kings 19).

JONAH, famous graduate of *"Whale University,"* had 120,000 converts in a single crusade. Yet, later, he begged God to take his life: "O Lord, take, I beseech Thee, my life from me; for it is better for me to die than to live" (Jon. 4:3).

As one of my longtime friends once stated: "Depression came when Jonah's personal *security* was more important than the *souls* of people."

Even the rich and wise *SOLOMON* confessed that he came to a place that he *"hated life"* (read Ecc. 2:17).

2. *Recognize The Danger Of Depression.* A nonchalant mother shocked me: "Oh, my teenager stays depressed. I guess it's the stage he's in."

We treat depression too lightly. Depression can *result* in broken homes, physical breakdown, suicides and attempts, spiritual breakdown and countless other sorrows.

Broken Homes: A depressed mate exaggerates the negative side of his marriage, thinking, "Maybe I made a mistake." The parade of home-wrecking thoughts can become endless.

Physical Breakdowns: The National Institute of Mental Health has estimated that 125,000 Americans are hospitalized annually with depression. Another 200,000 get aid from psychiatrists.

Suicide: Between 50,000 to 70,000 people commit suicide every year. It's estimated that over one million attempt it!

Two brokenhearted parents wrote me: "Our daughter attended church regularly. She appeared to be as happy as any normal 18 year old. Suddenly for a few days she became withdrawn. Last week we walked into her room and found her dead. *She took her own life.*"

Among all the persons being treated for depression in hospitals and clinics, nearly twenty percent are under 18. The suicide rate among 15 to 19 year olds has DOUBLED in the last ten ye*ars.* In a national survey of persons between 18 to 74 years of age, those under 29 showed the highest incidence of depression.

By the way, *listening* parents often mean the difference between life and death for their frustrated teenagers.

Spiritual Breakdown: Millions of Christians who wouldn't lie, cheat or kill are immobilized by frustrations and paralyzed in their pursuit of spiritual goals.

3. *Find The Basic Cause And Scriptural Solution To Your Depressions.* Though medical doctors speak of physical cycles and "highs and lows," *all depression is not necessarily physical.* Be honest with yourself. Pinpoint your CAUSE of stress and take it to God.

Unconfessed sin is like a rock in your shoe. *Get it out!* If hidden sin is bringing inner frustration, no vacation or doctor will heal it. "But your *iniquities* have separated between you and your God, and your sins have hid His face from you..." (Isa. 59:2).

Greed for gain will begin an avalanche of despondency. King Ahab's obsession for Naboth's vineyard affected the entire family: "He that is greedy of gain troubleth his own house..." (Prov. 15:27). Jesus knew the danger: "Beware of covetousness: for a man's life consisteth not in the abundance of the things which he possesseth" (Lk. 12:15).

Making comparisons is a sure road to frustration. One young pastor lamented, "When I hear a conference speaker share a personal success story, I feel like a *lawn mower* in a Cadillac showroom. Where is God when *I* pray?"

As one of my friends has said many times, *"Comparing* has brought more people unhappiness than they could ever imagine."

Taking criticism personally can bring depression to the person who forgets that "Poverty and shame shall be to him that refuseth instruction: but he that regardeth reproof shall be honoured" (Prov. 13:18).

Many years ago, while lunching with a pastor during a crusade in Dallas, Texas, he shared with me a wise observation: "Mike, our brethren help to keep us *balanced.*" I believe that. On the other hand, seeking *people approval* is a quick road to inner turmoil.

Fault-finding. One friend noted an inner depression when he indulged in revealing the flaws of others: "The words of a talebearer are as wounds..." (Prov. 18:8). God brought healing through the Word: "Whoso keepeth his mouth and his tongue keepeth his soul from troubles" (Prov. 21:23). Guard your conversations. *Your words can create death or life.*

Impatience has impoverished thousands. Despondent youth, blinded to the benefits of *waiting,* become runaways, dropouts, premature parents, and candidates for divorce.

An unforgiving attitude will drain your joy. David Wilkerson, author of "The Cross and the Switchblade," once said that a major problem he encountered among teens involved bitterness and hatred toward parents.

Many youth have found a *new world* of power and victorious living when a *forgiving spirit* was allowed to control their lives: "And when ye stand praying, *forgive,* if ye have ought against any: that your Father also which is in Heaven may forgive you your trespasses" (Mk. 11:25).

Fatigue is a major cause of depression. One renowned U.S. President refused to make major decisions at the end of the day. He insisted on a *rested* body and mind before committing himself on any issue.

Leaders have learned the power and strength of systematic recuperation.

"For 10 years I lived knowing I missed God's perfect plan," one pastor confessed. "Weariness and mental fatigue blinded me to the fruits of my labors in a pastorate. Impulsively, I resigned. A few weeks later I realized the serious mistake. *Complete rest and relaxation with my family would have changed everything.*"

If we refuse Christ's invitation to come apart and rest awhile, we usually *come apart!*

4. *Take Immediate Action!* In one of my crusades, one lady said that she had felt a cloud over her home for months. "Divorce," she had decided, "is the only answer." Unaware of her situation, I preached the message, "*Stay on Board.*" "If you think the '*Sea of Divorce*' is better than your '*Ship of Marriage,*' you're in for the heartache of your life." That sentence lodged in her mind. And the next one was revolutionary for her. "*Stay on board* and give God a chance to bring you to a harbor!"

Putting her doubts aside, she placed new faith in God and vowed new efforts to make her marriage work. *One week later her husband was wonderfully converted to Christ.*

You should *anticipate* and *plan* for personal victory! Sometimes what begins in tragedy ends in *triumph!*

Consider Daniel—from *lions' bait* to *honor.*

The Three Hebrew Children—from *fiery furnace* to *awe* and *approval.*

Joseph—from a *slave* to a *prime minister.*

Jesus—from the *Cross* to the *Resurrection.*

You can begin stepping out of depression now!

Enter into *joy.* Enter into *rest.*

Enter into the power-life.

Enjoy the Winner's World!

You are more than a conqueror. *You can!* Paul said, "*I can do ALL things through Christ which strengtheneth me*" (Phil. 4:13). God has assured us, "*...My grace is sufficient for thee...*" (2 Cor. 12:9).

Believe it! Do not let the words, the failures, the opinions of people crush you. Declare the promises of God. *Boldly. Aloud. Often.*

5. *Practice Three Secrets Of Power-Living Daily.*

Respect the opinions of God concerning your life. (Intake Scripture daily.)

Habitualize your morning talks with God. (Commit to one hour of prayer each day.)

Faith talk. (Repeat *aloud* the viewpoint of God.)

First: *Your Wisdom Hour.* Someone has said, "Many people can find the secret of a defeated life in a *neglected Bible.*" Of all activities, satan will attack this practice vehemently. *Just make up your mind to read the Word daily!* Start by *starting.* Do by *doing.*

Second: *Your Morning Talks With God.* Oswald J. Smith has said the happiest moments of his life were during prayer and Bible time called his "Morning Watch." His praying aloud prevented wandering thoughts. His walking insured against dozing!

In Calcutta, India, a renowned missionary friend of mine often stopped in the midst of our conversations to pray for various needs. This is the secret behind God's great work in Calcutta.

He who majors on *achievements* will find his thrills short-lived; but the child of God who majors on his *relationship* to the Father will find the well of joy endless...springing up with new victories daily.

Third: *Faith Talk And Word Declaration.* It simply means to say *aloud* what is *written* in the Word! Your conversations will develop problem-consciousness or create promise-awareness. Cultivate promise-awareness!

As I write these words, I am looking across famous Lake Victoria in Kisumu, Kenya, East Africa. Sitting here in the home of outstanding missionaries, it is easy to forget that they must encounter cultural barriers, endure separation from children in boarding schools, work alone without closest friends and confidants, prepare meals without the all-accommodating American supermarkets, and live with unbelievable delays and frustrating mechanical breakdowns.

THEIR SECRET?

They refuse the *oral confession* of defeat. They have learned to *activate Word power by praise.* With infectious laughter and practice of Proverbs 16:24: *"Pleasant words are...health to the bones."* This turns miserable experiences into *praise sessions.* Small wonder their lives have counted so beautifully for God here in East Africa!

So remember, you are the property of God! You will not lose to depression. *You will win over every circumstance as long as He is your Source and Focus.*

I sat at lunch recently in Lagos, Nigeria. My father and I were the guests in the home of my dear friend, Bishop David Oyedepo. He shared some changing truths that are influencing me greatly:

1. Gratitude Provokes Joy.
2. Joy Provokes Praise.
3. Praise Provokes Divine Presence.

Gratitude ultimately cures depression.

∼ 12 ∼

DISCIPLINE

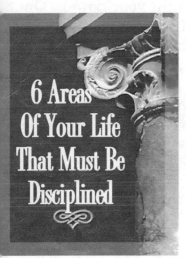

6 Areas Of Your Life That Must Be Disciplined

The Key To Victory, Power And Reward In Every Part Of Your Life Is Personal Discipline.

Every athletic champion and Olympic winner practices discipline. In fact, almost without exception, winners are successful because of discipline, which gives birth to *success-habits.*

Not only does discipline hone the mind and condition the body, it produces an important side effect—*security.* Just as a child, who receives discipline from its parents, feels secure in their love, so the person who practices self-discipline is confident that good things will happen to them instead of bad. Paul said, "...I keep under my body, and bring it into subjection..." (1 Cor. 9:27).

So the athlete knows what his body will do when he calls on it to perform in the contest. The scholar knows his mind will produce the answers he needs because he has *disciplined* it to be alert and prepared. And the Christian young person knows how he will react in the face of temptation because he has *disciplined* his moral and spiritual nature to *overcome* evil.

1. *Discipline Your Conversation.* Speak always in positive terms, from a position of faith and awareness of what God wants from you. Avoid negative words, such as "I can't...I'm weak...I always fail." Instead, say, "I can overcome all sin. I am getting stronger in the Lord. I can do all things through Christ, which strengtheneth me."

2. *Discipline Your Reading Habits.* Be sure you spend at least ten minutes each morning in the Word of God. There is no possibility of living the true victorious, happy life apart from a daily intake of the Scriptures. They will make you strong and keep you free: "The law of his God is in his heart; none of his steps shall slide" (Ps. 37:31). Be sure everything else you read contributes to your well-being.

3. *Discipline Your Prayer Life.* Stay in constant, personal

contact with God. Be sure you are on speaking terms with Him. Develop and cultivate an up-to-date prayer list.

4. *Discipline Your Friendships.* Refuse to associate with losers who pull you down. Choose friends who will be the kind of associates you'd like to spend your whole life with.

5. *Discipline Yourself With Regard To The Music You Listen To, The Television Programs You Watch And The Entertainment You Choose.* Control the circumstances that are within your power. One teenage girl finally admitted to me that she had schemed to find ways to be alone with her boyfriend when she knew she was too weak to say "no" to wrong. If you can't refuse temptation—at least you can *avoid* it. But it takes discipline.

6. *Finally, Discipline Your Church Attendance.* Develop inner strength by exposing yourself often to the atmosphere of a spiritual church service. Honor the spiritual mentors God places in your life.

Discipline is the first step to uncommon success.

RECOMMENDED BOOKS AND TAPES ON THIS TOPIC

B-17   Seeds of Wisdom on Overcoming (Book/$3)

TS-9   Secrets of the Greatest Achievers Who Ever Lived, Vol. 1 (Six tapes/$30)

TS-10   Secrets of the Greatest Achievers Who Ever Lived, Vol. 2 (Six tapes/$30)

TS-85   School of Wisdom, Vol. 1 - The Uncommon Life (Six tapes/$30)

❧ 13 ❧

DIVORCE

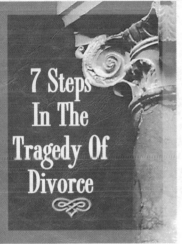

7 Steps
In The
Tragedy Of
Divorce

Divorce Destroys.

It has been said that divorce is the greatest emotional pain that the human heart can experience.

I believe it.

It destroys the *sense of worth* we desperately crave. It has brought heartache to millions. The scars are carried for a lifetime.

My purpose in this chapter is not to multiply the memories, or magnify the scars, nor to condemn. My purpose is to heal, to strengthen, to restore purpose and to aid in total recovery.

Jesus knew the intense pain divorce could bring. "For this cause shall a man leave his father and mother, and cleave to his wife; And they twain shall be one flesh: so then they are no more twain, but one flesh. What therefore God hath joined together, let not man put asunder" (Mk. 10:7-9).

Many divorced people write to me every week asking whether they are "living in sin,"...or whether they will have committed the "unpardonable sin" if they should remarry after divorce. Too many times ministers tend to either compromise or condemn because of lack of sufficient information, past prejudiced teaching or inexperience.

It often seems that those who *cause* the divorce *rarely* seek help. Seldom do they search for solid answers, consult consistently with counselors, nor do they assume personal responsibility for their conflicts. Yet, these people are almost always the *only* targets of the sermons preached to the divorced! The *victim* of divorce is often ignored and many times treated like the one who *caused* the divorce! It is like the *raped,* instead of the rapist, *being brought to trial!* For that reason, I want to focus on how to keep a *winning* attitude even when the stigma of divorce has touched your life.

At the age of 32, I had experienced a measure of success as a young evangelist who had traveled in more than 30 countries in crusades. I had been married for thirteen years and loved it. Quite frankly, I was quite critical of those who had unhappy marriages. Something was wrong with their personalities, I reasoned, or they really didn't try very hard, or they simply didn't exercise enough "positive thinking" and faith in God!

Then, suddenly, it happened to me. I was faced with a situation that was overwhelming. My emotions "went crazy." One minute I was full of faith; the next moment fear would seize my heart. I saw a lifetime of dreams evaporate before my very eyes.

And I felt totally helpless.

Of course, everyone around had good answers. (They had the same answers I had before I was *"there!"* It's always easier to tell the next man how to swim when you are not in the water with him!)

Oh, I knew God. I knew the *principles* taught in the Scriptures. I had spent years studying total success and victorious living.

But, I felt like an utter failure. It seemed that everything I had believed, lived and tried to teach had backfired. There was only one thing I knew to *do...stay connected to God.*

And somehow I did.

I might add, God does restore. Over 5,000 songs have been written from the various pages of that experience. Songs such as, "You Can Make It," "I Am Blessed," "God's Not Through Blessing You," and many others. I value God more than ever before. And I have cultivated more *discerning* to sense integrity, character and honesty. Oh, yes, and I've learned to *release* hostility, anger and bitterness *out* of my life.

I would like to share part of my experience with you. First, I found *me* blaming myself, Mike Murdock, for every single failure I could recall in my life! My thoughts were on *past* circumstances instead of *future* challenges! Everything I had ever done wrong was reprogrammed into my daily "diet of memories."

I chewed, and re-chewed old memories until I discovered the reason God gave us Isaiah 43:18,19: "Remember ye not the former things, neither consider the things of old. Behold, I will do a new thing; now it shall spring forth; shall ye not know it? I will even make a way in the wilderness, and rivers in the desert." *God gave me the power to break a mind-fixation on the past,* and increased my ability to picture the "blessings of tomorrow."

Have you been crushed by someone you *totally trusted?* Have you felt *devastated* and *ruined?* Are you overwhelmed by loneliness in *the midnight hours?* Do you feel as though your hands are completely tied? Does it anger you to see friends *lacking* understanding?

Do not become weary.

Your present circumstances will change.

You will rebuild. You will *grow.* You will not *stay* down.

You will win again.

It will take a little time.

You will have to invest some effort. And you may experience some pages of darkness in your "Diary of Success." But, you will start enjoying life *again,* loving *again* and learn the *real* secrets of inner power and peace.

Elizabeth Kubler-Ross, who did much work on how persons deal with the process of dying, discovered that many people process through different stages. I recognized some of these stages as descriptive of my own emotions following the breakup of my marriage.

1. *The Stage Of Denial.*

This is when we ignore or minimize what has happened to our marriage and home in hopes that it will just go away. We fear confrontation and refuse to face it. This is why many marriages fail. We won't go for help in hopes it will all just "work out in the end."

2. *The Stage Of Anger.*

What we do not understand, we fear.

What we fear, we fight.

What we fight, we fragment and destroy.

At this point, we make wild unchecked statements that are born out of emotional chaos such as "Good! I'm glad it's over! You just wait, I'll find someone who *really* loves me and appreciates me." *Divorce is a rejection.* Rejection means *devaluation.* Our self-confidence is attacked and *our defense is anger.*

3. *The Stage Of Bargaining.*

Anger will never create permanent cooperation from another. So, seeing the *futility* of anger, we deftly apply the technique of *bargaining,* or seeking a solution or compromise. We justify or use other means to find the ability to accept the tragedy of rejection, loss or failure.

4. *The Stage Of Depression.*

This happens at the most inappropriate times...special days, birthdays, anniversaries, at restaurants with friends, or at 2:00 a.m., when we just cannot go to sleep.

Depression is usually the result of introspection. The cure is to discipline our thoughts toward a goal in our future or to concentrate on helping *someone else* achieve a worthy goal. Use memories for *ministering* to others, not meditation! It is impossible to *think wrong... and feel good* at the same time.

5. *The Stage Of Acceptance.*

Believe it or not, acceptance *can* and eventually does come. When it does, you will almost feel a tinge of guilt for not feeling depressed and sad! It does not come because you lose compassion or caring for those in your "past chapters" of living, but because the beauty of your days *ahead* becomes more evident. *You see recovery.* You taste the sweetness of new achievements. A climate of *peace* evolves... *You enter your future.*

I have experienced two additional stages relative to divorce.

6. *The Stage Of Hope.*

Peace is a *present* need. Hope is the motivation for *tomorrow.* It says, "I will live and love again! My life is not over." *Purpose* is discovered. *Friendships* develop. You start growing rapidly. Emotionally, you age fast...and it becomes an *advantage.*

7. *The Stage Of Fulfillment.*

Whether it is a *new* relationship, a new career, or some particular achievement, God will see to it that you find fulfillment again. *Dare to believe that.* That is the place where complaining is never heard. Neither do we rehearse old memories of failure. We stop recycling our emotional "bandages" through the ears of friends. We are happier about tomorrow and everyone knows it.

Now, I do not know what particular stage you are presently experiencing. But, I assure you, that *you can start winning again.* You really can.

So, put your shoulders back. Hold your head up high. *Stop discussing* your moments of failure and start sharing your future successes, joys and triumphs. Your best days are *not* behind you, they are just *ahead.*

See it. *Feel* it. *Live* it.

RECOMMENDED BOOKS AND TAPES ON THIS TOPIC

B-02   Five Steps Out of Depression (Book/$3)
B-10   The Bridge Called Divorce (Book/$3)
B-19   Seeds of Wisdom on Warfare (Book/$3)
TS-69   Wisdom for Crisis Times (Six tapes/$30)

❧ 14 ❧

DREAMS AND GOALS

24 Facts About Uncommon Dreams ∞

God Talks Through Pictures.

He communicated through Abraham with a picture. "That in blessing I will bless thee, and in multiplying I will multiply thy Seed as the stars of the Heaven, and as the sand which is upon the sea shore; and thy Seed shall possess the gate of his enemies;" (Gen. 22:17).

He communicated to Joseph with a picture in a dream. "Behold, I have dreamed a dream more; and, behold, the sun and the moon and the eleven stars made obeisance to me" (Gen. 37:9).

At some time, God will birth within you an invisible picture of your future. That "Uncommon Dream" will be something you can *do,* something you can *become* or something you can *have.* God uses this Uncommon Dream to provide focus, progression and enthusiasm.

Satan will develop a strategy to *cloud* this picture and paralyze this Uncommon Dream.

You must recognize The Dream that God uses to stir hope, inspire direction and make you a blessing to others.

The Uncommon Dream Within You

1. *You Must Continually Visualize This Uncommon Dream In Your Heart And Mind.* "Write the vision, and make it plain upon tables, that he may run that readeth it" (Hab. 2:2).

2. *An Uncommon Dream Will Require Uncommon Patience.* "For the vision is yet for an appointed time, but at the end it shall speak, and not lie: though it tarry, wait for it; because it will surely come, it will not tarry" (Hab. 2:3).

3. *God Is Committed To The Uncommon Dream He Is Birthing, Whether You Embrace It Yet Or Not.* Peter made continuous mistakes.

But Jesus said, "I have prayed for thee, that thy faith fail not: and when thou art converted, strengthen thy brethren" (Lk. 22:32).

4. *An Uncommon Dream Is Often Birthed From Uncommon Pain.* Those raised in poverty often develop a passion for prosperity. Those with childhood disease become obsessed in helping others develop great health.

5. *An Uncommon Dream Will Require Uncommon Faith.* Read the biographies of uncommon men and women. Those with uncommon achievements nurtured the Seed of faith until it became a raging Force within them.

6. *The Uncommon Dream Must Be Born Within You, Not Borrowed From Others.* Others have opinions but you have direction. You alone will receive the confirmation from God for the achieving of the Dream He has birthed. Joseph had nobody else to encourage him—but he believed in his own Dream.

7. *The Uncommon Dream Will Require Uncommon Focus.* The Only Reason Men Fail Is Broken Focus. You will only succeed with something that consumes you. When God gives you The Uncommon Dream—it will require all of you—your time, your love and energy.

8. *The Uncommon Dream Will Require Uncommon Passion.* Passion is energy, enthusiasm and strength. Passion is a clue to the path the Holy Spirit has chosen for your life. Now, it is possible to have a passion for something that is unholy. But, it is important that you recognize that any uncommon achievement will require uncommon passion from God.

9. *The Uncommon Dream Will Require Uncommon Favor With Others.* Joseph received favor from Potiphar and Pharaoh. Esther received favor from the king. Ruth received favor from Boaz. When the hand of God is upon you, favor will come. Sow it. Expect it. Protect it. Respect it.

10. *The Uncommon Dream Will Require Uncommon Preparation.* Jesus prepared 30 years for 3½ years of ministry. Some call it— "short term pain for long term gain." Some vocations require many years of college before a person is prepared for it.

11. *The Uncommon Dream Will Qualify Those Who Deserve Access To You.* Many reach for you, but it is important that you *qualify* those who deserve access. Jesus never went home with Pharisees, yet had an entire meal with Zacchaeus, the tax collector.

12. *The Uncommon Dream Will Birth Uncommon Habits.* When a wealthy lady focused on developing the greatest company ever for

women, she started writing down her plans every morning. She selected six things in the order of their priority. At her death, her company was worth 1.3 billion dollars. You see, your Dream controls the habits you birth. When Muhammad Ali "saw himself" as heavyweight champion, he began to get up early in the morning for special roadwork. Champions are willing to do *daily* what ordinary men will only do *occasionally*.

13. *An Uncommon Dream Creates Uncommon Adversaries.* Nehemiah saw opposition erupt suddenly when God birthed within him the desire to rebuild the walls of Jerusalem. Whatever you decide to do, you will encounter opposition that will astound and shock you. It may come from your own family!

14. *The Uncommon Dream Will Determine What You Do First Each Morning.* Your obsession will determine the use of your time.

15. *The Uncommon Dream Is Usually The Opposite Of Your Present Circumstances.* Joseph was hated and despised by his brothers. They sold him into slavery for $12.80. Yet, The Uncommon Dream within his heart was that of his brothers submitting to him. It was the opposite of his present! Abraham and Sarah were too old to have children. Yet, The Uncommon Dream from God was Isaac, the beginning of millions. It was the opposite of their present.

16. *The Uncommon Dream Will Require The Miracles Of God.* God will never birth a Dream within you that is achievable without Him. He gives you The Dream to keep you connected to Him and to perpetuate His plans and desires. It will require Him to complete it.

17. *An Uncommon Dream Will Always Require The Assistance Of Others.* Keep a list of the top 12 people necessary to complete your Dream. God used 12 tribes to develop His Dream. Jesus used 12 disciples. The New Jerusalem even has 12 gates. Define your expectations of these 12. Plan a reward for their participation.

Dexter Yeager is one of the most uncommon men I have ever met. In his book, "Don't Let Anybody Steal Your Dream" he writes, "The successful person associates with those who *support* his Dream." Believe it. You must develop people around you who believe in your dream.

18. *The Uncommon Dream May Require Uncommon Negotiations With Others.* Sam Walton did this. When he wanted to create the number one store in America, he went to his vendors and negotiated for lower prices.

19. *The Uncommon Dream Will Require An Uncommon Plan.*

The command is not the plan. The command can take a *moment*. The plan can involve your *lifetime*. In a moment, God gave Noah an instruction to build the ark, but the instructions were specific and required precision.

20. *When You Announce Your Uncommon Dream, Those Who Believe In You Will Be Encouraged And Energized To Assist You.* You have given them a reason to function in your world. Define their position and release them to work!

21. *When You Announce An Uncommon Dream, Those Who Are Tempted To Oppose You May Decide To Join You Because Of Your Determination.*

Boldness is magnetic. It turns barriers into bridges. Weak people become strong in the presence of those who are bold.

22. *When You Announce An Uncommon Dream, You Make It More Difficult To Fail.* Your declaration removes the option to turn back and quit.

23. *When You Announce Your Uncommon Dream, You Will Create An Instant Bond With Those Who Have Had A Similar Desire And Goal.* Others want to assist you, because they believe in the same Dream.

24. *An Uncommon Dream Will Require Careful And Wise Use Of Your Time.* Great Dreams require much time. Become time-conscious. Make every hour produce a specific task for you.

Recognition Of A Divine And Uncommon Dream Birthed By God Will Unlock Your Greatest Ideas, Creativity And Energy To Create A Truly Uncommon Life.

RECOMMENDED BOOKS AND TAPES ON THIS TOPIC
B-08   Enjoying the Winning Life (Book/$3)
B-09   Four Forces That Guarantee Career Success (Book/$3)
B-11   Dream Seeds (Book/$9)
B-13   Seeds of Wisdom on Dreams and Goals (Book/$3)
B-22   Seeds of Wisdom on Prosperity (Book/$3)
B-28   The Blessing Bible (Book/$10)
B-65   Born to Taste the Grapes (Book/$3)
B-99   Secrets of the Richest Man Who Ever Lived (Book/$10)
B-104   7 Keys to 1000 Times More (Book/$10)
TS-11   Dream Seeds (Six tapes/$30)

❧ 15 ❧

ENEMIES

92 Facts
About
Your Enemies

Jesus Always Had Enemies.

Scriptures reveal this in His own words. Jesus Recognized His Enemies. "Why go ye about to kill Me?" (Jn. 7:19). Any Uncommon Achiever must recognize an adversary.

The Common resent *The Uncommon.*

The Impure despise *The Pure.*

The Unholy hate *The Holy.*

The Lazy despise *The Diligent.*

3 Facts Jesus Revealed About Enemies

1. *Jesus Expected His Disciples To Stir Up Enemies.* "And ye shall be hated of all men for My name's sake:" (Matt. 10:22). "The disciple is not above his master, nor the servant above his lord. It is enough for the disciple that he be as his master, and the servant as his lord. If they have called the master of the house Beelzebub, how much more shall they call them of his household?" (Matt. 10:24,25).

2. *Jesus Instructed His Disciples To Anticipate Enemies.* "Behold, I send you forth as sheep in the midst of wolves: be ye therefore wise as serpents, and harmless as doves" (Matt. 10:16).

3. *Jesus Warned His Disciples Ahead Of Time That Men Would Become Their Enemies.* "But beware of men: for they will deliver you up to the councils, and they will scourge you in their synagogues; And ye shall be brought before governors and kings for My sake, for a testimony against them and the Gentiles" (Matt. 10:17,18).

Jesus did not merely warn them of the devil.

Jesus warned them of *men.*

92 Facts About Your Enemies

1. *You Will Always Have An Enemy.* Jesus knew it. "And ye shall be hated of all men for My name's sake: but he that endureth to

the end shall be saved" (Matt. 10:22).

2. *Your Enemy Is Anyone Who Attempts To Sabotage The Assignment God Has For Your Life.* "Ye did run well; who did hinder you that ye should not obey the truth? This persuasion cometh not of Him that calleth you. A little leaven leaveneth the whole lump" (Gal. 5:7-9). "If thy brother, the son of thy mother, or thy son, or thy daughter, or the wife of thy bosom, or thy friend, which is as thine own soul, entice thee secretly, saying, Let us go and serve other gods, which thou hast not known, thou, nor thy fathers; Thou shalt not consent unto him, nor hearken unto him; neither shall thine eye pity him, neither shalt thou spare, neither shalt thou conceal him: But thou shalt surely kill him; thine hand shall be first upon him to put him to death, and afterwards the hand of all the people" (Deut. 13:6,8,9).

3. *Your Enemy Is Any Person Who Resents Your Desire For Increase And The Rewards It Brings.* David experienced this from his oldest brother. "And Eliab his eldest brother heard when he spake unto the men; and Eliab's anger was kindled against David, and he said, Why camest thou down hither? and with whom hast thou left *those few sheep* in the wilderness? I know thy pride, and the naughtiness of thine heart; for thou art come down that thou mightest see the battle" (1 Sam. 17:28).

4. *Your Enemy Is Anyone Unhappy Over Your Progress.* Nehemiah faced this. Ezra faced this. They "hired counsellors against them, to frustrate their purpose" (Ezra 4:5).

Accusations are hurled and often believed.

Letters are written and often believed.

"Now when the copy of king Artaxerxes letter was read before Rehum, and Shimshai the scribe, and their companions, they went up in haste to Jerusalem unto the Jews, and made them to cease by force and power. Then ceased the work of the house of God which is at Jerusalem" (Ezra 4:23,24).

5. *Your Enemy Is Anyone Who Increases Or Strengthens A Personal Weakness God Is Attempting To Remove From Your Life.* Delilah breathed life into the weakness of Samson. She was his Enemy (read Judges 16).

6. *Your Enemy Is Anyone That Attempts To Kill The Faith That God Is Birthing Within You.* God may be birthing your ministry. Your vision may be exploding. Your Enemy is any person who makes any attempt to abort the emergence of that Dream, Calling or Assignment.

7. *Your Enemy Is Anyone Who Would Rather Discuss Your Past*

Than Your Future. Yesterday is over. "Remember ye not the former things, neither consider the things of old. Behold, I will do a new thing; now it shall spring forth; shall ye not know it? I will even make a way in the wilderness, and rivers in the desert" (Isa. 43:18,19).

When Jesus stood at the scene of the woman caught in adultery, revelation exploded. Men were present, obsessed with her mistake, ready to stone her. But, Jesus was looking at her *future.* With one single stroke of mercy, He *removed* her past: "Neither do I condemn thee" (Jn. 8:11). Then, in a masterful stroke of the Master Artist, He painted a portrait of her *future:* "Go, and sin no more" (Jn. 8:11).

8. *Your Enemy Is Anyone Who Weakens Your Passion For Your Future And Your Dream.* The ten spies were used by the Enemy to weaken the resolve of Moses to enter Canaan. The crowd instructed the blind man to be quiet. "And many charged him that he should hold his peace: but he cried the more a great deal, Thou Son of David, have mercy on me" (Mk. 10:48).

9. *Your Enemy Is Anyone Who Attacks The Weak Around You.* Some in your life are too weak to discern a trap. They are blinded by personality, looks or even financial blessing.

10. *Your Enemy Is Sometimes Those Of Your Own Household.* "And a man's foes shall be they of his own household" (Matt.10:36).

11. *Your Enemy Should Not Be Feared.* "And fear not them which kill the body, but are not able to kill the soul: but rather fear Him which is able to destroy both soul and body in hell" (Matt. 10:28).

12. *The Perfect Will Of God Is Your Deliverance From Your Enemy.* "And that we may be delivered from unreasonable and wicked men: for all men have not faith" (2 Thess. 3:2).

13. *The Holy Spirit Will Provide Answers Concerning Your Enemy.* "But when they deliver you up, take no thought how or what ye shall speak: for it shall be given you in that same hour what ye shall speak. For it is not ye that speak, but the Spirit of your Father which speaketh in you" (Matt. 10:19,20).

14. *Your Enemy Is Often Discerned Ahead Of Time By Your Mentor.* Jesus prepared Peter. "And the Lord said, Simon, Simon, behold, satan hath desired to have you, that he may sift you as wheat: But I have prayed for thee, that thy faith fail not: and when thou art converted, strengthen thy brethren" (Lk. 22:31,32).

15. *Your Fasting Can Move The Hand Of God In Destroying Your Enemy.* The Old Testament prophets knew this. "Blow the trumpet in Zion, sanctify a fast, call a solemn assembly:...And I will no more make

you a reproach among the heathen:...But I will remove far off from you the northern army, and will drive him into a land barren and desolate, with his face toward the east sea, and his hinder part toward the utmost sea, and his stink shall come up, and his ill savour shall come up, because he hath done great things" (Joel 2:15,19,20).

16. *God Will Fight For You Against Your Enemy.* "For the Lord your God is He that goeth with you, to fight for you against your enemies, to save you" (Deut. 20:4).

17. *Your Enemy Will Not Be Allowed By God To Win.* "The Lord is on my side; I will not fear: what can man do unto me?" (Ps. 118:6).

18. *Your Enemy Is A Natural And Necessary Part Of Your Life.* "If the world hate you, ye know that it hated Me before it hated you. If ye were of the world, the world would love his own: but because ye are not of the world, but I have chosen you out of the world, therefore the world hateth you. Remember the word that I said unto you, The servant is not greater than his lord. If they have persecuted Me, they will also persecute you; if they have kept My saying, they will keep yours also. But all these things will they do unto you for My name's sake, because they know not Him that sent Me" (Jn. 15:18-21).

19. *Satan Is Your Eternal Enemy.* "For we wrestle not against flesh and blood, but against principalities, against powers, against the rulers of the darkness of this world, against spiritual wickedness in high places" (Eph. 6:12).

20. *You Cannot Defeat Your Enemy In Your Own Strength.* "Not that we are sufficient of ourselves to think any thing as of ourselves; but our sufficiency is of God; Who also hath made us able ministers of the new testament;" (2 Cor. 3:5,6).

21. *God Expects You To Prepare Your Defense Against Your Enemy.* "Finally, my brethren, be strong in the Lord, and in the power of His might. Put on the whole armour of God, that ye may be able to stand against the wiles of the devil" (Eph. 6:10,11).

22. *Overcoming Your Enemy Is The Key To Your Rewards.* "He that overcometh, the same shall be clothed in white raiment; and I will not blot out his name out of the book of life, but I will confess his name before My Father, and before His angels. Him that overcometh will I make a pillar in the temple of My God, and he shall go no more out: and I will write upon him the name of My God, and the name of the city of My God, which is New Jerusalem, which cometh down out of Heaven from My God: and I will write upon him My new name" (Rev. 3:5,12).

23. *The Spoils Of War, Not Your Enemy, Must Always Remain Your Focus.* "To him that overcometh will I grant to sit with Me in My throne, even as I also overcame, and am set down with My Father in His throne" (Rev. 3:21). "But rejoice, inasmuch as ye are partakers of Christ's sufferings; that, when His glory shall be revealed, ye may be glad also with exceeding joy. If ye be reproached for the name of Christ, happy are ye; for the Spirit of glory and of God resteth upon you; on their part He is evil spoken of, but on your part He is glorified" (1 Pet. 4:13,14).

24. *You Will Always Have A Warfare-Companion During Every Battle With Your Enemy.* "Fear not: for I have redeemed thee, I have called thee by thy name; thou art Mine. When thou passest through the waters, I will be with thee; and through the rivers, they shall not overflow thee: when thou walkest through the fire, thou shalt not be burned; neither shall the flame kindle upon thee" (Isa. 43:1,2).

25. *Your Enemy Provides God An Opportunity To Reveal His Commitment To You.* "And He said unto me, My grace is sufficient for thee: for My strength is made perfect in weakness. Most gladly therefore will I rather glory in my infirmities, that the power of Christ may rest upon me. Therefore I take pleasure in infirmities, in reproaches, in necessities, in persecutions, in distresses for Christ's sake: for when I am weak, then am I strong" (2 Cor. 12:9,10).

26. *The Wisdom For Conquering Your Enemy Will Be Imparted In Your Secret Place Of Prayer.* "For in the time of trouble He shall hide me in His pavilion: in the secret of His tabernacle shall He hide me; He shall set me up upon a rock. And now shall mine head be lifted up above mine enemies round about me: therefore will I offer in His tabernacle sacrifices of joy; I will sing, yea, I will sing praises unto the Lord" (Ps. 27:5,6).

27. *You Should Never Disclose Publicly The Amount Of Any Damage Done By Your Enemy.* "A fool uttereth all his mind: but a wise man keepeth it in till afterwards" (Prov. 29:11).

28. *An Uncommon Enemy Will Require Uncommon Wisdom.* "If any of you lack Wisdom, let him ask of God, that giveth to all men liberally, and upbraideth not; and it shall be given him" (James 1:5). "Thou through Thy commandments hast made me wiser than mine enemies: for they are ever with me" (Ps. 119:98).

29. *You Should Never Reveal Your Strategy Against Your Enemy To Those Uncommitted To You And Your Cause.* "A fool uttereth all his mind: but a wise man keepeth it in till afterwards" (Prov. 29:11).

30. *Your Warfare With An Enemy Is Always Seasonal.* "To every thing there is a season, and a time to every purpose under the Heaven:...A time to kill, and a time to heal; a time to break down, and a time to build up; A time to love, and a time to hate; *a time of war,* and a time of peace" (Ecc. 3:1,3,8).

31. *Your Greatest Weapon Against Your Enemy Is The Word Of God.* "And take the helmet of salvation, and the sword of the Spirit, which is the Word of God:" (Eph. 6:17).

32. *The Holy Spirit Will Teach You The Principles Of Warfare Against Your Enemy.* "Blessed be the Lord my strength, which teacheth my hands to war, and my fingers to fight:" (Ps. 144:1).

33. *You Must Enter Every Battle Against Your Enemy For The Purpose Of Bringing Glory To God.* "Then said David to the Philistine, Thou comest to me with a sword, and with a spear, and with a shield: but I come to thee in the name of the Lord of hosts, the God of the armies of Israel, whom thou hast defied. This day will the Lord deliver thee into mine hand; and I will smite thee, and take thine head from thee; and I will give the carcases of the host of the Philistines this day unto the fowls of the air, and to the wild beasts of the earth;...And all this assembly shall know that the Lord saveth not with sword and spear: for the battle is the Lord's, and He will give you into our hands" (1 Sam. 17:45-47).

34. *You Should Expect To Win Every Battle Against Your Enemy.* "This day will the Lord deliver thee into mine hand; and I will smite thee, and take thine head from thee; and I will give the carcases of the host of the Philistines this day unto the fowls of the air, and to the wild beasts of the earth; that all the earth may know that there is a God in Israel" (1 Sam. 17:46).

35. *Your Enemy Will Be Opposed By God Even When You Feel Unable To Defend Yourself.* "For the battle is not yours, but God's. Ye shall not need to fight in this battle: set yourselves, stand ye still, and see the salvation of the Lord with you, O Judah and Jerusalem: fear not, nor be dismayed; tomorrow go out against them: for the Lord will be with you" (2 Chr. 20:15,17). "The Lord is a man of war: the Lord is His name" (Ex. 15:3).

36. *The Holy Spirit Will Demoralize And Weaken Your Enemy With Fear Towards You Before The Battle Even Begins.* He did it for Rahab. "And she said unto the men, I know that the Lord hath given you the land, and that your terror is fallen upon us, and that all the inhabitants of the land faint because of you. And as soon as we had heard these things, our hearts did melt, neither did there remain any

more courage in any man, because of you: for the Lord your God, He is God in Heaven above, and in earth beneath" (Josh. 2:9,11).

37. *Your Enemy Is Often Ignorant Of Your Past Victories, Which Makes Them Vulnerable And Unprepared For You.* Goliath was ignorant of David's fight with the lion and the bear. The Pharisees knew nothing of the power of Jesus. Your Enemy is *not* ready for you. Be strengthened by that.

38. *Your Enemy, When Aware Of Your Past Victories, Becomes Even More Fearful Of You.* In Jericho, they were aware of the parade of victories, and as Rahab said, "For we have heard how the Lord dried up the water of the Red sea for you, when ye came out of Egypt; and what ye did unto the two kings of the Amorites, that were on the other side Jordan, Sihon and Og, whom ye utterly destroyed" (Josh. 2:10).

39. *The Holy Spirit Will Reveal Any Snare Prepared By Your Enemy.* "Lest satan should get an advantage of us: for we are not ignorant of his devices" (2 Cor. 2:11).

40. *The Holy Spirit Within You Is More Powerful Than Any Enemy That You Will Ever Face.* "Greater is He that is in you, than he that is in the world" (1 Jn. 4:4).

41. *Your Enemy Will Never Discern The Protective Wall Of Angels Surrounding You During Battle.* "The angel of the Lord encampeth round about them that fear Him, and delivereth them" (Ps. 34:7).

42. *Your Enemy Cannot Withstand The Weapon Of Praise During Times Of Battle.* "His praise shall continually be in my mouth" (Ps. 34:1).

43. *Your Enemy Reveals By His Attacks That He Is Fully Persuaded Of Your Ability To Obtain Your Goal.* Your Enemy would not waste the time, ammunition, finances and effort if your dreams were impossible. Paul said, "I can do all things through Christ which strengtheneth me" (Phil. 4:13). If your Enemy believes in your future, why shouldn't you?

44. *Your Enemy Will Attack You At The Birth Of Any Significant Season In Your Life.* When Jesus began His *ministry,* satan launched his greatest temptations (see Matt. 4 and Lk. 4). The crisis may occur when there is the *birth of a champion* in your household, like the birth of Moses. His birth activated the killing of all the newborn children in Egypt. It may be the *birth of a miracle* about to occur in your personal life (see Dan. 9). Attack Is Merely Proof That Your Enemy Considers Your Assignment Very Achievable.

45. *Jesus Instructed His Disciples To Sow Seeds Of Love, Prayer*

And Acts Of Kindness Into Their Enemy. "But I say unto you, Love your enemies, bless them that curse you, do good to them that hate you, and pray for them which despitefully use you, and persecute you; That ye may be the children of your Father which is in Heaven: for He maketh His sun to rise on the evil and on the good, and sendeth rain on the just and on the unjust" (Matt. 5:44,45).

46. *Loving Your Enemies Will Create A Great Reward.* "For if ye love them which love you, what reward have ye? do not even the publicans the same?" (Matt. 5:46). "But love ye your enemies, and do good, and lend, hoping for nothing again; and your reward shall be great, and ye shall be the children of the Highest: for He is kind unto the unthankful and to the evil" (Lk. 6:35).

47. *Any Legal Entanglement With Your Enemy Should Be Avoided Whenever Possible.* "Agree with thine adversary quickly, whiles thou art in the way with him; lest at any time the adversary deliver thee to the judge, and the judge deliver thee to the officer, and thou be cast into prison. Verily I say unto thee, Thou shalt by no means come out thence, till thou hast paid the uttermost farthing" (Matt. 5:25,26).

48. *An Enemy Causes Movement In Your Life.* Without a Pharaoh, the Israelites would have adapted to Egypt. The Promised Land would have become a mere fantasy instead of a fact.

49. *When God Has Used Up The Benefits Of Your Present Season, He Assigns An Enemy To Become Your Exit From That Season.* Remember—The Enemy causes movement. God moves you to your next season...through an adversary, like a Pharoah.

50. *Your Enemy Is An Announcement From God That Your Present Season Has Come To A Conclusion.* When Goliath entered the picture, David changed seasons from shepherd boy to warrior. His victory was an announcement that yesterday was coming to a close. Tomorrow was being birthed.

51. *Your Enemy Unleashes Your Imagination.* When Pharaoh increased the pain and burden on the Israelites, they began to *picture* their future...where they *wanted* to be. Canaan became their focus. The Promised Land became their new target. Pain in your present is often necessary to give birth to the dream God is developing.

52. *Your Enemy Exposes Your Weaknesses.* Awareness of your weakness births humility. Humility is the magnet that attracts God and angels.

53. *Your Enemy Reveals Your Limitations.* When you recognize your personal limitations, you begin looking for the solution in those

near you. Whatever you lack, God has carefully stored in someone near you. When your Enemy comes, he often exhausts your strength, your creativity and your ideas. This usually launches your search to find the Heavenly *treasure* God has stored in *earthen* vessels near you. Remember—love is the secret code map to the treasure!

54. *Your Enemy Unifies Your Friends.* When the newspapers attacked me, I heard from some lawyers and partners who I did not really know even cared! Some wanted to sue, offering their legal services for free!

55. *The Holy Spirit Will Often Bring Conviction On Your Enemies.* "Who will have all men to be saved, and to come unto the knowledge of the truth" (1 Tim. 2:4). The jailor of Paul experienced this. "Then he called for a light, and sprang in, and came trembling, and fell down before Paul and Silas, And brought them out, and said, Sirs, what must I do to be saved?" (Acts 16:29,30).

"The Lord is not slack concerning His promise, as some men count slackness; but is long suffering to us-ward, not willing that any should perish, but that all should come to repentance" (2 Pet. 3:9). Before he became the Apostle Paul, Saul was an Enemy to the church, but God turned his heart. He can do the same with your Enemy.

56. *Your Enemy Today Could Possibly Become Your Greatest Ally Tomorrow.* It happened when the *tormentor* of the early church (Saul) became the *mentor* of the early church. "Then Ananias answered, Lord, I have heard by many of this man, how much evil he hath done to Thy saints at Jerusalem:...But the Lord said unto him, Go thy way: for he is a chosen vessel unto Me, to bear My name before the Gentiles, and kings, and the children of Israel" (Acts 9:13,15).

57. *Your Enemy May Be Suddenly And Dramatically Confronted By The Holy Spirit.* He did it to Saul, before he became Paul. "And as he journeyed, he came near Damascus: and suddenly there shined round about him a light from Heaven: And he fell to the earth, and heard a voice saying unto him, Saul, Saul, why persecutest thou Me? And he said, Who art Thou, Lord? And the Lord said, I am Jesus Whom thou persecutest: it is hard for thee to kick against the pricks" (Acts 9:3-5).

58. *Your Enemy Can Experience A Sudden Change Of Heart.* Saul became Paul...quickly. "And he trembling and astonished said, Lord, what wilt Thou have me to do? And the Lord said unto him, Arise, and go into the city, and it shall be told thee what thou must do" (Acts 9:6).

59. *Your Enemy Can Completely Turn Around Because Of One*

Tragedy Or Crisis. "And Saul arose from the earth; and when his eyes were opened, he saw no man: but they led him by the hand, and brought him into Damascus. And he was three days without sight, and neither did eat nor drink" (Acts 9:8,9).

60. *Your Enemy Is A Door, Not A Wall, To Your Next Season.* It happened for Esther. It happened for Daniel. It happened for Job. "The Lord gave Job twice as much as he had before" (Job 42:10).

61. *The Only True Difference Between A Nobody And A Somebody Is The Enemy They Decided To Conquer.* David went from a nobody to a *Somebody...through* Goliath. "And it came to pass as they came, when David was returned from the slaughter of the Philistine, that the women came out of all cities of Israel, singing and dancing to meet king Saul, with tabrets, with joy, and with instruments of musick. And the women answered one another as they played, and said, Saul hath slain his thousands, and David his ten thousands" (1 Sam. 18:6,7).

62. *Your Enemy Is The Difference Between Obscurity And Significance.* Heavyweight champions have gone from unknown to world champions...in a single fight. When Evander Holyfield sees Mike Tyson walk through the door, he doesn't grab his ear! He grabs his checkbook! No friend of Evander Holyfield has ever given him $22 million...It *took an Enemy!* It happened to David (see 1 Sam. 18:6,7). Even bronco riders desire a mean bull so the judges can accurately assess their skills!

63. *The Size Of Your Enemy Will Determine The Size Of Your Rewards.* "And there went out a champion out of the camp of the Philistines, named Goliath, of Gath, whose height was six cubits and a span. And he had an helmet of brass upon his head, and he was armed with a coat of mail; and the weight of the coat was five thousand shekels of brass. And he had greaves of brass upon his legs, and a target of brass between his shoulders. And the staff of his spear was like a weaver's beam; and his spear's head weighed six hundred shekels of iron: and one bearing a shield went before him. And the men of Israel said, Have ye seen this man that is come up? surely to defy Israel is he come up: and it shall be, that the man who killeth him, the king will enrich him with great riches, and will give him his daughter, and make his father's house free in Israel" (1 Sam. 17:4-7,25).

64. *Your Enemy Forces Any Judas In Your Life To Reveal Himself.* Judas is not your Enemy. Everybody has a Judas. Even

Judases! Judases are *intimidated* by you. They work *undercover.* They betray you *behind your back.* A Judas is weak, spineless and intimidated. It is possible to live around a Judas for years and never discern it. They will not confront you. They attempt to weaken your influence with others through their words, their actions and conduct.

A Judas resents the love and loyalty expressed by others toward you.

A Judas is someone who believes your Enemy has a right to be heard. A Judas plays both parts: in your presence, a friend. In *their* presence, a friend.

When your Enemy enters, he will bond with the Judas in your Circle of Confidantes. Your Judas will be exposed quickly when an Enemy links with him.

Do not fear—when Judas is revealed, you are only *three days* from the *resurrection* of your whole life and future.

65 *Anything Good Always Has An Enemy.* *Evil* despises righteousness. *Fear* despises faith. *Weakness* despises strength.

Jesus was the very Son of God—yet the religious crowd despised Him.

66. *You Will Only Be Remembered For The Enemy You Destroy Or The One Who Destroys You.* Samson is remembered because Delilah deceived him. David is remembered for the Goliath he killed.

67. *Your Enemy Can Not Abort Your Future—He Is Merely The Announcement That Your Future Is Being Born.* When Goliath roared, David was receiving the announcement that his shepherd days were concluding. Kingship was being born.

68. *Your Enemy Is As Necessary As Your Friend.* Your friend gives you *comfort,* but your Enemy gives you a *future.*

69. *Your Enemy Is Your Opportunity To Reveal Your Difference From Others.* The brothers of David were angry, fearful and intimidated. *Nobody* would have discerned the *difference* in David... without Goliath. Your Enemy is an opportunity to reveal what you truly believe.

70. *When You Discover Your Assignment, You Will Discover Your Enemy.* Demonic warfare is a clue that satan has discovered the intentions of God toward you.

Demons are *not* omnipresent. They cannot be everywhere simultaneously. They receive *geographical* Assignments. This is apparent when the angel, answering the prayers of Daniel, mentions the warfare and the attempted interception of the message. He indicated that God had heard Daniel when he prayed. He was released and dispatched from Heaven. But, it took him 21 days to arrive. "Then said he unto me, Fear not, Daniel: for from the first day that thou didst set thine heart to understand, and to chasten thyself before thy God, thy words were heard, and I am come for thy words. But the prince of the kingdom of Persia withstood me one and twenty days: but, lo, Michael, one of the chief princes, came to help me; and I remained there with the kings of Persia" (Dan. 10:12,13).

Where do we assign a security guard? Fifty miles from a bank vault? Of course not. He is assigned *where the treasure is located.* So, when you feel demonic activity around you, get excited. Satan is anticipating a miracle package arriving at your house. Warfare is his attempt to break your focus and abort your interest in the miracle.

71. *The Favorite Entry Point Used By Your Enemy Will Usually Be Through Someone You Have Chosen To Trust.* Your future depends on the weakness of the person you trust. Everybody trusts somebody. And, that person you are trusting is usually trusting someone you would not dream of trusting! Adam trusted Eve who opened the door to the serpent. Samson trusted Delilah. Your Enemy will always use someone you have chosen to trust.

72. *The Enemy You Fail To Destroy Will Eventually Destroy You.* The Prophet Samuel instructed Saul to kill the Amalekites utterly. He refused. He left king Agag alive with the best of the sheep and so forth. So, at Saul's death, the man who accepted the credit for finishing the suicidal attempt of Saul cried, "I am an Amalekite" (read 2 Sam. 1:8,10). What You Refuse To Conquer Will Eventually Conquer You.

73. *You Will Never Outgrow Your Enemy—You Must Simply Learn To Fight.* Many youth think that someday they will simply outgrow their desire to sin. Yet, the desire to sin is forever available. You must simply learn to fight back.

74. *Struggle Is The Proof That You Have Not Yet Been Conquered By Your Enemy.* You may be tired of fighting. Battle may weary you. But, struggle is still the proof that your Enemy has not yet won.

75. *Your Enemy Must Be Destroyed, Not Understood.* Conversation is often the Door to Annihilation. It happened in the Garden of Eden. Satan moved Eve to the negotiation table to prepare them for alienation. Negotiate with *friends,* but *destroy* your Enemy.

76. *Your Enemy Will Not Seek To Understand You, But To Discredit You.* When I received bad press, they requested that I answer questions. I was happy to do so, but I requested their written

verification that my entire answers would be printed...under the question asked.

They refused.

77. *When God Completes A Season In Your Life, He Hardens The Heart Of An Enemy Toward You.* Pharaoh's heart was hardened toward the Israelites. Why? It softened their heart about the move that God desired. In my little town here in Texas, I experienced the most incredible movements against the ministry. During my first partner meeting, police began to tow cars away during the service... though the little building we bought had been a Baptist church for over 30 years. Parking spaces had been used for years, but God *hardened* their heart...to move our ministry to another location.

What you think is an Enemy trying to stop you is God's way of "boot kicking you" into the next season of your life.

78. *Your Enemy Causes Good People To Find You.* Many times, ministers have become unnoticed and unrecognized. But, during a season of attack, people who discerned truth became aware of them and bonded with them.

Bad Times Always Bring Good People Together.

79. *Your Enemy Causes Unused And Dormant Gifts To Emerge.* Adversity will expose hidden greatness within you. The brothers of David were totally blind to his *difference* from them.

80. *Any Uncontested Enemy Will Flourish.* Ignoring an Enemy does not remove him. Hoping your Enemy will leave does not remove him. You must contest your Enemy. "Resist the devil, and he will flee from you" (James 4:7).

81. *Your Enemy Will Often Vary The Weapons And Strategy He Uses Against You.* What he uses when you are a teenager may be completely different than what he uses when you are older.

82. *The Reaction Of Your Enemy Is Proof Of Your Progress.* When your Enemy gets anxious, he knows his time is limited.

83. *Any Move You Make In The Right Direction Will Be Instantly Addressed By Your Enemy.*

84. *Your Enemy Will Ultimately Reveal The Greatness Of God To You.* Your heart may doubt. Your mind may be confused. But, in a crisis, God will expose His power and love toward you. An Enemy gives Him an opportunity to do so.

85. *Your Enemy May Enter Your Life Under the Disguise Of Friendship.* An Enemy may enter silently, quietly and begin to weaken your life like termites in a building. One evening, some years ago, my manager informed me that a young man had been sitting for

hours in the staff sanctuary. He insisted on an appointment. I explained to her that he needed to schedule through my secretary. He replied to her that he had driven several hundred miles and wanted more than anything in the world to "just be the protégé of Dr. Murdock...whatever it takes." He came in crying, weeping and begging for an opportunity to be an "armor-bearer." Within weeks, he had started a slander campaign against me on my own staff. It was shocking. But, he had *entered* sweetly and quietly as a friend.

86. *An Enemy Will Often Ignore Protocol And The Established Chain Of Authority.* Rebellion is at the heart of an Enemy. He despises the *order* of God. I mentioned earlier about the young man who had wanted an appointment. He refused to accept the counsel of my manager to schedule with me the next day. I misread his aggressiveness.

Aggressiveness is not always proof of desire.

Aggressiveness is often rebellion to protocol.

My manager informed him that I could not see him that day. He replied, "I am determined to see him."

Later he cried to me, "You are what I have wanted to be around my entire life. I want you to become my mentor. I will do anything to become your protégé. Nobody has ever given me a chance. Just give me a chance. I believe in you." Within weeks, he sowed more discord and strife into my staff than anyone in the history of my ministry.

He ignored *protocol.*

I ignored the signal.

87. *Your Enemy Must Be Exposed.* When there is a liar in your circle, expose them. You owe that to those under your protection. That's why Peter exposed Ananias and Sapphira (read Acts 5:1-11).

You are responsible for any person you destroy. You are also responsible for any person you *permit* to be destroyed. One young staff member affected by another disgruntled staff member became a complete emotional wreck. She eventually left our ministry. She had been so loyal, so sweet and loving toward the things of God. Within days, he had confused her and left her shattered.

88. *Your Enemy Will Attempt To Involve You In Unnecessary Battles Which Promise Little Or No Reward.* Battles drain your energy. They break your focus and empty your resources.

89. *Your Enemy Should Be Confronted In The Timing Of The Spirit And With The Right Spiritual Weaponry.* This enables you to predict his strategy and conduct. The motivation of Peter to protect Jesus by cutting off the ear of the soldier is admirable, but it was not

Spirit led.

90. *An Uncommon Enemy Can Be Defeated Through Uncommon Endurance.* God requires endurance. "And ye shall be hated of all men for My name's sake: but he that endureth to the end shall be saved" (Matt. 10:22).

91. *It Is Wisdom To Avoid Confrontation With Your Enemy When Possible.* Jesus did this. "But when they persecute you in this city, flee ye into another:" (Matt. 10:23). Fleeing does not demonstrate fear, but Wisdom to sustain your life and ministry and retain your focus.

92. *It Is Wise to Make Peace With Your Enemy When Possible.* "But I say unto you, That ye resist not evil: but whosoever shall smite thee on thy right cheek, turn to him the other also. And if any man will sue thee at the law, and take away thy coat, let him have thy cloak also. And whosoever shall compel thee to go a mile, go with him twain. Give to him that asketh thee, and from him that would borrow of thee turn not thou away" (Matt. 5:39-42).

Never use a tank to kill a mosquito.

Enemies are Bridges, not barricades.

Recognition Of The Enemy God Uses To Promote You Can Prevent Destruction, Protect Your Life And Those You Love.

RECOMMENDED BOOKS AND TAPES ON THIS TOPIC

B-07   Battle Techniques for War Weary Saints (Book/$3)
B-17   Seeds of Wisdom on Overcoming (Book/$3)
B-19   Seeds of Wisdom on Warfare (Book/$3)
B-21   Seeds of Wisdom on Adversity (Book/$3)
B-40   Wisdom for Crisis Times (Book/$9)
B-82   31 Reasons People Do Not Receive Their Financial Harvest
        (Book/$12)
B-92   Secrets of the Journey, Vol. 1 (Book/$5)
B-93   Secrets of the Journey, Vol. 2 (Book/$5)
B-94   Secrets of the Journey, Vol. 3 (Book/$5)
B-95   Secrets of the Journey, Vol. 4 (Book/$5)
B-96   Secrets of the Journey, Vol. 5 (Book/$5)
B-102   Secrets of the Journey, Vol. 6 (Book/$5)
B-103   Secrets of the Journey, Vol. 7 (Book/$5)
TS-5   How to Walk Through Fire (Six tapes/$30)
TS-40   Wisdom for Crisis Times (Six tapes/$30)

The Atmosphere
You Permit
Determines
The Product
You Produce.

-MIKE MURDOCK

❧ 16 ❧

ENTHUSIASM

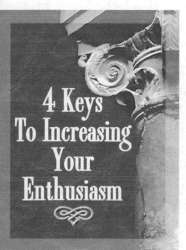

It Intrigues The World. It is almost a phenomenon. What am I talking about?

An enthusiastic, happy person! There is something magnetic and powerful about a victorious Christian. People are drawn to a consistent, excited believer!

Many write me and ask me in the crusades and seminars: "With today's problems—68,000 youth get V.D. every day; 1,200 new alcoholics every day!—how can you keep your spirit *high* in a down world?"

Believe me, *you can.* It is possible. Regardless of your family situation, your financial status, or past failures, you can step *up* into a Victory Zone and stay excited about life. Ephesians 2:6 says, God "hath raised us up together, and made us sit together in Heavenly places in Christ Jesus."

God intended for us to be *"up."* He provided a plan to get us there. Spiritually. Mentally. Emotionally.

4 Things You Must Do To Increase Enthusiasm

1. *Rebuild Your Concept Of God.* What is your idea and opinion of God? Is He a harsh dictator or a loving Father? Read Luke 15 and you will find a description of the Father *Jesus knew.*

The total obedience and respect Jesus had for His Father indicates His "God-picture" resulted in *trust.* Go beyond what you have heard or imagined about Him. *Read the Gospels.* The nature, the compassion, the love of the *Father* is reflected through the *activities and attitudes of Jesus Christ.* Jesus took time to talk to an immoral woman...little children...a tax collector in a tree. *People mattered to Jesus.*

Spend time developing the proper concept of God. Rebuild the mind-photo that strengthens your faith toward Him. By reading books, listening to cassette tapes and *sharing* your love with others, you will *correct* and *enlarge* your picture of God.

2. *Recognize The Limitations Of Satan.* Certainly, there is a need to understand the damage of demonic influence. However, through the *Word* you will understand the *limitations* of their efforts. Satan is a liar. A deceiver. A manipulator. I might add that he is a loser. He is an ex-employee of Heaven who got "fired." He is headed for total destruction. *He* is *under* the dominion of the believer, who is a joint-heir with Christ, who has "...put all things under His feet" (Eph. 1:22). Satan, and the demon forces, are *beneath us.* "We are *more than conquerors*" (Rom. 8:37). *Remember,* you are the winner! When you feel you are at your lowest, you are still "on *top* of the devil!"

3. *Understand The Needs Of Others.* Two classes of people who received attention from Christ were: First, people who *received* His ministry and His work. Good examples are Zacchaeus in Luke 19:2 and the Samaritan woman in John 4:9. Secondly, people who *ministered* to Him. Mary and Martha illustrate this in Luke 10:38.

Jesus' dealing with the Pharisees reveals they had a contempt, *an* irritation and absolutely no real respect for Him. They *neither ministered* to Him *nor received ministry* from Him. Jesus saw people as *needs* that He could meet. If they received it, miracles happened. If rebellion surfaced, He detached Himself from them. He knew how to say no when necessary.

Cultivate discernment of people in your life. If you are a *positive* influence on them, it will show. If you are not lifting them, chances are, they are a negative influence on you. "He that walketh with wise men shall be wise: but a companion of fools shall be destroyed" (Prov. 13:20). Jesus could not spend time with *everyone.* He never gave "Zacchaeus Time" to be abused by the Pharisees. Develop the ability to listen to God in the part someone is to play in your life.

4. *Rebuild A Good Picture Of Yourself.* Parents, schooling, and friends condition us. We become failure-conscious. Sometimes we become more problem-oriented than *possibility-oriented.* We concentrate on our weaknesses and lose confidence and self-respect. *Begin to concentrate on your strong points.* Sometimes what you consider a weakness is actually a God-implanted gift.

Let me illustrate. I've always loved to talk. My father was and is a very quiet man. I admired that. So I tried with little success to re-train my mouth to be quiet! I memorized Scriptures about talking too much. I suppressed my opinions in conversations. Oh, I admired and tried to emulate shy, timid, quiet friends. *Impossible.* I *had* to talk! Then, through my mother and father's gentle and tender nurturing, they helped me see that God had given me a gift to express myself and make truths clear. I could study and work to make my words *edifying* and uplifting—a *strong point.* Since then, I've simply asked the Lord to give me words that will bless those around me!

Stop talking about your lacks. *Be thankful for gifts God has given to you!*

Listen to a preacher who wrote one-half of the New Testament: "I can do all things through Christ..." (Phil. 4:13). "Nay, in all these things we are more than conquerors..." (Rom. 8:37).

Paul had the right concept of *God.*

Paul had the right concept of *satan.*

Paul had the right concept of *people.*

Paul had the right concept of *himself.*

The Apostle Paul: God's idea of a winner. And Paul stayed *up...in* a down world!

RECOMMENDED BOOKS AND TAPES ON THIS TOPIC

B-01   Wisdom for Winning (Book/$10)

B-99   Secrets of the Richest Man Who Ever Lived (Book/$10)

TS-85   School of Wisdom, Vol. 1 - The Uncommon Life (Six tapes/$30)

Your Rewards In Life Are Determined By The Problems You Solve For Others.

-MIKE MURDOCK

≈ 17 ≈

FAVOR

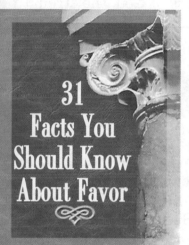

31 Facts You Should Know About Favor

Uncommon Favor Births Uncommon Success.

Uncommon Favor moved Joseph from the prison to the palace of Pharaoh *in one day.* Nothing is more glorious or more miraculous. Nothing else can create ecstasy like a single experience of Uncommon Favor.

Favor is the secret, hidden and unspoken dream of every human living today. We strive for it, pray for it and even beg for it.

Favor can turn tragedy into *triumph... within moments.*

1. *Uncommon Favor Is When God Causes Someone To Desire To Become A Problem Solver In Your Life.* It may be a relative, your boss, or a stranger. According to the Scripture, God is the catalyst for linking you to the Golden Connection with someone who blesses you.

2. *Uncommon Favor Is A Gift From God That Can Stop If It Is Not Recognized And Celebrated.* God does not owe you. Others are not obligated to you. *Men* cannot stop it. "He that openeth, and no man shutteth;" (Rev. 3:7).

3. *Uncommon Favor Is Only Guaranteed To Those Who Qualify Through Acts Of Obedience.* "If thou shalt hearken diligently unto The Voice of the Lord thy God...all these blessings shall come on thee, and overtake thee" (Deut. 28:1,2).

4. *Uncommon Success Will Require Uncommon Favor From Someone.* You cannot work hard enough to get everything you deserve. You cannot work long enough to be debt-free. It will require Uncommon Favor to take giant steps into an Uncommon Dream. "The Lord thy God shall bless thee in all thine increase, and in all the works of thine hands," (Deut. 16:15).

5. *Uncommon Favor Is An Attitude Of Goodness Toward You, Not An Exchange Or Payment For Something You Have Done.* The

world uses "favors" as a substitute for Favor.

A congressman may say to a lobbyist, "I will pass this bill through if you will give me $25,000 for another project." That is an *exchange*. It is a *transaction*. You intimidate and obligate others...through *favors,* not *Favor.* That is the satanic *substitution* for the divine plan of *Favor.*

You will always resent anyone you owe. Satan has always attempted to imitate God. He envies the success of God, the strength of God, and the love that God has generated toward Himself. So, he emulates God. Favor is the *divine* way, not the substitute.

6. *Uncommon Favor Is An Exception To The Rule, Not A Normality.* Millions struggle without seeing significant progress. "Except the Lord build the house, they labour in vain that build it:" (Ps. 127:1).

7. *Uncommon Favor Must Begin As A Seed From You Before It Returns As A Harvest To You.* "Be not deceived; God is not mocked: for whatsoever a man soweth, that shall he also reap" (Gal. 6:7).

8. *When You Sow Seeds Of Favor Consistently, You Will Reap The Harvest Of Favor Consistently.* Erratic Seeds produce erratic Harvests. Seeds of Love, Patience and Forgiveness will begin to grow in your own life.

9. *The Seed Of Uncommon Favor Can Grow Over A Period Of Time.* Jesus "grew in favor with God and man" (Lk. 2:52).

10. *Uncommon Favor Can Make You Wealthy In A Single Day.* Ruth experienced this. "So Boaz took Ruth, and she was his wife:" (Ruth 4:13). The wealth of Abraham was transferred to Rebekah through Isaac...in a single day.

11. *Uncommon Favor Can Silence A Lifetime Enemy Forever.* Haman was hung after the king showed Esther and Mordecai Uncommon Favor.

12. *Uncommon Favor Can Make You A Household Name In 24 Hours.* The king chose Esther to be his queen and a nobody became a somebody...in a single day (see Esth. 2:16).

13. *Uncommon Favor Can Double Your Financial Worth In The Midst Of Your Worst Tragedy.* It happened to Job. "The Lord gave Job twice as much as he had before...So the Lord blessed the latter end of Job more than his beginning:" (Job 42:10-12).

14. *Uncommon Favor Can Accelerate The Timetable Of Your Assignment And Destiny.* Joseph became Prime Minister within 24 hours...even after false accusations.

15. *One Day Of Favor Is Worth A Lifetime Of Labor.* Ruth was a peasant woman. She worked hard for her living. She toiled, she sweated and remained poor, but in a single day, Boaz accepted her as his wife.

16. *Uncommon Favor Comes When Uncommon Intercessors Pray For You.* Peter experienced this. He was in prison, but the church prayed. God became involved. The doors of the prison opened. Peter was released (see Acts 12:5).

17. *Uncommon Favor Always Begins When You Solve An Uncommon Problem For Someone.* Joseph interpreted the dream for the butler. Two years later, his gift made room for him in the palace of Pharaoh (see Gen. 41:42-44).

18. *Currents Of Favor Always Flow When You Solve The Problem Nearest You.* But, many who experience profound waves of Favor have found them suddenly stopped. Their progress is paralyzed. Tragedies break across their life. That is why it is important that you understand this Law of Recognition—recognizing the Dominant Source of Favor God has chosen to bless your life.

19. *Uncommon Favor Will Usually Come Through Someone Observing You Who Is Capable Of Greatly Blessing You.* Your parents. Your boss. Your neighbors. Someone you do not even yet know.

20. *Uncommon Favor Is Not An Accident, But A Deliberate Design By God To Reward You For Acts Of Obedience Invisible To Others.* "If ye be willing and obedient, ye shall eat the good of the land:" (Isa. 1:19).

21. *Uncommon Favor Will Stop When You Deliberately Ignore An Instruction From God.* Saul ignored the instructions of Samuel to destroy King Agag, and all the Amalekites. Favor stopped. Saul was removed from kingship and David became the king (read 1 Sam. 15:9-11,26).

22. *The Flow Of Uncommon Favor Is Often Paralyzed Through The Development Of Arrogance And Self-Sufficiency.* When Nebuchadnezzar sneered at the authority of God because of his uncommon success, God permitted him to live like a beast in the field...until his humility returned (see Dan. 5:20,21).

23. *Uncommon Favor Can Stop A Tragedy Instantly In Your Life.* It moved Joseph from the prison to Pharaoh's palace in a single day (see Gen. 41:39,40). Esther had Favor with the king and saved an entire nation.

24. *The River Of Uncommon Favor Will Dry Up When God*

Observes Greed. "Will a man rob God? Yet ye have robbed Me. But ye say, Wherein have we robbed Thee? In tithes and offerings. Ye are cursed with a curse: for ye have robbed Me, even this whole nation" (Mal. 3:8,9). It is a tragedy, an absurdity and futility to try to breathe Favor into a family or a man who God has chosen to curse *because of their greed.*

25. *Uncommon Favor Is A Seed That Anyone Can Sow Into The Life Of Another.* It does not require money, nor genius nor uncommon skill. It requires love, attentiveness and time.

26. *Uncommon Favor Should Be Pursued, Requested And Celebrated.* When the servant of Abraham knelt and asked God to show him favor, it was appropriate. God is the Source of Favor. He responds to faith and pursuit. Within hours, Rebekah was en route back to Isaac because of the Favor of God.

27. *Uncommon Favor Is Often The Only Exit From A Place Of Captivity And Bondage.* Joseph knew this. He *requested* Favor from the butler. It eventually came.

28. *Uncommon Favor Will Cease When Not Received With Thankfulness.* Loss is the quickest cure for ingratitude. *Anything Unrecognized Becomes Unrewarded...And Will Ultimately Exit Your Life.*

Who has God used the most during your lifetime to bring provision, encouragement or protection to you?

29. *Honoring Your Parents Is The First Clue In Understanding The Law Of Favor.* The first commandment with a promise was to honor your parents. God promised that it would go well with you all the days of your life. Think for a moment. Your parents paid your bills, fed you, clothed you, sheltered you, educated and trained you, endured your immaturity, tolerated your stumbling and learning days...yet are usually the last to receive your respect, your gifts and your spoken evidences of love.

It is common for a young man to spend more money on his new girlfriend within 90 days than he has given to his mother and father in the first 20 years of his life.

Refusing to honor and bless your parents is suicidal. It will destroy you. God guarantees it.

30. *Uncommon Men Always Sow Favor.* David sowed into Absalom. Abraham sowed into Lot. Boaz sowed into Ruth. Joseph sowed into Potiphar.

31. *The Favor Of God Will Always Create Favor With Men.* God

respected Abraham. That favor gave him favor with kings. Stop for a moment. Identify the *Dominant* Source of Favor in your life. Have you written a note of appreciation? Have you sown Favor to your own family?

What you fail to *recognize*, you stop *celebrating*.

What you stop *celebrating*, you stop *rewarding*.

Anything unrewarded will *exit* your life.

Recognition Of Your Dominant Source Of Favor Will Solve A Thousand Problems In Your Life.

RECOMMENDED BOOKS AND TAPES ON THIS TOPIC

B-99   Secrets of the Richest Man Who Ever Lived (Book/$10)

B-57   Thirty-One Secrets of an Unforgettable Woman (Book/$9)

TS-57   Thirty-One Secrets of an Unforgettable Woman (Six tapes/$30)

TS-99   Secrets of the Richest Man Who Ever Lived (Six tapes/$30)

TS-89   School of Wisdom, Vol. 4 - Unleashing Uncommon Favor (Six tapes/$30)

Money
Is Merely A Reward
For Solving A Problem.

-MIKE MURDOCK

～ 18 ～

FINANCES

Your Life Is On Display!

There Are 3 Major Reasons God Delights In Blessing You Financially

1. To Serve As An Example.

God wants your success to serve as an example of what His love and power can do in a person's life.

By sending success into the lives of His children, God can demonstrate to an unbelieving world both His *nature* and His *power.*

The Apostle Paul wrote: *"God* hath chosen the weak things of the world to confound the things which are mighty" (1 Cor. 1:27). He also testified that God dealt with him and said: "...My strength is made perfect in weakness" (2 Cor. 12:9).

Have you ever known people who seemed to be the model of success in every area of life—spiritually, physically and mentally? Their life appeared almost perfect. Their financial condition was stable. Their family and social life was an example of all that is wholesome, healthy and desirable.

Yet, as you studied those individuals, you found it hard to pinpoint the secret of their success. Do you know what I mean? There seemed to be no outstanding abilities or resources within these people for them to draw from. Maybe you have looked at people like this and wondered what their real secret was.

The Master Key to any truly successful life is Daily Obedience. For instance, Abraham's *obedience* brought the blessings of God in abundance. "And he said, I am Abraham's servant. And the Lord hath blessed my master greatly; and he is become great: and he hath given him flocks, and herds, and silver, and gold, and menservants, and maidservants, and camels, and asses. And Sarah my master's wife bare a son to my master when she was old: and unto him hath he given all that he hath" (Gen. 24:34-36).

He served as an example to each of us of what God wants for His children. "And if ye be Christ's, then are ye Abraham's Seed, and heirs according to the promise" (Gal. 3:29).

"Now to Abraham and his Seed were the promises made. He saith not, And to Seeds, as of many; but as of one, And to thy Seed, which is Christ. For ye are all the children of God by faith in Christ Jesus. For as many of you as have been baptized into Christ have put on Christ. There is neither Jew nor Greek, there is neither bond nor free, there is neither male nor female: for ye are all one in Christ Jesus. And if ye be Christ's, then are ye Abraham's Seed, and heirs according to the promise" (Gal. 3:16,26-29).

2. *To Provide For Your Family*.

God wants to give you success to enable you to provide for your family's needs.

The Bible makes it explicitly clear that we must provide for their material needs as well as their spiritual needs: "But if any provide not for his own, and specially for those of his own house, he hath denied the faith, and is worse than an infidel" (1 Tim. 5:8).

God gets no glory if your family has to live in a rat-breeding, roach-infested tenement. He is not pleased if your family never has enough to eat, and your children wear "hand-me-downs" and go without shoes. He is a God of an abundance of blessings. He wants you and your family to have plenty...and to spare.

3. *To Carry Out The Great Commission*.

The reason God wants you successful is to *financially support and undergird the work of God.* As God sends prosperity into your life, He not only meets your needs, but also makes it possible for you to help carry out the Great Commission.

Someone has said that money in the hands of an unbeliever is a *snare,* but money in the hands of a believer is a *tool* to do God's will.

As Christians prosper financially and use their resources for God's work, good things start happening. Churches are built, mission stations are established, gospel radio and television programs are aired, soul winning ministries are launched to share the message of salvation with those who have not yet been born again. All these things cost money. So God prospers His people that there will be no shortage of funds to do His work.

Thousands of people have misunderstood God's attitude toward success and prosperity. Somewhere they have gotten the idea that it is wrong to want to be successful. In fact, some even feel that prosperity is of the devil. Nothing could be further from the truth! Don't be misled. God *does* want you successful! His Word *does* say: "...thou shalt make thy way prosperous, and then thou shalt have good success" (Josh. 1:8).

Your financial success matters to God.

Never forget it.

RECOMMENDED BOOKS AND TAPES ON THIS TOPIC

B-22   Seeds of Wisdom on Prosperity (Book/$3)

B-82   31 Reasons People Do Not Receive Their Financial Harvest (Book/$12)

B-99   Secrets of the Richest Man Who Ever Lived (Book/$10)

When Satan
Wants To Destroy You
He Sends A Person
Into Your Life.

-MIKE MURDOCK

≈ 19 ≈

FOOLS

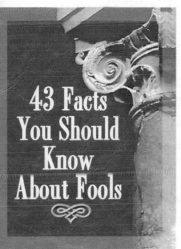

The Wise Recognize Fools.

Fools are everywhere. There are fools in the educational institution, in the world of religion, in the political arena and even among your relatives.

Fools *break* your focus.

Fools *waste* valuable time and energy.

Fools *slow* your life down.

Fools *rob* you of precious moments.

I mentioned a statement by former President Richard Nixon in one of my books, "Secrets of the Richest Man Who Ever Lived." He commented that Lee Iacoca, the legendary leader of Chrysler, had one major problem—no tolerance for fools. Nixon further explained that his attitude created two more problems! First, there are so many fools and second, some people that you think are fools really are not!

1. *A Fool Is Anyone Who Despises Wisdom, Instruction And Correction From A Proven Mentor.* "The fear of the Lord is the beginning of knowledge: but fools despise Wisdom and instruction" (Prov. 1:7).

2. *A Fool Is Anyone Who Attempts To Destroy The Reputation Of A Proven Champion Through Lying And Misrepresentation.* "He that uttereth a slander, is a fool" (Prov. 10:18).

3. *A Fool Is Anyone Who Refuses To Depart From Evil, Even Though Corrected.* "But it is abomination to fools to depart from evil" (Prov. 13:19).

4. *A Fool Is Anyone Who Does Not Take The Danger Of Sin Seriously.* "Fools make a mock at sin: but among the righteous there is favour" (Prov. 14:9).

5. *A Fool Is Anyone Who Reveals Confidences That Should Be Kept Private.* "Wisdom resteth in the heart of him that hath

understanding: but that which is in the midst of fools is made known" (Prov. 14:33).

6. *A Fool Is Any Son That Disregards The Wisdom Of His Father.* "A fool despiseth his father's instruction: but he that regardeth reproof is prudent" (Prov. 15:5).

7. *A Fool Is Any Son Who Shows Disrespect Toward The Mother That Brought Him Into The World.* "A wise son maketh a glad father: but a foolish man despiseth his mother" (Prov. 15:20).

8. *A Fool Is Anyone Whose Conduct Does Not Change Even After Experiencing Painful Consequences From It.* "A reproof entereth more into a wise man than an hundred stripes into a fool" (Prov. 17:10).

9. *A Fool Is Anyone Who Considers Any Pursuit Of Wisdom To Be A Wasted Effort.* "Wherefore is there a price in the hand of a fool to get Wisdom, seeing he hath no heart to it?" (Prov. 17:16).

10. *A Fool Is Anyone Who Continually Expresses His Discontent With God.* "The foolishness of man perverteth his way: and his heart fretteth against the Lord" (Prov. 19:3).

11. *A Fool Is Anyone Who Refuses To Embrace Peace.* "It is an honour for a man to cease from strife: but every fool will be meddling" (Prov. 20:3).

12. *A Fool Is Any Man Who Spends More Money Than He Is Willing To Earn For His Family.* "There is treasure to be desired and oil in the dwelling of the wise; but a foolish man spendeth it up" (Prov. 21:20).

13. *A Fool Is Anyone Who Creates His Own Belief System, Contrary To The Word Of God.* "He that trusteth in his own heart is a fool: but whoso walketh wisely, he shall be delivered" (Prov. 28:26).

14. *A Fool Is Anyone Who Refuses To Pay His Debts.* "When thou vowest a vow unto God, defer not to pay it; for he hath no pleasure in fools: pay that which thou hast vowed. Better is it that thou shouldest not vow, than that thou shouldest vow and not pay" (Ecc. 5:4,5).

15. *A Fool Is Anyone Who Makes Financial Increase His Life Focus Rather Than God.* "But God said unto him, Thou fool, this night thy soul shall be required of thee: then whose shall those things be, which thou hast provided? So is he that layeth up treasure for himself, and is not rich toward God" (Lk. 12:20,21).

16. *A Fool Is Someone Who Wants Something He Has Not Yet Earned.* Ahab's wife, queen Jezebel, was also a fool. Her husband's bitter words concerning the man with the vineyard angered her heart. Why? She wanted something she had not yet earned.

17. *A Fool That Keeps Silent Often Remains Undetected.* "Even a fool, when he holdeth his peace, is counted wise: and he that shutteth his lips is esteemed a man of understanding" (Prov. 17:28).

18. *A Fool Is Always At The Center Of Strife And Contention.* "A fool's lips enter into contention, and his mouth calleth for strokes. A fool's mouth is his destruction, and his lips are the snare of his soul" (Prov. 18:6,7).

19. *Any Companion To Fools Will Ultimately Be Destroyed.* "He that walketh with wise men shall be wise: but a companion of fools shall be destroyed" (Prov. 13:20).

20. *The Wise Always Leave The Presence Of Fools When They Perceive A Lack Of Desire For Knowledge.* "Go from the presence of a foolish man, when thou perceivest not in him the lips of knowledge" (Prov. 14:7).

21. *Liars Are Fools.* "He that hideth hatred with lying lips...is a fool" (Prov. 10:18). A liar destroys his trustworthiness with a single sentence. He will trade a lifetime relationship for a single falsehood. Without a doubt, he is a fool.

22. *A Fool Is Usually Only Changed By Correction During His Childhood.* "Foolishness is bound in the heart of a child; but the rod of correction shall drive it far from him" (Prov. 22:15).

23. *A Fool Cannot Be Changed Through Counsel.* "Speak not in the ears of a fool: for he will despise the Wisdom of thy words" (Prov. 23:9).

24. *A Fool Should Never Be Given A Position Of Leadership Over Others.* "Wisdom is too high for a fool: he openeth not his mouth in the gate" (Prov. 24:7). In the ancient days, the wise elders of the city met at the gates of the city. Fools were never welcomed or given position of influence there.

25. *The Continuous Threat Of Pain Is The Only Influence That Keeps A Fool In His Place.* "A whip for the horse, a bridle for the ass, and a rod for the fool's back" (Prov. 26:3).

26. *A Fool Who Is Trusted Ultimately Destroys Those Who Trusted Him.* "He that sendeth a message by the hand of a fool cutteth off the feet, and drinketh damage" (Prov. 26:6).

27. *A Fool Remains Unaffected Or Changed By Any Wisdom He Quotes From Others.* "The legs of the lame are not equal: so is a parable in the mouth of fools" (Prov. 26:7).

28. *A Fool, When Given A Position Of Honor Or Power, Becomes Deadly To Those Within His Influence.* "As he that bindeth a stone in

a sling, so is he that giveth honour to a fool" (Prov. 26:8).

29. *Every Fool Will Eventually Taste The Consequences Of His Attitude And Rebellion.* "The great God that formed all things both rewardeth the fool, and rewardeth transgressors" (Prov. 26:10).

30. *A Fool Is Someone Who Makes The Same Mistakes Repeatedly.* "As a dog returneth to his vomit, so a fool returneth to his folly" (Prov. 26:11).

31. *A Fool Uses His Anger To Threaten To Create Problems For Others.* "A stone is heavy, and the sand weighty; but a fool's wrath is heavier than them both" (Prov. 27:3).

32. *A Fool Exposed Is More Destructive Than Wild Animals Disturbed.* "Let a bear robbed of her whelps meet a man, rather than a fool in his folly" (Prov. 17:12).

33. *No Amount Of Wisdom Or Counsel Can Create A Peaceful Relationship With A Fool.* "If a wise man contendeth with a foolish man, whether he rage or laugh, there is no rest" (Prov. 29:9).

34. *A Fool Tells Everything He Knows And Feels To Others.* "A fool uttereth all his mind: but a wise man keepeth it in till afterwards" (Prov. 29:11).

35. *A Fool Talks Too Much And Is Known By His Torrent Of Words.* "A fool also is full of words: a man cannot tell what shall be; and what shall be after him, who can tell him?" (Ecc. 10:14). "A fool's voice is known by multitude of words" (Ecc. 5:3).

36. *A Fool Never Believes That He Is Wrong.* "Keep thy foot when thou goest to the house of God, and be more ready to hear, than to give the sacrifice of fools: for they consider not that they do evil" (Ecc. 5:1).

37. *The Parents Of A Fool Will Live In Sorrow Their Entire Lifetime.* "He that begetteth a fool doeth it to his sorrow: and the father of a fool hath no joy" (Prov. 17:21). "A foolish son is a grief to his father, and bitterness to her that bare him" (Prov. 17:25).

38. *Any Atheist Is A Fool.* "The fool hath said in his heart, There is no God" (Ps. 14:1; see also Ps. 53:1).

39. *A Fool Does Not Learn From His Observation Nor Experiences Enough To Make Changes.* "Wisdom is before him that hath understanding; but the eyes of a fool are in the ends of the earth" (Prov. 17:24).

40. *Any Conversation With Fools Should Be Avoided.* Association is defiling. Correction is useless. Solomon understood this. "Answer not a fool according to his folly, lest thou also be like unto him" (Prov. 26:4). He refused to enter into any relationship or conversation.

41. *A Fool Perpetuates His Offenses To Others Around Him.* He wants others to feel his pain. He arouses an army of protesters against someone who offended him, rather than exhibiting a desire to settle the offense.

42. *A Fool Refuses To Admit His Mistakes Even When His Pain Is The Obvious Result.*

43. *A Fool Refuses To Reach For Counsel From Accessible Champions.* When I heard several complaints over financial problems, I offered to pay the registration to "The Uncommon Millionaire's Conference." I brought in six multi-millionaires to advise on financial blessing for three days. Those who had been complaining of their *finances...never even attended* the 21 hours of teaching at the conference, though some lived less than 5 minutes away.

Recognition Of A Fool Will Enable You To Avoid A Thousand Heartbreaking Experiences In Your Life.

RECOMMENDED BOOKS AND TAPES ON THIS TOPIC

B-14   Seeds of Wisdom on Relationships (Book/$3)

B-46   31 Facts About Wisdom (Book/$5)

B-64   Seven Obstacles to Abundant Success (Book/$3)

B-82   31 Reasons People Do Not Receive Their Financial Harvest (Book/$12)

TS-99   Secrets of the Richest Man Who Ever Lived (Six tapes/ $30)

Giving Is Proof
That You
Have Conquered Greed.

-MIKE MURDOCK

❧ 20 ❧

GIVING

12 Facts You Should Know About Giving

Giving Is God's Cure For Greed.

1. *The Major Difference Between Satan And God Is That Satan Is A Taker And God Is A Giver.* Satan *takes* joy, peace, love. God *gives* joy, peace, love. Jesus said, "I am come that they might have life, and that they might have it more abundantly" (Jn. 10:10). *Jesus was a Giver:* Of life; Of health; Of love.

2. *Giving Is A God-Characteristic.* "For God so loved...that He GAVE..." (Jn. 3:16).

3. *Giving Impresses God.* Proverbs 3:9, 10 interprets an offering as a public honoring of Himself. To God, *an offering is faith in action.* So, *the danger of greed is solved through the act of giving.* The need and importance of money is not ignored.

4. *God Promises Response To Giving.* "Give, and it shall be given unto you; good measure, pressed down, and shaken together, and running over, shall men give into your bosom. For with the same measure that ye mete withal it shall be measured to you again" (Lk. 6:38).

"Bring ye all the tithes into the storehouse, that there may be meat in Mine house, and prove Me now herewith, saith the Lord of hosts, if I will not open you the windows of Heaven, and pour you out a blessing, that there shall not be room enough to receive it. And I will rebuke the devourer for your sakes, and he shall not destroy the fruits of your ground; neither shall your vine cast her fruit before the time in the field, saith the Lord of hosts" (Mal. 3:10,11).

Why? *God always reacts to faith.*

Jesus marveled at faith. It impresses all of Heaven!

5. *Giving An Offering Is An Eternal Proof Of Your Real Faith!* (see Mal. 3:10,11). When you sow your Seeds into God's work, your offering is evidence that you possess:

...*a generous* heart (willingness to *share);*

...a *thankful* heart (willingness to *remember*);

...a *faith-filled* heart (willingness to *trust);*

...a *confident* heart (willingness to *expect).*

Your money represents you. It is your time, your sweat, your energy, your mental abilities, your toil—a major part of you. It is the *power* part of *you.* With it, you bargain—exchange your way through life. You trade it for food. For shelter. For clothing. You talk with your money. You tell your children you can care through your provision.

6. *When You Give It To God, It Is A Public Expression That He Is Important To You.* He knows that. You release your money. That's faith in *Him.* That indicates your confidence in *Him.* You activate an *exchange* principle:

You give your *sins* to Him...

He gives *forgiveness* (1 Jn. 1:9).

You give your *confused mind...*

He gives you *peace of mind* (Jn. 14:27).

You give your *unclean heart...*

He gives you a *new one* (Ezek. 36:26).

You *release what you have...*

He *releases what He has for you* (Lk. 6:38).

7. *Your Giving Is Your Love In Action.* It is the *power principle of total prosperity. Giving Is A God Characteristic.* "If ye then, being evil, know how to give good gifts unto your children, how much more shall your Father which is in Heaven give good things to them that ask him? (Matt. 7:11).

8. *Godly Giving Is To Express Our Appreciation..* "A gift is as a precious stone in the eyes of him that hath it..." (Prov. 17:8).

9. *Everyone Has A Need To Give.* "...freely ye have received, freely give" (Matt. 10:8).

10. *Everyone Has Something To Give.* "As every man hath received the gift, even so minister the same one to another..." (1 Pet. 4:10). It may be a spoken word of *thanks,* a small bouquet of *flowers,* an hour of *time,* a bag of *groceries,* a *commendation* for a job well done, use of your special gift or *ability.* Don't give what you don't have—*give what you have.*

11. *Do Not Let Rejection Of Your Gift Stop Your Continued Giving.* Jesus kept giving though "...His own received Him not" (Jn. 1:11). Your gift may be rejected if: 1) It is not *really needed;* 2) It is not *valued;* 3) Its purpose is not *discerned.*

12. *God Treasures The Giver.* He sees His own nature in you and

honors it with the *promise of prosperity:*

"And now, behold, I have brought the firstfruits of the land, which Thou, O Lord, hast given me. And thou shalt set it before the Lord thy God:...And thou shalt rejoice in every good thing which the Lord thy God hath given unto thee, and unto thine house," (Deut. 26:10,11).

"Every good gift and every perfect gift is from above, and cometh down from the Father of lights, with Whom is no variableness, neither shadow of turning. Of His own will begat He us with the word of truth, that we should be a kind of firstfruits of His creatures" (James 1:17,18).

Sow with great expectation today. "Give, and it shall be given unto you..." (Lk. 6:38). *What You Make Happen For Others, God Will Make Happen For You.*

Your Uncommon Seed Will Always Create An Uncommon Harvest.

RECOMMENDED BOOKS AND TAPES ON THIS TOPIC

B-22   Seeds of Wisdom on Prosperity (Book/$3)

B-24   Seeds of Wisdom on Faith-Talk (Book/$3)

B-82   31 Reasons People Do Not Receive Their Financial Harvest (Book/$12)

TS-82   31 Reasons People Do Not Receive Their Financial Harvest (Six tapes/$30)

The Proof Of Desire
Is
Pursuit.

-MIKE MURDOCK

∼ 21 ∼

GOAL-SETTING

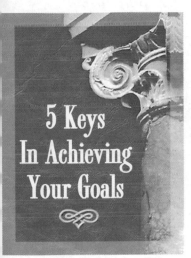

5 Keys
In Achieving
Your Goals

One Of The Major Causes Of Failure Is The Unwillingness To Take The Time To Determine Your True Goals.

It is also a very misunderstood practice. Some think that the Bible teaches against planning ahead, using Matthew 6:25 and James 4:13-15 as their basis. However, the concern Matthew dealt with was worry, not the setting of goals. James was referring to the setting of goals without God's involvement.

4 Reasons Some Never Set Goals

1. *Some Have Not Tasted The Joy That Goal-Setting Produces.*
2. *Some Have Not Been Taught To Write These Goals Down With Clarity.*
3. *Some Are Afraid Of Possible Failure.* If we do not set a goal, there is no guilt or negative feelings of not reaching it!
4. *Some Fail To Set Goals Because Memories Of Previous Failures Intimidate Them.* Perhaps their goals were too unreasonable.

At any rate, I want to help you understand the wonderful victories accomplished through *written* goals.

In the Old Testament, Abraham's father, Terah, set a goal of making Canaan his residence. Later, Abraham accomplished this with his nephew, Lot (read Gen. 11,12). In the New Testament, the Apostle Paul planned to "winter" with the Corinthians (see 1 Cor. 16:6), and to spend another winter in Nicopolis (see Titus 3:12). In Proverbs 16:9 we are told: "We should make plans...counting on God to direct us" (TLB). Proverbs 14:8 says: "The wise man looks ahead..." (TLB).

Planning cures disorder.

One outstanding lesson on planning ahead is given in Luke 14:28-30: "For which of you, intending to build a tower, sitteth not down first, and counteth the cost, whether he have sufficient to finish it? Lest haply, after he hath laid the foundation, and is not able to finish it, all that behold it begin to mock him, Saying, This man began to build, and was not able to finish."

The setting up of specific goals is one good way of fulfilling the *purpose* God has for your life. For instance, you might *purpose* to be a better Christian this year. That is general. To fulfill that purpose, your daily goal would be to read a specific amount of chapters in the Bible *each day,* set up a *morning prayer time,* and so on.

Goal setting takes time, discipline, courage and patience.

There are temptations along this line. Sometimes we let others dictate our personal goals instead of deciding for ourselves. Some people become comfortable in a particular job and stay with it for 20 years even though *they may be missing a Divine position God is wanting to transfer them to.* Financial security to them is their job, not their Heavenly Father.

1. *You Must Decide For Yourself What You Really Want Out Of Life.* Nobody else can decide for you. If you do not care what happens to your life, no one else will.

2. *Get Alone With God And His Word.* This enables you to understand His plan and what He desires. This is getting "in agreement" with His will and purpose. This helps you to *avoid* setting the *wrong* goals.

3. *Write Down On A Sheet Of Paper Every Single Dream, Goal And Desire That Is Presently Important To You.* Write down anything that you have ever wanted to *do, become* or *possess.* It may be spiritual, physical, mental, financial or have to do with family. It is important that you *write* it down. (Do not leave it in your mind!) The shortest pencil is better than a long memory. As my brother John has said, "Faintest line is better than strongest mind."

4. *Choose The Top Three Goals Out Of The Long List.* Now write down at least *five* actions you can do *now* toward accomplishing that *big* priority goal. Remember, a *big success* is simply several little successes linked together.

5. *Be Alert To The People God Will Send Into Your Life To Help You Fulfill His Purpose, And Be Responsive To Obey God When He Directs Your Talents To Help Fulfill The Dreams Of Others.* This simply restates my basic motto that God gave me during a five-day fast in 1977: "What You Make Happen For Others, God Will Make Happen For You."

Taking time to determine and set your true goals can prevent a wasted lifetime.

≈ 22 ≈

GOD

Tomorrow Contains More Joy Than Any Yesterday You Can Recall.

God Wants To Bless You!

"But without faith it is impossible to please Him: for he that cometh to God must believe that He is, and that He is a rewarder of them that diligently seek Him" (Heb. 11:6).

"Fear not, little flock; for it is your Father's good pleasure to give you the kingdom" (Lk. 12:32).

Here Are 12 Benefits You Can Count On Receiving From God

1. *You Can Expect His Ready Ear To Listen.*

"Lord, Thou hast heard the desire of the humble: Thou wilt prepare their heart, Thou wilt cause Thine ear to hear" (Ps. 10:17).

"He that planted the ear, shall He not hear? He that formed the eye, shall He not see?" (Ps. 94:9).

"And this is the confidence that we have in Him, that, if we ask any thing according to His will, He heareth us: And if we know that He hear us, whatsoever we ask, we know that we have the petitions that we desired of Him" (1 Jn. 5:14,15).

2. *You Can Expect His Watchful Eye.*

"Behold, the eye of the Lord is upon them that fear Him, upon them that hope in His mercy;" (Ps. 33:18).

"He that planted the ear, shall He not hear? He that formed the eye, shall He not see?" (Ps. 94:9).

"Neither is there any creature that is not manifest in His sight: but all things are naked and opened unto the eyes of Him with Whom we have to do" (Heb. 4:13).

3. *You Can Expect His Forgiveness.*

"For Thou, Lord, art good, and ready to forgive; and plenteous in mercy unto all them that call upon Thee" (Ps. 86:5).

"For God so loved the world, that He gave His only begotten Son, that whosoever believeth in Him should not perish, but have everlasting life. For God sent not His Son into the world to condemn the world; but that the world through Him might be saved" (Jn. 3:16,17).

"For all have sinned, and come short of the glory of God; Being justified freely by His grace through the redemption that is in Christ Jesus: Whom God hath set forth to be a propitiation through faith in His blood, to declare His righteousness for the remission of sins that are past, through the forbearance of God;" (Rom. 3:23-25).

"If we confess our sins, He is faithful and just to forgive us our sins, and to cleanse us from all unrighteousness" (1 Jn. 1:9).

4. *You Can Expect His Guidance.*

"And the Lord shall guide thee continually, and satisfy thy soul in drought, and make fat thy bones: and thou shalt be like a watered garden, and like a spring of water, whose waters fail not" (Isa. 58:11).

"I will instruct thee and teach thee in the way which thou shalt go: I will guide thee with Mine eye" (Ps. 32:8).

"Through the tender mercy of our God; whereby the Dayspring from on high hath visited us, To give light to them that sit in darkness and in the shadow of death, to guide our feet into the way of peace" (Lk. 1:78,79).

"Howbeit when He, the Spirit of truth, is come, He will guide you into all truth: for He shall not speak of Himself; but whatsoever He shall hear, that shall He speak: and He will shew you things to come" (Jn. 16:13).

"For as many as are led by the Spirit of God, they are the sons of God. For ye have not received the spirit of bondage again to fear; but ye have received the Spirit of adoption, whereby we cry, Abba, Father. The Spirit itself beareth witness with our spirit, that we are the children of God:" (Rom. 8:14-16).

5. *You Can Expect Inner Peace In Your Heart.*

"Peace I leave with you, My peace I give unto you: not as the world giveth, give I unto you. Let not your heart be troubled, neither let it be afraid. Ye have heard how I said unto you, I go away, and come again unto you. If ye loved Me, ye would rejoice, because I said, I go unto the Father: for My Father is greater than I" (Jn. 14:27,28).

"I will not leave you comfortless: I will come to you. Yet a little while, and the world seeth Me no more; but ye see Me: because I live, ye shall live also. At that day ye shall know that I am in My Father, and ye in Me, and I in you. He that hath My commandments, and keepeth them, he it is that loveth Me: and he that loveth Me shall be loved of My Father, and I will love him, and will manifest Myself to him" (Jn. 14:18-21).

"I have told you these things, so that in Me you may have peace. In this world you will have trouble. But take heart! I have overcome the world" (Jn. 16:33 NIV).

"Be careful for nothing; but in every thing by prayer and supplication with thanksgiving let your requests be made known unto God. And the peace of God, which passeth all understanding, shall keep your hearts and minds through Christ Jesus. Finally, brethren, whatsoever things are true, whatsoever things are honest, whatsoever things are just, whatsoever things are pure, whatsoever things are lovely, whatsoever things are of good report; if there be any virtue, and if there be any praise, think on these things" (Phil. 4:6-8).

6.   *You Can Expect Inner Joy In Your Spirit.*

"I will praise the Lord, Who counsels me; even at night my heart instructs me. I have set the Lord always before me. Because He is at my right hand, I will not be shaken. Therefore my heart is glad and my tongue rejoices; my body also will rest secure...You have made known to me the path of life; You will fill me with joy in Your presence, with eternal pleasures at Your right hand" (Ps. 16:7-11 NIV).

"These things have I spoken unto you, that My joy might remain in you, and that your joy might be full" (Jn. 15:11).

"Then was our mouth filled with laughter, and our tongue with singing: then said they among the heathen, The Lord hath done great things for them. The Lord hath done great things for us; whereof we are glad. Turn again our captivity, O Lord, as the streams in the south. They that sow in tears shall reap in joy. He that goeth forth and weepeth, bearing precious Seed, shall doubtless come again with rejoicing, bringing his sheaves with him" (Ps. 126:2-6).

"Therefore with joy shall ye draw water out of the wells of salvation. And in that day shall ye say, Praise the Lord, call upon His name, declare His doings among the people, make mention that His name is exalted. Sing unto the Lord; for He hath done excellent things: this is known in all the earth. Cry out and shout, thou inhabitant of Zion: for great is the Holy One of Israel in the midst of thee" (Isa. 12:3-6).

"So they read in the book in the Law of God distinctly, and gave the sense, and caused them to understand the reading...for this day is holy unto our Lord: neither be ye sorry; for the joy of the Lord is your strength" (Neh. 8:8-10).

7. *You Can Expect His Protection.*

"Keep me as the apple of the eye, hide me under the shadow of Thy wings, From the wicked that oppress me, from my deadly enemies, who compass me about" (Ps. 17:8,9).

"He that dwelleth in the secret place of the Most High shall abide under the shadow of the Almighty. I will say of the Lord, He is my refuge and my fortress: my God; in Him will I trust...He shall cover thee with His feathers, and under His wings shalt thou trust: His truth shall be thy shield and buckler...A thousand shall fall at thy side, and ten thousand at thy right hand; but it shall not come nigh thee. Only with thine eyes shalt thou behold and see the reward of the wicked. Because thou hast made the Lord, which is my refuge, even the Most High, thy habitation; There shall no evil befall thee, neither shall any plague come nigh thy dwelling" (Ps. 91:1-10).

8. *You Can Expect New Power To Overcome Sin.*

"Ye are of God, little children, and have overcome them: because greater is He that is in you, than he that is in the world" (1 Jn. 4:4; also see Eph. 3:20).

"For this cause I bow my knees unto the Father of our Lord Jesus Christ, Of Whom the whole family in Heaven and earth is named, That He would grant you, according to the riches of His glory, to be strengthened with might by His Spirit in the inner man; That Christ may dwell in your hearts by faith; that ye, being rooted and grounded in love, May be able to comprehend with all saints what is the breadth, and length, and depth, and height; And to know the love of Christ, which passeth knowledge, that ye might be filled with all the fulness of God. Now unto Him that is able to do exceeding abundantly above all that we ask or think, according to the power that worketh in us, unto Him be glory in the church by Christ Jesus throughout all ages, world without end. Amen" (Eph. 3:14-21).

"The sting of death is sin; and the strength of sin is the law. But thanks be to God, which giveth us the victory through our Lord Jesus Christ" (1 Cor. 15:56-58).

"For I delight in the law of God after the inward man: But I see another law in my members, warring against the law of my mind, and bringing me into captivity to the law of sin which is in my members. O wretched man that I am! who shall deliver me from the body of this death? I thank God through Jesus Christ our Lord. So then with the mind I myself serve the law of God; but with the flesh the law of sin" (Rom. 7:22-25).

"Everyone who sins breaks the law; in fact, sin is lawlessness. But you know that He appeared so that He might take away our sins. And in Him is no sin. No one who lives in Him keeps on sinning. No one who continues to sin has either seen Him or known Him...No one who is born of God will continue to sin, because God's Seed remains in him; he cannot go on sinning, because he has been born of God" (1 Jn. 3:4-6,9 NIV).

"We know that anyone born of God does not continue to sin; the one who was born of God keeps him safe, and the evil one cannot harm him. We know that we are children of God, and that the whole world is under the control of the evil one. We know also that the Son of God has come and has given us understanding, so that we may know Him Who is true. And we are in Him Who is true—even in His Son Jesus Christ. He is the true God and eternal life. Dear children, keep yourselves from idols" (1 Jn. 5:18-21 NIV).

9. *You Can Expect Physical Healing In Your Body.*

"And said, If thou wilt diligently hearken to the voice of the Lord thy God, and wilt do that which is right in His sight, and wilt give ear to His commandments, and keep all His statutes, I will put none of these diseases upon thee, which I have brought upon the Egyptians: for I am the Lord that healeth thee" (Ex. 15:26).

"That it might be fulfilled which was spoken by Esaias the prophet, saying, Himself took our infirmities, and bare our sicknesses" (Matt. 8:17).

"Who His own self bare our sins in His own body on the tree, that we, being dead to sins, should live unto righteousness: by Whose stripes ye were healed. For ye were as sheep going astray; but are now returned unto the Shepherd and Bishop of your souls" (1 Pet. 2:24,25).

"Bless the Lord, O my soul, and forget not all His benefits: Who forgiveth all thine iniquities; Who healeth all thy diseases; Who redeemeth thy life from destruction; Who crowneth thee with lovingkindness and tender mercies; Who satisfieth thy mouth with good things; so that thy youth is renewed like the eagle's" (Ps.103:2-5).

10. *You Can Expect Inner Healing In Your Broken Heart.*

"O Lord, open my lips; and my mouth will declare Your praise. You do not delight in sacrifice, or I would bring it; You do not take pleasure in burnt offerings. The sacrifices of God are a broken spirit; a broken and contrite heart, O God, You will not despise. In Your good pleasure make Zion prosper; build up the walls of Jerusalem" (Ps. 51:15-18 NIV).

"He healeth the broken in heart, and bindeth up their wounds" (Ps. 147:3).

"The Lord is nigh unto them that are of a broken heart; and saveth such as be of a contrite spirit" (Ps. 34:18).

"For thus saith the high and lofty One that inhabiteth eternity, Whose name is Holy; I dwell in the high and holy place, with him also that is of a contrite and humble spirit, to revive the spirit of the humble, and to revive the heart of the contrite ones. For I will not contend for ever, neither will I be always wroth: for the spirit should fail before Me, and the souls which I have made" (Isa. 57:15,16).

"Thus saith the Lord, The Heaven is My throne, and the earth is My footstool: where is the house that ye build unto Me? and where is the place of My rest? For all those things hath Mine hand made, and all those things have been, saith the Lord: but to this man will I look, even to him that is poor and of a contrite spirit, and trembleth at My word" (Isa. 66:1,2).

"Having therefore, brethren, boldness to enter into the holiest by the blood of Jesus, By a new and living way, which He hath consecrated for us, through the veil, that is to say, His flesh; And having an high priest over the house of God; Let us draw near with a true heart in full assurance of faith, having our hearts sprinkled from an evil conscience, and our bodies washed with pure water" (Heb. 10:19-22).

11. *You Can Expect His Consistency And Faithfulness.*

"Know therefore that the Lord thy God, He is God, the faithful God, which keepeth covenant and mercy with them that love Him and keep His commandments to a thousand generations;" (Deut. 7:9).

"But the Lord is faithful, who shall stablish you, and keep you from evil" (2 Thess. 3:3).

"I am with you alway, even unto the end of the world" (Matt. 28:20).

"There hath no temptation taken you but such as is common to man: but God is faithful, Who will not suffer you to be tempted above that ye are able; but will with the temptation also make a way to escape, that ye may be able to bear it" (1 Cor. 10:13).

"Jesus Christ the same yesterday, and to-day, and for ever" (Heb. 13:8).

"I the Lord do not change. So you, O descendants of Jacob, are not destroyed. Ever since the time of your forefathers you have turned away from My decrees and have not kept them. Return to Me, and I will return to you, says the Lord Almighty. But you ask, 'How are we to return?' Will a man rob God? Yet you rob Me. But you ask, 'How do we rob You?' In tithes and offerings. You are under a curse—the whole nation of you—because you are robbing Me. Bring the whole tithe into the storehouse, that there may be food in My house. Test Me in this, says the Lord Almighty, and see if I will not throw open the floodgates of Heaven and pour out so much blessing that you will not have room enough for it" (Mal. 3:6-10 NIV).

"O give thanks unto the Lord; for He is good: because His mercy endureth for ever" (Ps. 118:1).

12. *You Can Expect His Wisdom For Living.*

"But of Him are ye in Christ Jesus, Who of God is made unto us Wisdom, and righteousness, and sanctification, and redemption:" (1 Cor. 1:30).

"God is faithful, by Whom ye were called unto the fellowship of His Son Jesus Christ our Lord" (1 Cor. 1:9).

"Verily, verily, I say unto you, The hour is coming, and now is, when the dead shall hear the voice of the Son of God: and they that hear shall live. For as the Father hath life in Himself; so hath He given to the Son to have life in Himself; And hath given Him authority to execute judgment also, because He is the Son of man" (Jn. 5:25-27).

"The thief cometh not, but for to steal, and to kill, and to destroy: I am come that they might have life, and that they might have it more abundantly" (Jn. 10:10).

"He that loveth not knoweth not God; for God is love. In this was manifested the love of God toward us, because that God sent His only begotten Son into the world, that we might live through Him. Herein is love, not that we loved God, but that He loved us, and sent His Son to be the propitiation for our sins" (1 Jn. 4:8-10).

"And we have known and believed the love that God hath to us. God is love; and he that dwelleth in love dwelleth in God, and God in him. Herein is our love made perfect, that we may have boldness in the day of judgment: because as He is, so are we in this world. There is no fear in love; but perfect love casteth out fear: because fear hath torment. He that feareth is not made perfect in love. We love Him, because He first loved us" (1 Jn. 4:16-19).

"Hear, O Israel: The Lord our God is one Lord: And thou shalt love the Lord thy God with all thine heart, and with all thy soul, and with all thy might" (Deut. 6:4,5).

Make a commitment to God. He made one to you in the person of His Son, Jesus Christ. Calvary was commitment. The blood and cross of Jesus was commitment. Gethsemane was commitment.

Our Prayer Together...

"Father, I need You. And I believe You exist. Forgive me for every sin I've ever committed. I commit my life and heart to Your control. Cleanse my mind, free my heart to serve You. I make You Savior and Lord of my life. I accept Your forgiveness, peace and mercy with joy and a thankful heart. Use me to touch another with Your special love. I love You with all my mind, my heart and body. In the Name of Your Son, Jesus, I pray. Amen."

RECOMMENDED BOOKS AND TAPES ON THIS TOPIC

B-15   Seeds of Wisdom on Miracles (Book/$3)

B-26   The God Book (Book/$10)

B-27   The Jesus Book (Book/$10)

❧ 23 ❧

HAPPINESS

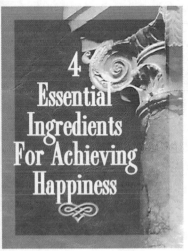

4 Essential Ingredients For Achieving Happiness

Happiness Is The Fragrance Of An Obedient Life.

Happiness is *feeling good* about the *happenings* in your life. Do not confuse this with popularity, which simply means *others* feel good about you. But what you think about yourself, your character, and your own accomplishments determines your real sense of worth and value.

I hate to see people unhappy. I hate to see people hurting inside. "I don't know what is wrong," an attractive lady sobbed at a recent crusade. "My husband is so good to me. We live in a beautiful home...but I feel so frustrated. What do you think is wrong with me?"

What Is Happiness?

Life is not a schedule of defeats, but a parade of miracles. It wasn't meant to be an endurance of trials, but an enjoyment of triumphs. We *decide.* Jesus said, "These things have I spoken unto you, that My joy might remain in you, and that your joy might be full" (Jn. 15:11).

While many believers live in the joy and the power of the Jesus-life, others do not. Why are so many living in fear and defeat? Is happiness released by a Sunday morning walk to a church altar? Or repeating the "sinner's prayer" after a television pastor? Or by time spent with a marriage counselor?

Too many are looking to someone else to bring their happiness to them. "But let every man prove his own work, and then shall he have rejoicing in himself alone, and not in another" (Gal. 6:4).

Happiness does not start *around* you, it begins *inside* you. *Stop waiting for flowers to arrive.* It is the growing of the Seed *inside* you this very moment. *Start growing the Seeds inside.*

Do You Feel Good About Yourself?

If not, *why not?* What bad news have you believed about yourself? Satan is the accuser of the brethren (see Rev. 12:10). Is he using a *past failure* in your life to destroy your faith?

One day I was praying. Suddenly, a mental photograph of a past failure leaped on the stage of my mind. It wasn't the first time satan had reminded me of that failure. I cried out, "Father, why does he keep using that same failure over and over and over?" My Heavenly Father spoke so gently, "He's running out of material!"

Don't let past hurts and memories chain you to the *prison* of *defeat. Smash* the locks of your prison. Dare to resist the hurts and disappointments of yesterday. "Remember ye not the former things, neither consider the things of old. Behold, I will do a new thing; now it shall spring forth; shall ye *not* know it? I will even make a way in the wilderness, and rivers in the desert" (Isa. 43:18,19).

Happiness is feeling good about yourself. Your sense of worth and value determines how good you really feel. Feeling good (or *happiness)* depends on *two* things:

Your relationships.

Your achievements.

You were built for connection. Your heart requires fellowship. Your mind demands negotiation. Your mouth longs for an ear that understands.

The Creator established your need for relationships. Relationships satisfy two huge needs of the human heart: 1) The need to *receive* love, and 2) The need to *release* love.

You have an inborn craving to make contact. That's why the wounded divorce victim still reaches out another time to risk love again, at the cost of emotional havoc. *Something in you always reaches for another...* even when your memory is screaming "anger!"

Relationships are a risk. They demand time, energy, attention and discipline. Like tender plants, they require patience before strength. Millions of people wither in loneliness, refusing to labor on the monument of love.

4 Essential Ingredients

1. *Your Relationship With God Is A Must.*
He created you. He knows you so well. He has read every single

sentence in your mind before you even think it.

God requires honesty. As well as holiness. In fact, *every miracle is preceded by the ache and agony of need.*

Like a child who rams the car into the telephone pole while trying to impress his father with his driving abilities, you sometimes have to splatter before you succeed. *You need Him.* I'd rather be His, *drawn* by His *blessing,* than *driven* by His *wrath. Jesus cried,* "...how often would I have gathered thy children together, as a hen doth gather her brood under her wings, and ye would not!" (Lk. 13:34).

2. *Your Family Relationships Are Vital.*

Your family relationships are vital to your happiness. The *Winner* is one who sees the *needs* of each member and strives to help fill that emptiness. *Time spent with your family is never wasted.* Wipe out criticism and sarcasm from the climate of your home.

Be a confidence-builder. "Withhold not good from them to whom it is due, when it is in the power of thine hand to do it" (Prov. 3:27).

3. *Friendships Are Greater Than Gold.*

They satisfy the inner part of us. Discern those orchestrated by the Holy Spirit and build them carefully, consistently and wisely.

4. *Setting Goals Is Important To Achieving Your Happiness.*

Everyone needs to feel they have achieved something with their lives. When you stop producing, loneliness and laziness will choke all enthusiasm from your living. What would you like to be doing? What job could turn on the excitement inside you? What are you doing about it?

Get started on a project in your life. Start building on your dreams. Resist those who would control and change your personal goals. You decide the goals God intended.

Get going today! When you do, you will start feeling good about your life.

Happiness Is The Fragrance Of An Obedient Life

"Blessed are the poor in spirit: for theirs is the kingdom of Heaven.

Blessed are they that mourn: for they shall be comforted.

Blessed are the meek: for they shall inherit the earth.

Blessed are they which do hunger and thirst after righteousness: for they shall be filled.

Blessed are the merciful: for they shall obtain mercy.

Blessed are the pure in heart: for they shall see God.

Blessed are the peacemakers: for they shall be called the children of God.

Blessed are they which are persecuted for righteousness' sake: for theirs is the kingdom of Heaven.

Blessed are ye, when men shall revile you, and persecute you, and shall say all manner of evil against you falsely, for My sake" (Matt. 5:3-11).

RECOMMENDED BOOKS AND TAPES ON THIS TOPIC

B-01   Wisdom for Winning (Book/$10)
B-101   The 3 Most Important Things in Your Life (Book/$10)
B-114   The Law of Recognition (Book/$10)
TTS-11 Strategy of Hourly Obedience (Six tapes/$30)
TS-14   How to Stay Motivated (Six tapes/$30)
TS-19   Wisdom for Winning (Six tapes/$30)

~ 24 ~

HOLY SPIRIT

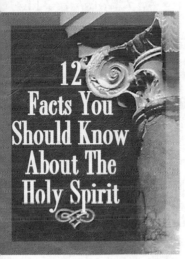

The Holy Spirit Is The Greatest Secret Of The Universe.

The Holy Spirit is the Mystery for which everyone is searching. I would trade every experience of my lifetime for what I have discovered about the Holy Spirit. If your spiritual encounter does not bond you with the Holy Spirit, it has merely been an encounter.

1. *The Holy Spirit Is A Person, Not Fire, Wind Or A White Dove.* "And I will pray the Father, and He shall give you another Comforter, that He may abide with you for ever;" (Jn. 14:16).

2. *The Holy Spirit Created You.* "The Spirit of God hath made me, and the Breath of the Almighty hath given me life" (Job 33:4). The Apostle Paul wrote, "But the Spirit giveth life" (2 Cor. 3:6).

Jesus taught it. "The Spirit gives life" (Jn. 6:63 NIV).

3. *The Holy Spirit Authored The Word Of God.* "For the prophecy came not in old time by the will of man: but holy men of God spake as they were moved by the Holy Ghost" (2 Pet. 1:21).

The Apostle Paul taught it. "All scripture is given by inspiration of God, and is profitable for doctrine, for reproof, for correction, for instruction in righteousness: That the man of God may be perfect, throughly furnished unto all good works" (2 Tim. 3:16,17).

4. *The Holy Spirit Selects The Gifts And Skills Given To You By The Father.* "Now there are diversities of gifts, but the same Spirit. And there are differences of administrations, but the same Lord...For to one is given by the Spirit the word of Wisdom; to another the word of knowledge by the same Spirit; To another faith by the same Spirit; to another the gifts of healing by the same Spirit;" (1 Cor. 12:4-9).

5. *The Holy Spirit Determines To Whom You Are Assigned, For A Moment, Or Your Lifetime.* "Then the Spirit said unto Philip, Go near, and join thyself to this chariot" (Acts 8:29).

6. *The Holy Spirit Knows The Geographical Location Where Your Gifts Will Flourish And Be Celebrated.* "So they, being sent forth by the Holy Ghost, departed unto Seleucia; and from thence they sailed to Cyprus" (Acts 13:4).

7. *The Holy Spirit Births An Uncommon Love For Those To Whom You Are Called.* "Because the love of God is shed abroad in our hearts by the Holy Ghost which is given unto us" (Rom. 5:5).

8. *The Holy Spirit Is Pleasured By Singing And Worship.* "The Lord thy God in the midst of thee is mighty; He will save, He will rejoice over thee with joy; He will rest in His love, He will joy over thee with singing" (Zeph. 3:17).

His Rules of Conduct include entering His presence with singing. "Come before His presence with singing" (Ps. 100:2).

9. *The Holy Spirit Intercedes For You Every Moment.* "Likewise the Spirit also helpeth our infirmities...but the Spirit (Himself) maketh intercession for us" (Rom. 8:26).

10. *The Holy Spirit Is Easily Offended.* "Let no corrupt communication proceed out of your mouth, but that which is good to the use of edifying, that it may minister grace unto the hearers. And grieve not the Holy Spirit of God, whereby ye are sealed unto the day of redemption. Let all bitterness, and wrath, and anger, and clamour, and evil speaking, be put away from you," (Eph. 4:29-31).

11. *When The Holy Spirit Is Offended, He Withdraws His Manifest Presence.* "I will go and return to My place, till they acknowledge their offence, and seek My face: in their affliction they will seek Me early" (Hos. 5:15). Depression is the proof.

12. *Joy Is The Proof The Holy Spirit Is Present.* "In Thy presence is fulness of joy; at Thy right hand there are pleasures" (Ps. 16:11). The greatest discovery of my lifetime is the habitual companionship of the Holy Spirit, The One Who Stayed.

Recognition Of The Voice Of The Holy Spirit Is The Master Secret Of Life.

RECOMMENDED BOOKS AND TAPES ON THIS TOPIC
B-100   The Holy Spirit Handbook, Vol. 1 (Book/$10)
TS-100   The Holy Spirit Handbook, Vol. 1 (Six tapes/$30)
TS-59   Songs from The Secret Place, Vol. 1 (Six music tapes/$30)

≈ 25 ≈

IDEAS

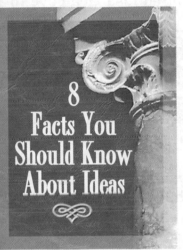

8
Facts You
Should Know
About Ideas

Ideas Are Golden Gates To Change.

An idea is a thought, divinely planted by God, that could solve a problem for someone. The Scriptures excite us with the promise of *"witty inventions."* "I Wisdom dwell with prudence, and find out knowledge of witty inventions" (Prov. 8:12).

Methods for creating wealth are guaranteed to the obedient. "But thou shalt remember the Lord thy God: for it is He that giveth thee power to get wealth, that He may establish His covenant which He sware unto thy fathers, as it is this day" (Deut. 8:18).

Many years ago, I planted an incredible Seed in Columbus, Ohio. Six weeks later, I was in Houston, Texas, staying at the Hyatt Regency Hotel. It was Tuesday morning, 7:15 a.m., during my second hour of prayer. Suddenly, the Holy Spirit *birthed an idea.* I saw in my spirit a special Bible for mothers. It would contain 2,000 scriptures to help mothers locate within ten seconds the scripture appropriate for solving an immediate problem they faced. I called it, *"The Mother's Topical Bible."* Then, I saw one in my mind called *"The Father's Topical Bible,"* especially for fathers going through difficult places in their life.

Then *"The Businessman's Topical Bible"* exploded in my heart. Then, I saw one especially designed for teenagers who did not understand how to find scriptures in the *Bible..."The Teenager's Topical Bible."*

I called a friend "in the publishing business."

He was elated. "Mike, we will print 60,000 leather-bound editions and see how they sell in the bookstores. You will receive a small royalty from each one that sells."

Within months, 1,300 bookstores purchased *every copy* of those Bibles. Eventually, paperbacks were printed. Different translations such as The Living Bible and New International Version were made available.

That *idea* unlocked hundreds of thousands of dollars. Someone told me that almost two million of those topical Bibles have gone throughout the earth.

That idea produced blessings for millions.

I recognized it was from God. It was *given* to me. Yes, others have copied it and imitated it. It was a divinely inspired idea God gave to me.

But, *I had to recognize it. Several years ago, while in prayer, the Holy Spirit gave me another little Bible idea. It is called the "One-Minute Pocket Bible."* Anyone can carry it in their shirt pocket. The small *"One-Minute Pocket Bible"* has gone throughout America. One of the greatest television ministries today purchased thousands for their partners. Every Mother's Day, pastors give these pocket Bibles and topical Bibles to ladies in their church.

Good ideas are interesting but are not commands.

God ideas are actually God commands. They awaken you in the middle of the night, becoming your obsession.

Oral Roberts once explained that when God promised you more than you *"have room to receive,"* He was speaking of ideas, insights and concepts. He instructed the people to *review* any idea, insight or concept God had given them, then, present it to God for blessing.

One man listened with great faith. Years prior, he had had an idea. It was repeatedly rejected. He became demoralized and discouraged with it. He had stored it in boxes in his attic. After hearing Brother Roberts, he decided that the idea was from God. Satan had simply paralyzed his expectations and faith.

He went home, crawled into his attic and brought the boxes back down. Today, he is worth over one hundred million *dollars...because of that idea.*

Are you sitting on a million-dollar idea? Are you chasing pennies...when God gave you a million-dollar concept?

Years ago, I was speaking in Dothan, Alabama. When I finished preaching, I asked the people to give their Seed an Assignment as they planted the Seed in the offering. "Write on your check where you most need to see your Harvest today," I instructed.

Some months later, I returned to the church. The pastor was exhilarated.

"I want you to meet this couple. Do you remember asking the people to give their Seed an Assignment? You told them to write on the check where they would like to see God produce their Harvest the most."

He explained that within 90 days from the time they had planted their Seed, an idea that had been ignored and rejected was suddenly accepted by a major grocery chain. Their *first* check for the their first order was for *2.4 million dollars. Their idea was worth 2.4 million dollars.* Ross Perot, the famed billionaire, reportedly said, "*One Good Idea Can Enable A Man To Live Like A King The Rest Of His Life.*"

Enter God's presence to receive His *commands.*
Stay in God's presence to receive His *plan.*
God is talking to you.
Are you listening?

8 Facts About Ideas

1.   An Uncommon Idea Comes Through Observation Of What Is Around You.

2.   An Uncommon Idea Will Help People.

3.   An Uncommon Idea From God Will Solve Problems For Somebody.

4.   An Uncommon Idea Is A Solution That Eliminates Stress And Increases Enthusiasm And Joy.

5.   An Uncommon Idea Can Come To You Whether It is Respected By Those Around You Or Not. Walt Disney was fired from a newspaper because he was "not creative enough."

6.   An Uncommon Idea Can Create Uncommon Wealth.

7.   An Uncommon Idea Requires Uncommon Attention.

8.   An Uncommon Idea Can Create A Lifetime Of Provision.

Recognition Of A God-Inspired Idea Can Provide A Lifetime Income For Your Family.

RECOMMENDED BOOKS AND TAPES ON THIS TOPIC

B-11   Dream Seeds (Book/$9)
B-99   Secrets of the Richest Man Who Ever Lived (Book/$10)
B-100   The Holy Spirit Handbook, Vol. 1 (Book/$10)
B-104   7 Keys to 1000 Times More (Book/$10)
TS-11   Dream Seeds (Six tapes/$30)
TS-29   The Double Diamond and Gifts, Goals and Guts (Six tapes/$30)
TS-100   The Holy Spirit Handbook (Six tapes/$30)
TS-99   Secrets of the Richest Man Who Ever Lived (Six   tapes/$30)

One Hour In The Presence Of God Will Reveal Any Flaw In Your Most Carefully Laid Plan.

-MIKE MURDOCK

❦ 26 ❦

INTERCESSION

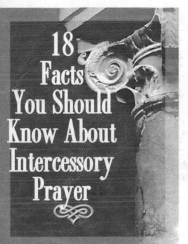

Prayer Is The Greatest Weapon Of Life.

Lost battles are evidences that The Weapon was unused. When you pray, your spirit is fed the essential "bread of life." Prayer is as necessary for your spirit as food is for your body. Prayer changes *your inner world*. The peace and presence of God fills you. It changes your *external circumstances* also.

1. *God Commanded Us To Pray.* "Men ought always to pray, and not to faint;" (Lk. 18:1).

2. *Prayer Pleasures The Heart Of God.* "And there I will meet with thee, and I will commune with thee from above the mercy seat, from between the two cherubims which are upon the ark of the testimony, of all things which I will give thee in commandment unto the children of Israel" (Ex. 25:22).

3. *Prayer Will Pleasure Your Own Spirit.* "Come unto Me, all ye that labour and are heavy laden, and I will give you rest" (Matt. 11:28).

4. *Prayer Affects The Lives Of Others.* "I exhort therefore, that, first of all, supplications, prayers, intercessions, and giving of thanks, be made for all men;" (1 Tim. 2:1).

"Confess your faults one to another, and pray one for another, that ye may be healed. The effectual fervent prayer of a righteous man availeth much" (James 5:16).

5. *Prayer Births Uncommon Miracles.* "Call unto Me, and I will answer thee, and shew thee great and mighty things, which thou knowest not" (Jer. 33:3).

6. *Your Prayer Requests Should Be Made Directly To The Father.* "And in that day ye shall ask Me nothing. Verily, verily, I say unto you, Whatsoever ye shall ask the Father in My name, He will give it you" (Jn. 16:23).

7. *Every Prayer Request Should Be Made In The Name Of Jesus.* "Whatsoever ye shall ask in My name, that will I do, that the Father may be glorified in the Son. If ye shall ask any thing in My name, I will do it. If ye love Me, keep My commandments" (Jn. 14:13-15).

8. *Prayer Reveals Humility.* It reveals confidence and faith in God. It is the proof of your respect for God. "Therefore I say unto you, What things soever ye desire, when ye pray, believe that ye receive them, and ye shall have them" (Mk. 11:24).

9. *Intercessors Are Those Called To Pray For You.* As Samuel said, "Moreover as for me, God forbid that I should sin against the Lord in ceasing to pray for you..." (1 Sam. 12:23).

10. *Intercession Was The Habit Of Jesus.* "And it came to pass in those days, that He went out into a mountain to pray, and continued all night in prayer to God" (Lk. 6:12).

11. *Intercessors Are Sought Out By God.* "And I sought for a man among them, that should make up the hedge, and stand in the gap before Me for the land, that I should not destroy it: but I found none" (Ezek. 22:30).

12. *Intercessors Are Needed By Every One Of Us.* Peter needed intercessors. While he was in prison, others interceded for him. "Peter therefore was kept in prison: but prayer was made without ceasing of the church unto God for him" (Acts 12:5). God sent an angel, released him from prison, *because of intercessors.*

13. *Intercession Is The Habit Of Uncommon Champions Of God.* The Apostle Paul was brilliant. He knew scripture. He knew the art of persuasion. But, he also understood the incredible force that his prayers had. He wrote to Timothy, "I thank God, Whom I serve from my forefathers with pure conscience, that without ceasing I have remembrance of thee in my prayers night and day;" (2 Tim. 1:3).

14. *Intercession Is Occurring Right Now In Heaven For You.* Jesus is your Intercessor. "It is Christ that died, yea rather, that is risen again, Who is even at the right hand of God, who also maketh intercession for us" (Rom. 8:34).

15. *Intercession Occurs Daily For You By The Holy Spirit Within You.* "Likewise the Spirit also helpeth our infirmities: for we know not what we should pray for as we ought: but the Spirit (Himself) maketh intercession for us with groanings which cannot be uttered. And He that searcheth the hearts knoweth what is the mind of the Spirit, because He maketh intercession for the saints according to the will of God" (Rom. 8:26,27).

16. *The Intercession Of Jesus Protected Peter From Spiritual*

Destruction. "And the Lord said, Simon, Simon, behold, satan hath desired to have you, that he may sift you as wheat: But I have prayed for thee, that thy faith fail not: and when thou art converted, strengthen thy brethren" (Lk. 22:31,32). Peter would not fail, because of the intercession of Jesus for him. Jesus expected His prayers to produce results.

17. *Intercessors Prevent Tragedies From Occurring In Our Lives.* Lot experienced this. When the sin of Sodom and Gomorrah infuriated God, He came down to destroy those two wicked cities. Lot, his wife and family lived in those cities. Abraham interceded to God on behalf of them. The mercies of God were released. Lot and his two daughters *escaped...because of the prayers of Abraham* on behalf of that city. "And it came to pass, when God destroyed the cities of the plain, that God remembered Abraham, and sent Lot out of the midst of the overthrow, when he overthrew the cities in the which Lot dwelt" (Gen. 19:29). It was not the goodness of Lot that created his deliverance. It was the memory of God regarding Abraham's intercession.

18. *When You Recognize The Intercessors God Has Assigned To Your Life, Your Respect For Them Will Bring Great Results.* "For this cause we also, since the day we heard it, do not cease to pray for you, and to desire that ye might be filled with the knowledge of His will in all Wisdom and spiritual understanding; That ye might walk worthy of the Lord unto all pleasing, being fruitful in every good work, and increasing in the knowledge of God; Strengthened with all might, according to His glorious power, unto all patience and longsuffering with joyfulness; Giving thanks unto the Father, which hath made us meet to be partakers" (Col. 1:9-12).

Every month, I send thousands of Faith Agreement Pages to my friends and partners. Some simply throw them away. However, many rush those Faith Agreement Pages back and experience miracles!

When You Respect Your Intercessors, Your Life Will Experience The Greatest Parade Of Miracles You Ever Dreamed Possible.

RECOMMENDED BOOKS AND TAPES ON THIS TOPIC
B-23   Seeds of Wisdom on Prayer (Book/$3)
B-69   Wisdom Keys for a Powerful Prayer Life (Book/$3)
B-115   Seeds of Wisdom on The Secret Place (Book/$5)

The Questions You Ask
Determine
The Answers You Discover.

-MIKE MURDOCK

❧ 27 ❧

JOBS

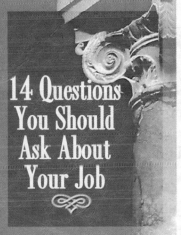

14 Questions
You Should
Ask About
Your Job

Your Work Is Important.

Happiness depends on feeling good about yourself. It is based on your relationships and achievements. When your gifts and abilities are developed and utilized through your life's work, you grow in confidence and strength.

If you are unhappy at work, it will affect your family life, even your health. Take time to plan your career and life's work.

Your work is a gift from God. "To rejoice in his labour, this is the gift of God" (Ecc. 5:19). "The Lord shall make thee plenteous in goods...and...bless all the work of thine hand:" (Deut. 28:11,12).

God has given you your life's work to bring you personal fulfillment. It is a vital key to your self-esteem and significance. If you are investing forty miserable hours each week on a job you do not like, two hours of church on *Sunday will not necessarily* cure it.

1. *Are You Really Happy With What You Are Presently Doing?* Your personal excitement and enthusiasm about your productivity each day is so important. Nobody else can answer this but *You.*

2. *Is Your Present Job Actually A Short-Range Or A Long-Range Goal?* For instance, high school or college students may not intend to work their entire lifetimes at fast food restaurants. So their "after school" job is a *short-range goal.* They are gaining education, experience and basic financial provision.

Likewise, you should clarify in your own mind the *real* reasons why you have chosen to work where you are presently working or where you desire to work.

3. *Are Your God-Given Gifts And Strongest Talents Being Developed?* Prosperity and promotion usually come to those who totally focus on their most significant skills.

4. *Are You Working Just To Pay Your Bills And Have Fun Or To*

Truly Express A Contribution To Life And To This Work? Prominent achievers go the *extra mile*.

5. *Do You Feel That God Is Satisfied With What You Are Doing Now?* I remember one tremendous guitarist who left a nightclub band after honestly answering this question. Though he loved his music, he felt God did not want him sowing his talents in such an environment.

6. *Do You Feel That You Are Doing The Highest Quality Of Work That You Are Capable Of Doing?* Millions cultivate the habit of mediocrity in their daily duties. If you are not striving for total excellence, you either have the wrong job or the wrong *attitude*.

7. *Do You Feel Like You Are Working "As Unto The Lord?"* You must see the work you do for your boss as work you are doing for *God*. If not, you will soon resent your boss and the time you spend on his work. This attitude will eventually cause you to feel unfulfilled and unproductive.

Seriously consider the above questions. Then, ask the Lord for His instructions regarding your career.

8. *How Much Income Do You Personally Feel That You Need To Consider Yourself Financially Successful?* Each of us have different needs. Some have 5 x 7 dreams. Others have 16 x 20 dreams. Neither is right or wrong. The key is to establish a true picture of your personal desires.

9. *What Kind Of Problems Do You Really Love To Solve?* You can determine this by your favorite topic of conversation, favorite books and magazines that you enjoy. What would you *enjoy* talking about *the most? These things reveal your true interests.*

10. *What Kind Of Environment Do You Find Most Enjoyable?* Some people discover that they need many people around them to be most productive. Others prefer solitude.

11. *What Are Your Social Needs?* If your job deprives you of important relationships, it will become a source of discomfort and depression. You must diagnose the personal leisure and social needs that your happiness requires.

12. *What Kind Of Family Life Or Time Do You Feel Is Necessary?* Obviously, a bachelor schedules his life differently from a family man with five children or a divorced mother of an infant. The job that is right for you should provide adequate time for sharing with those you love.

13. *What Level Of Social Approval And Respect Do You Need?* Each of us wants to be accepted by our friends. Never work for a

company of which you are ashamed.

One man admitted to me that he had no confidence in the products he was promoting. Consequently, he experienced very little success. He left that job and went to work with a company he could honestly support. It made all the difference in his happiness.

14. *What Kind Of Financial Future Is Necessary For Your Peace Of Mind?* While very few jobs offer a lifetime guarantee, every one of us needs a sense of predictable income. *Tomorrow does come.*

You must find *where* God wants you *to be and what* He wants you to be doing, and *move* as quickly as possible in that direction. Paul wrote, "With good will doing service, as to the Lord, and not to men" (Eph. 6:7).

The Questions You Ask Determine The Answers You Discover. Review These Questions And Your Success Will Explode!

RECOMMENDED BOOKS AND TAPES ON THIS TOPIC

B-44   31 Secrets for Career Success (Book/$10)

B-99   Secrets of the Richest Man Who Ever Lived (Book/$10)

B-118   Seeds of Wisdom on Problem Solving (Book/$5)

TS-99   Secrets of the Richest Man Who Ever Lived (Six tapes/$30)

TS-85   School of Wisdom, Vol. 1 - The Uncommon Life (Six tapes/ $30)

Loneliness
Is Not
The Loss Of Affection,
But
The Loss Of Direction.

-MIKE MURDOCK

❧ 28 ❧

LONELINESS

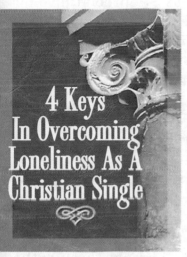

4 Keys In Overcoming Loneliness As A Christian Single

Loneliness Is Not The Loss Of Affection, But The Loss Of Direction.

I read somewhere that there are more than 55 million single adults living in the U.S.A. today.

Many have experienced marriage and have lost their partner through divorce or death. For both, the transition to single life is often traumatic. Readjustment of schedules, loss of friendships.

Sudden aloneness can trigger an unbelievable crisis. It is an inside battle that requires time, and often painful, *spiritual* "surgery." An interesting statement comes from a famous "single." The missionary, Apostle Paul, said, *"Art thou loosed from a wife? seek not a wife"* (1 Cor. 7:27). At first glance, it seems to contradict Genesis 2:18 which says, *"It is not good that the man should be alone..."*

Paul is simply saying, *"Concentrate on the present advantages."* Unpack and live where you are! Stop reliving yesterday. Memories are photographs of experiences. What we concentrate on, we *feel*. What we feel, we begin to perform. And our performance determines our sense of worth and self-esteem.

It is satan's weapon to destroy the productivity of the present by forcing our concentration on the *past*.

Get involved with *present* opportunities. Develop your mind. Discipline your body. Open your heart to those around you. My compassion for singles runs deep. I have experienced their emotional cycles, the sense of loss, the overwhelming loneliness. But I also know that during the pressure zone, God becomes very real. That pressure zone is also a *growth* zone.

1.   *Anticipate Emotional Cycles And Mood Swings.*

Singles usually experience constantly changing emotional cycles. Sometimes we sit in our apartment or home thinking, "God, when are

You going to send *somebody* I can share my dreams and plans with? *Please,* God!" Then the very next day, "Whew! I'm glad nobody's here to hassle me!"

It is part of maturing. What we *think* we need and what we actually need are often two different things.

2. *Recognize That Greatness Is A Process.*

Your experience with *emptiness...prepares* you for the *filling.*

Your experience of *loneliness...develops* appreciation for *companionship.*

The experience *of doubt...forces* us to dig for what we *really* believe.

The testing of *sincerity* in others...develops *your discerning* abilities.

Timing is the Golden Word in the World of Wisdom. It will be the Key to the treasures you dream of unlocking. There is a time to be *aggressive.* There is a time to be *gentle.*

"To every thing there is a season, and a time to every purpose under the Heaven" (Ecc. 3:1).

"The Lord is good unto them that wait for Him..." (Lam. 3:25).

3. *Pursue Success Secrets Of The Singles Who Have Succeeded.*

The most powerful force in the world is love. It breaks through the barricades of prejudice, tradition and selfishness. It is the basis for motivation: the labors of a father, the toils of a mother are rooted in that invisible ingredient called love.

To love someone is to place high value on them. "Falling in love" is the mental picture that illustrates *dethronement* of self and the *elevation* of another.

An important question every *single* should ask is, "Why am I really attracted to this person? Is it simply good looks? Talents? Mutual interests?" Many times we actually love a characteristic or *quality* in someone *rather than the person.* Memories of past harsh treatment will accentuate and magnify the gentleness of a new friend. Financial pressures will exaggerate the attractiveness of financial security.

Many singles have accepted *less* than God's very best simply because of loneliness.

4. *Discern That Loneliness Can Cloud Your Judgment.*

Be honest with yourself. *Discern the dominant basis of attraction.* Name it. *If* the person in your life now is a spiritual strength or simply helps you to "climb socially," *name it for what it is.* If it is simply feeding physical desires, to deceive yourself, it will be *costly.*

Stay strong. *Don't let temporary loneliness create a permanent problem.*   And remember, "Blessed is the man that endureth temptation: for when he is tried, he shall receive the crown of life, which the Lord hath promised to them that love Him" (James 1:12).

RECOMMENDED BOOKS AND TAPES ON THIS TOPIC

B-17   Seeds of Wisdom on Overcoming (Book/$3)

B-29   The Survival Bible (Book/$10)

TS-8   Life as a Christian Single (Six tapes/$30)

TS-39   The Double Diamond Principle (Six tapes/$30)

The Proof Of Love
Is The
Investment Of Time.

-MIKE MURDOCK

≈ 29 ≈

LOVE

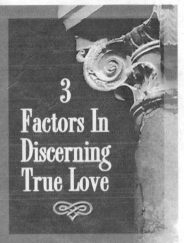

3 Factors In Discerning True Love

The Most Powerful Force In The World Is Love.

"And now these three remain: faith, hope and love. But the greatest of these is love" (1 Cor. 13:13).

It breaks through barricades. It is the basis for motivation: the labors of a father, the toils of a mother are rooted in that invisible ingredient called love.

To love someone is to place high value on them. "Falling in love" is the mental picture that illustrates *dethronement* of self and the *elevation* of another.

An important question every *single* should ask is, "Why am I really attracted to this person? Is it simply good looks? Talents? Mutual interests?"

Many times we actually love a characteristic or *quality* in someone *rather than the person.* Memories of past harsh treatment will accentuate and magnify the gentleness of a new friend. Financial pressures will exaggerate the attractiveness of financial security.

Many singles have accepted *less* than God's very best simply because of loneliness.

How do we discern *true love?* How do we know when we are "in love?" How can we have the assurance that someone truly loves *us?*

Many argue over this thing of "falling in love," but let's avoid quibbling and admit: God has to give you *a very special desire* and love for that person who excites your desire for *commitment.*

3 Proofs Of Uncommon Love

1. *Uncommon Love Does Not Fear.* Fear is distrust and lack of confidence. "There is no fear in...love; but perfect love casteth out fear: because fear hath torment. He that feareth is not made perfect in

love" (1 Jn. 4:18). Something is missing when fear is present. It may be evidence of the wrong person or the wrong timing. Be cautious.

2. *Uncommon Love Wants To Give.* Love wants to contribute to another's needs: "For God so loved the world that He *gave* His only begotten Son, that whosoever believeth in Him should not perish, but have everlasting life" (Jn. 3:16). True love results in the investment of time, effort and even finances in another. Ministering to someone you love should become a joy.

3. *Uncommon Love Anticipates The Needs Of Others.* Jesus proved this with Zacchaeus, and with the Samaritan woman at the well: "...for your Heavenly Father knoweth that ye have need of all these things. But seek ye first the kingdom of God, and His righteousness; and all these things shall be added unto you" (Matt. 6:32,33).

As you sow your love into those around you, expect God to bless you beyond your greatest expectations.

What You Make Happen For Others, God Will Make Happen For You (see Eph. 6:8).

Do not give to others in proportion to your capacity or ability to give. *Discern the size of their cup, and give according to their capacity to receive.* A gallon poured into a pint container is not only *waste,* but drowns those who receive, and *weakens the "ability" of the giver to "sow" again.*

Love is worthy of scrutiny.

Unleash the River of Love within you and it will come back to you 1000 times over!

RECOMMENDED BOOKS AND TAPES ON THIS TOPIC

B-14   Seeds of Wisdom on Relationships (Book/$3)

TS-85   School of Wisdom, Vol. 1 - The Uncommon Life (Six tapes/ $30)

❧ 30 ❧

MENTOR

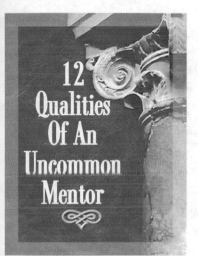

Mentors Are Trusted Teachers.

Various teachers will enter and exit your life. The Holy Spirit is your dominant and most important Mentor of all (see Jn. 14:15, 16). But, a Mentor is *trusted*.

Wisdom determines the success of your life. There are two ways to receive Wisdom: 1) Mistakes; 2) Mentors.

Mentors are the difference between poverty and prosperity; decrease and increase; loss and gain; pain and pleasure; deterioration and restoration.

1. *An Uncommon Mentor Is The Master Key To The Success Of A Protégé.* "Wisdom is the principal thing" (Prov. 4:7).

2. *An Uncommon Mentor Transfers Wisdom Through Relationship.* "He that walketh with wise men shall be wise: but a companion of fools shall be destroyed" (Prov. 13:20). Joshua knew this. "And Joshua the son of Nun was full of the spirit of Wisdom; for Moses had laid his hands upon him:" (Deut. 34:9).

3. *An Uncommon Mentor Guarantees Your Promotion.* "Exalt her, and she shall promote thee: she shall bring thee to honour, when thou dost embrace her. She shall give to thine head an ornament of grace: a crown of glory shall she deliver to thee" (Prov. 4:8,9).

4. *An Uncommon Mentor Can Determine Your Wealth.* "Riches and honour are with me; yea, durable riches and righteousness" (Prov. 8:18).

5. *An Uncommon Mentor Can Paralyze Your Enemies Against You.* "For I will give you a mouth and Wisdom, which all your adversaries shall not be able to gainsay nor resist" (Lk. 21:15).

6. *An Uncommon Mentor Can Cause Influential People To Listen To You.* "And Joshua the son of Nun was full of the spirit of Wisdom; for Moses had laid his hands upon him: and *the children of*

Israel hearkened unto him..." (Deut. 34:9).

7. *An Uncommon Mentor Will Require Your Pursuit.* He does not need what you know. You need what he knows. Elijah never pursued Elisha. Elisha desired what was in him. *The Proof Of Desire Is Pursuit.*

8. *An Uncommon Mentor Is More Interested In Your Success Than Your Affection.* His focus is not the celebration of you, but the correction of you.

9. *An Uncommon Mentor Is Not Necessarily Your Best Friend.*
▶ Your Best Friend loves you *the way you are.*
Your Mentor loves you *too much* to *leave you* the way you are.
▶ Your Best Friend is comfortable with your *past.*
Your Mentor is comfortable with your *future.*
▶ Your Best Friend *ignores* your weakness.
Your Mentor *removes* your weakness.
▶ Your Best Friend is your *cheerleader.*
Your Mentor is your *coach.*
▶ Your Best Friend sees what you do *right.*
Your Mentor sees what you do *wrong.*

10. *An Uncommon Mentor Sees Things You Cannot See.* He sees weaknesses in you before you experience the pain of them. He sees an enemy before you discern him. He has already experienced the pain of a problem you are about to create.

11. *An Uncommon Mentor Will Become An Enemy To The Enemies Of His Protégé.* Jesus proved this. "Simon, Simon, behold, satan hath desired to have you, that he may sift you as wheat: But I have prayed for thee, that thy faith fail not: and when thou art converted, strengthen thy brethren" (Lk. 22:31,32). An Uncommon Mentor will fight against any philosophy, pitfalls or prejudices that would rob the protégé of experiencing complete success in his life.

12. *An Uncommon Mentor Can Create An Uncommon Protégé.* Jesus took a fisherman and turned Peter into a master preacher. Everything you know will come through Mentorship, by experience or a person.

Invest everything to spend time and moments with an Uncommon Mentor God has chosen to sow into your life.

Recognition Of An Uncommon Mentor Will Prevent A Thousand Heartaches.

❦ 31 ❧

MINISTERS

20 Important Facts About Ministers

You Are A Captive Or A Deliverer.
Ministers are *Deliverers.*

They are those who have *recognized* the authority of God and submitted. They have recognized the *plan* of God and cooperated. They have recognized the *consequences of disobeying* their God, and obeyed.

Deliverers hate *doubt* and *unbelief.*

Deliverers *fear God.*

Deliverers keep *His commandments.*

Deliverers are obsessed with doing the will of God on the earth. Yet, like the Pharisees, millions do not recognize Ministers assigned to bring change and revolution to their life.

The *counsel* of *pastors* is often *ignored.*

The *predictions* of *prophets* are *treated lightly.*

Late night talk show hosts scoff at Ministers.

Scorners do not recognize them.

The *rebellious refuse* to recognize them.

The *ignorant belittle* their counsel.

Two classes of people exist on the earth: *Deliverers* and *Captives.* Captives are those imprisoned by sin, habits, error, philosophy or anything that prevents them from entering excellence, perfection and a life in the Spirit.

Deliverers think differently than captives.

Captives *discuss* pain.

Deliverers *destroy* pain.

Captives think Deliverers do not care.

Deliverers care enough to fight.

Captives crave *attention.*

Deliverers crave *freedom.*

Deliverers Are Anointed To Set Captives Free. "The Spirit of the Lord God is upon Me; because the Lord hath anointed Me to preach good tidings unto the meek; He hath sent Me to bind up the brokenhearted, to proclaim liberty to the captives, and the opening of the prison to them that are bound;" (Isa. 61:1).

The Anointing causes Deliverers to assess the Enemy accurately. That's why Deliverers hate chains and bondage and want to set Captives free.

I remember when one of my dogs had a thorn embedded in its paw. But, when I tried to help it, it moved away from me, yelping. My dog *needed* help. But, the pain had become its focus so much that it did not appreciate my desire and ability to help. That reminds me a lot of hurting people. They are so obsessed with pain, memories and burdens that when a Deliverer arrives, they are often blinded to him.

1. *True Ministers Are Different Because Their Assignments Are Different.* John the Baptist had a different Assignment than the Apostle Paul. Billy Graham has a different Assignment than Benny Hinn. God uses our differences in background, personality and viewpoint to achieve His desired end.

2. *Ministers Do Not Always Understand Each Other.* Peter and Paul had their differences. Throughout history, great men have not always been in agreement. Job said, "Great men are not always wise:" (Job 32:9).

3. *Ministers Sometimes Experience Failure, Too.* Jonah is not the only disobedient man of God in history. Micah is not the only disappointed and discouraged prophet who ever lived. Elijah was not the last prophet who wanted to commit suicide.

Ministers are a barometer for those to whom they are assigned. They feel their pain. They have tasted disappointment. That increases their effectiveness in relating to others.

4. *Ministers Sometimes Rebel Against Their Assignment.* Jonah did (read Jon. 1-4).

5. *Ministers Often Exude The Authority Of God That Intimidates Some While Invigorating Others.* Stephen's message brought anger to many, and yet deliverance to others.

6. *Ministers Are The Most Gentle Tools God Uses To Deal With People.* The Israelites rebelled against Moses. He taught. He cried. He begged. But, when they ignored the Voice of Ministers, judgment followed. God opened up the earth and swallowed some. Fire scorched others.

7. *Ministers May Not Be Packaged Like You Anticipated.* John the Baptist might not be accepted today. But, God was with him.

8. *Ministers Do Not Always Have Comfortable And Enjoyable Personalities.* Isaiah and Ezekiel might not be very popular with most Christians today.

9. *Ministers Do Not Always Use The Words Of Academic Excellence And Higher Education.* God often uses the heart of the humble over the silken voice of the gifted (see 1 Cor. 2:1-4).

10. *Ministers Do Not Always Recognize When God Has Spoken To Another Minister.* They simply must respect the fact that they, too, are Ministers. "Believe in the Lord your God, so shall ye be established; believe His prophets, so shall ye prosper" (2 Chr. 20:20).

11. *Ministers Are Not Always Adapted Socially.* God uses foolish things to confound the wise.

12. *The Decisiveness Of Ministers Is Often Unsettling To The Uncertain* (see Jn. 19:11,12).

13. *The Holiness Of Ministers Agitates The Unholy* (see Acts 7:54-59).

14. *The Courage Of Ministers Often Enrages The Manipulators* (read Acts 16:17-24).

15. *The Price Paid For Ignoring A Minister Is Often Devastating.* Remember Ananias and Sapphira lying to Peter?

16. *Ignoring Ministers Who Fuel Your Faith Can Create A Lifetime Of Losses.* When the Israelites ignored the faith of Moses, Joshua and Caleb, they spent 40 more years of tears, wandering in the wilderness.

17. *When You Disrespect Or Disdain A Minister, Tragedy May Result.* It happened when the children of Israel laughed at the prophet Elisha, calling him an old "bald head."

18. *Disrespect Of A Minister Will Create A Loss Of Relationship With Him.* The Pharisees sneered at Jesus. You never saw Him eating supper with them, either. But, when Zacchaeus, the ungodly tax collector, respected Jesus, Jesus provided him access. Their meal together changed the course of the tax collector's life.

19. *The Ungodly Sometimes Recognize A Minister Before The Religious Crowd Does.* Zacchaeus recognized Jesus while the Pharisees did not. Pharaoh, the leader of Egypt, saw the Spirit of God in Joseph (read Gen. 42).

20. *Recognition Of A Minister Often Creates Access To Him.* Saul disrespected David. David fled. But, his son Jonathan, who recognized the mantle on David, received complete access to David.

Ministers Are Uncommon Gifts From An Uncommon God.

You Are Never
As Far From A Miracle
As It First Appears.

-MIKE MURDOCK

❧ 32 ❧

MIRACLES

You Are Never As Far From A Miracle As It First Appears.

Everybody wants a miracle.

Some will drive 500 miles to see one. Someone else will fly 3,000 miles to *experience* one for themselves.

Some do not even believe they exist. Others believe they only happen by *accident.*

The truth *is...miracles are not accidents.*

They are not the Master's manipulations of human "mannequins." Nor are they the performances of an egotistical, divine "show off."

Miracles happen to people who *need* them, *want* them and *reach* for them.

1. *Name Your Desired Miracle. You cannot find* until you *define.* Jesus asked the blind man to explain what he wanted. Jesus was not ignorant. He simply needed a *commitment* to establish the contract! (see Matt. 18:18,19). *Many people do not like where they are, but they have never decided where they want to be.*

I fly up to 20,000 miles per month. The airlines do not sell me tickets based on point of departure, but rather on my desired *destination. I can't leave until I've decided where I want to land.* My treasured friend, Nancy Harmon, wrote it in her great song, *"Name It and Claim It."*

You Will Never Leave Where You Are Until You Decide Where You Would Rather Be.

2. *Confirm Your Scriptural Grounds For Pursuing Your Desired Miracle. Search* the Word. *Stand* on the promise God inspires. *Avoid* any justification of failure. Do you want to really impress God? *Then believe* what He said. "God is not a man, that He should lie;" (Num. 23:19).

3. *Ask For The Miracle.* "Ask, and it shall be given you...For every one that asketh receiveth..." (Matt. 7:7,8). Make a demand on the ability of God. Jesus said once that someone had touched Him...for

a desired reason and purpose. Be persistent. Reach for your miracle.

4. *Don't Feed Your Friendships With Doubters.* Some "friends" may criticize you. They may even suggest that you lower or "accept things as they are." Dare to resist. *Climb,* don't crawl! He made you. *Feed your mind* on the Word. Surround yourself with tapes and books that fuel the fire of your faith within you.

5. *Talk Faith-Talk Daily.* Stop talking defeat. Stop discussing your fears, doubts and unbelief. Talk your *expectations,* not your disappointing experiences. When others plant Seeds of fear, speak aloud and boldly what God *has spoken in His Word.* You were born to win. You were *born to taste the grapes of God's blessings!*

6. *Visualize Yourself With The Completed Miracle.* Never underestimate the power and influence of your God-given mind-machine. It is a "camera." The photo file it compiles is almost unbelievable.

The picture that stays in your mind will happen in time. In Mark 5, the sick woman said: "If I can touch the hem of His garment, I know I'll be healed." She had a *mental picture* of her effort...and the actual healing resulting.

When Abraham saw stars, he *visualized his children* to come. Jesus, for the joy that was set *before* Him, endured the cross. He pictured the resurrection, the ascension, the return to the Father...it *energized Him to endure the crucifixion.*

7. *Never Let Go In The Night What God Has Promised In The Light.* Miracles are for the *persistent,* not the wisher. Hold on to what God wants you to have. You are Heaven's favorite product. God's entire promotional program is geared to *you.*

The book of Ephesians says that you are *chosen,* you are *blessed,* you are *predestinated,* you are *accepted,* you are *quickened,* you are *seated* in Heavenly places (Eph. 1:3-8).

God established the miracle-system. He wants it to work for *you.* Go ahead...reach for your miracle!

You Were Born To Taste The Grapes!

RECOMMENDED BOOKS AND TAPES ON THIS TOPIC

B-15   Seeds of Wisdom on Miracles (Book/$3)

B-28   The Blessing Bible (Book/$10)

B-47   The Covenant of Fifty-Eight Blessings (Book/$8)

B-104   7 Keys to 1000 Times More (Book/$10)

≈ 33 ≈

MISTAKES

15 Keys
For Turning
Your Mistakes
Into Miracles

All Men Fall.
The Great Ones Simply Get Back Up.
This is a human world. You will find that mistakes are just a part of your daily life. Mistakes happen on the job, in your choice of friends and even in financial decisions.

Yesterday's failure can become *today's* success. *Tragedies* can become *triumphs.*

Though some mistakes can be devastating, the majority of your mistakes can be turned around for your good!

You can change the direction of your life! *You* can step *out* of failure and into a victorious and successful life. God, your Creator and Heavenly Father, has anticipated your problem areas and has laid out a *plan* for turning your mistakes into miracles!!

Proverbs 24:16: "For a just man falleth seven times, and riseth up again:"

Psalm 37:23,24: "The steps of a good man are ordered by the Lord: and He delighteth in his way. Though he fall, he shall not be utterly cast down: for the Lord upholdeth him with His hand."

Here Are 15 Powerful Keys

1. *Accept Your Humanity. You are not God.* Neither do you have "angel wings!" The possibilities of your making a mistake are 100 percent. *The nature* of your mistakes and *what you do about them* determine your success.

God anticipated your weaknesses. "Like as a father pitieth his children, so the Lord pitieth them that fear Him. For He knoweth our frame; He remembereth that we are dust" (Ps. 103:13,14).

True, some use the flimsy comment, "I'm just human," as a "cop-out" and cover-up instead of a motivation for higher principles.

Thousands who learn to *accept* themselves learn to *enjoy* life!

2. *Admit Your Mistake.*

▶ *Recognize and confess it to yourself.* Do not justify it. Do not lie to yourself. The Scriptures say: "He that covereth his sins shall not prosper: but whoso confesseth and forsaketh them shall have mercy" (Prov. 28:13).

▶ *Confess your mistake to God.* "If we confess our sins, He is faithful and just to forgive us our sins, and to cleanse us from all unrighteousness" (1 Jn. 1:9).

▶ *Confess your mistake to others who were damaged by your mistake.* "And when ye stand praying, forgive, if ye have aught against any: that your Father also which is in Heaven may forgive you your trespasses" (Mk. 11:25).

Caution: there are exceptions. When your confession would do more to *destroy* faith and confidence in the mind of another, confess to God *alone.* "In the multitude of words there wanteth not sin: but he that refraineth his lips is wise" (Prov. 10:19).

3. *Assign The Responsibility Of The Mistake To Those Truly Responsible.* If others are involved, you must allow them to accept their own share of the blame. Assuming all responsibility for others opens the door to bitterness, resentment and self-pity. Besides, you add to their own success by forcing them to account for themselves. Parents who always "cover" for little Johnny or Susie destroy their children's chances for maturity. "Chasten thy son while there is hope, and let not thy soul spare for his crying" (Prov. 19:18).

"I've got to go get my husband out of the bar tonight, he's drinking again," a heartbroken lovely lady told me one night.

I replied, "Why?"

She looked surprised. "Well...uh...he...uh."

I said, "If you keep cushioning the fall, he'll never quit jumping. *You've got to let him hit the bottom.* Then, and only then, will he want to reach for the top."

4. *Review The Other Possible Alternatives Available To You At The Time Of Your Mistake.* Obviously, you made a wrong move. What were the options at the time? Could you have done it differently? Did you do your very best? "For which of you, intending to build a tower, sitteth not down first, and counteth the cost, whether he have sufficient to finish it?" (Lk. 14:28).

Sometimes what *appears* to be a mistake was the *only* possible decision at the time! Don't waste valuable time on unavoidable past circumstances. Perhaps a mistake wasn't made at all!

On the other hand, by carefully evaluating the past, you will avoid making the same mistake again.

5. *Name The People Or Circumstances That Were Influencing You When You Made Your Mistake.*

A minister friend once told me, "Mike, I missed God's perfect will during ten long years of my life."

"What caused it?" I asked.

"I got overtired," he said. "I overreacted to criticism from a disgruntled deacon. I just up and resigned from my church before God was finished with my ministry there. It was the biggest mistake of my entire life."

▶ *Fatigue* warped his judgment.

Are you watching too much television? Neglecting consistent church attendance? Involved in unhealthy friendships? Is it your ego? Be honest!

Your dreams and goals can be destroyed by listening to the wrong advice. Even *sickness* can greatly affect your decision-making.

▶ *A frustrated friend may be creating a climate of discontent for you.* "He that walketh with wise men shall be wise: but a companion of fools shall be destroyed" (Prov. 13:20).

6. *Be Willing To Taste The Pain Of Your Mistake.* There are times God wants us to *feel* the *hurt* of our wrongs. In Luke 15, the prodigal son *"came to himself"* when he became so hungry. "He would fain have filled his belly with the husks that the swine did eat:" (verse 16). *Pain can motivate you.* God may allow you to crash! *If He cushioned every blow, you would never grow.*

However, I assure you, your Heavenly Father will not allow your suffering and aching to be a permanent feeling. He will use it to develop a *humility,* a *compassion* for others and a *reminder* of why Jesus Christ died on Calvary for the sins of the world: "But He knoweth the way that I take: when He hath tried me, I shall come forth as gold" (Job 23:10).

The Psalmist said: "It is good for me that I have been afflicted; that I might learn Thy statutes" (Ps. 119:71).

Hebrews 5:8 says: "Though He were a Son, yet learned He obedience by the things which He suffered;"

7. *Write A List Of The Personal Lessons You Have Learned And Any Current Alternatives.* Take a sheet of paper and "Write the vision and make it plain..." (Hab. 2:2). Ask yourself these questions.

▶ "What *weaknesses in myself* does this mistake reveal?"
▶ "What have I learned about *others* during this time?"

▶ "What do the *Scriptures* teach in regard to my mistake?"

Take time to *think...to hear* with your *heart* what you can understand through this time of learning. Read and study the lives of people who made the same mistake and how they recovered. Focus on what you can do *now,* and begin taking the necessary steps toward recovery.

8. *Stop Talking To Everyone About Your Mistake.* A few choice friends will gladly lend an ear as you release your pent-up hurt. You may need it...with the *right* people. However, it is even more effective to discuss it with God. "In the day when I cried Thou answeredst me, and strengthenedst me with strength in my soul" (Ps. 138:3). "I sought the Lord, and He heard me, and delivered me from all my fears" (Ps. 34:4).

You see, too many times we display our weaknesses *unnecessarily.* It magnifies our mistakes and puts ammunition in the hands of our enemies. Stop putting yourself down! Make up your mind you are *not* losing, you are *learning*!

"He that hath knowledge spareth his words..." (Prov. 17:27). "Give instruction to a wise man, and he will be yet wiser: teach a just man, and he will increase in learning" (Prov. 9:9). *Be kind but firm in refusing others the liberty to focus on your past failures.* "Brethren, I count not myself to have apprehended: but this one thing I do, forgetting those things which are behind...I press toward the mark for the prize of the high calling of God in Christ Jesus. Let us therefore, as many as be perfect, be thus minded: and if in any thing ye be otherwise minded, God shall reveal even this unto you" (Phil. 3:13-15).

I suggest you actually memorize Isaiah 43:18,19: "Remember ye not the former things, neither consider the things of old. Behold, I will do a new thing; now it shall spring forth; shall ye not know it? I will even make a way in the wilderness, and rivers in the desert."

9. *Make Restitution With Those You Have Wronged Or Hurt.* True repentance involves restitution—mending broken fences. One definition of restitution is "the *final restoration* of all things and persons to be in harmony with God's will." Restitution is a *faith-releasing* principle that purifies your conscience. It unties the hands of God to work freely on your behalf. "If a man shall steal an ox, or a sheep, and kill it, or sell it; he shall restore five oxen for an ox, and four sheep for a sheep" (Ex. 22:1). "And Zacchaeus stood, and said unto the Lord; Behold, Lord, the half of my goods I give to the poor; and if I have taken any thing from any man by false accusation, I restore him fourfold" (Lk. 19:8).

Several years ago, a man was having marital problems, stomach pains and could not sleep at night. He broke down and confessed to me that he had embezzled money from his company.

"You must make it right," I insisted. "Go to your president and totally level with him. Admit your mistake."

Though he feared losing his job, the man truly recognized the value of restitution. Guess what happened? *Not only was he permitted to keep his job, but later received a promotion from the president who respected his openness and new convictions!*

Pain is merely a passage to a miracle.

10. *Allow A Season Of Time For Your Recovery.* It is natural to want an *"instant"* change in your circumstances. Take for instance, the emotional cycle following a divorce...loneliness, anger, depression, bitterness, frustration, emptiness, guilt, past memories. How do you cope with these? It is not always as easy as glib-tongued friends may try to make it appear.

It *simply* takes time *for total healing*.

Of course, there are things you can do to *hasten* the healing, just as it is possible to *slow* your healing process.

The wisest man who ever lived said: "To every thing there is a season, and a time to every purpose" (Ecc. 3:1).

But, do not weary of waiting for your complete miracle. Give yourself space: "And let us not be weary in well doing: for in due season we shall reap, if we faint not" (Gal. 6:9).

Meanwhile, during your "Recovery Zone," learn all you can, cultivate compassion, exercise faith, and develop control in all areas of your life.

11. *Help Someone Else Receive Their Miracle.* Jesus Christ is our master example of concentrating on the success of *others*. He literally is a Success-Maker. He reprogrammed the mentality of losers.

Jesus Cared About Others.

He took the time:

...to compliment (see Matt. 8:10);

...to heal the sick (see Matt. 8:16);

...to forgive sin (see Matt. 9:2);

...to advise ministers (see Matt. 10:1-42);

...to teach the unlearned (see Matt. 5,6,7);

...to expose frauds (see Matt. 23).

He created *success situations* for people.

Look around you! What can you do now to be a better employee on your job? A better husband or wife? A better friend? Proverbs 3:27 says: "Withhold not good from them to whom it is due, when it is in the power of thine hand to do it."

"Render therefore to all their dues: tribute to whom tribute is due; custom to whom custom; fear to whom fear; honour to whom honour" (Rom. 13:7).

"Knowing that whatsoever good thing any man doeth, the same shall he receive of the Lord, whether he be bond or free" (Eph. 6:8). Never forget the greatest Wisdom Principle in scriptural success: "What You Make Happen For Others, God Will Make Happen For You!"

12. *Develop The Winner's Mentality. You become what you think.* So, start hanging "success photographs" on the walls of your own mind!

Picture yourself in *health.*

Picture yourself in *prosperity.*

Picture yourself in a *happy marriage.*

Picture yourself as an *overcomer.*

Picture yourself as *victorious.*

When you control your thoughts, you control your life: "Whatsoever things are true...honest...just...pure...lovely...of good report; if there be any virtue, if there be any praise, *think on these things"* (Phil. 4:8).

Visualize what you want to *materialize!* Some time ago I bought a car. With it, I received an owner's handbook on how to operate it, how to solve possible problems. It was to help me enjoy driving my new car, and avoid some frustrating situations.

God, the Creator, provided the same service to you and me to enjoy living in His world. That Success Handbook is called the Bible. It is your source for How To Live On Planet Earth. Without it, you may easily sabotage your life.

Read the Bible often. It will place positive and powerful mind-photographs in your thinking. You will begin to understand God, others and yourself in a beautiful new light!

13. *Celebrate Even Your Smallest Accomplishments!* When you find a parking space exactly where you wanted...a dress you wanted on sale for half price...a gasoline station open when your tank shows empty—*talk about it!* Immediately verbalize a big, *"Thanks, Father!"* Tell your friends!

Learn to appreciate these "little" blessings! Cultivate the "attitude of gratitude!" Look for the good in others. Look for the good in yourself! Recognize your own accomplishments no matter how insignificant they may appear.   Jesus told a great truth in Matthew 25 when the principle of recognition and rewards was given: "...thou hast been faithful over a few things, I will make thee ruler over many things..." (verses 21,23).

Express thanksgiving for the "little" blessings, and you will see those "bigger blessings" begin to follow.

14. *Begin This Very Moment. Start today. God put you and this book together. God is a now God.* He wants you to become a *Winner* this very day.

Right now, pray this prayer aloud: "Father, I need You. I want You. Forgive me of every mistake I have made with my life. I accept Jesus Christ as the Lord and Master of my life.   I now receive Your forgiveness, and believe that You will begin to fill my heart and life with peace and joy from this very moment. Fill me with Your Holy Spirit as I enter the winner's world! I place all the memories of yesterday's mistake at the cross of Calvary. I thank You for sending the right people into my life this week to help me develop and grow into a powerful winner for You. In Jesus' name, Amen."

15. *Never, Never, Never Quit.* You've started. You have read this book this far through which shows you have what it takes to be a winner! *You can make it!* You may experience a few setbacks, a few moments of doubt and confusion. This is normal and will not linger. Immediately, say aloud, "I am not a quitter, I am a winner! Nothing can stop me."

Make this your confession: "I can do all things through Christ which strengtheneth me:" (Phil. 4:13).   Remember 1 John 4:4: "...greater is He that is in you, than he that is in the world."

"The Lord upholdeth all that fall, and raiseth up all those that be bowed down" (Ps. 145:14).

Your mess will become your message.

Your pain will become your pulpit.

Your burden will become your blessing.

Your weakness will become your weapon.

RECOMMENDED BOOKS AND TAPES ON THIS TOPIC

B-17   Seeds of Wisdom on Overcoming (Book/$3)

B-40   Wisdom for Crisis Times (Book/$9)

TS-40   Wisdom for Crisis Times (Six tapes/$30)

TS-83   School of Wisdom, Vol. 3 - What I'd Do Differently If I Could Begin My Life Over Again (Six tapes/$30)

Money Does Not Change You-
It Simply Makes More
Of Whatever You Really Are.

-MIKE MURDOCK

～ 34 ～

MONEY

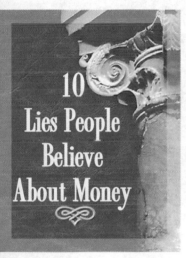

10 Lies People Believe About Money

Prosperity Is Simply Having Enough Of God's Provision To Complete His Instruction For Your Life.

One of the needs people write me about most is their financial problems. I know what it means to prosper and I also know what it means to be completely wiped out financially.

One of the tools satan uses to destroy incentive, goals and joy of accomplishment is financial difficulty. Read this chapter with an open mind toward God and how you can become a winner in the financial area of your life.

Lies are deadly. I thought of this when I read a recent account of an airplane crash. Chilling screams of terror tore into the cold night air. The explosion of metal. Helpless cries of torment and desperation. Families wiped out. Lifetime dreams shattered like glass upon concrete. Emotional scars forever engraved on the soul. Havoc. Destruction. Chaos. All in a matter of minutes.

Because somebody lied.

In the rush, the plane mechanics had failed to notice the tiny malfunction. Signaled that all was well, the pilot proceeded down the runway. *He accepted the opinion and judgment of others.*

It cost him his life.

Your happiness depends on something you are believing. Success or failure depends on your believing a lie or the truth. In marriage, in health, in spiritual matters and even in finances, what you believe makes *all* the difference. From Santa Claus to tooth fairies, all of us can remember moments we believed a lie. Sometimes harmless, sometimes devastating.

One of the greatest needs of life is *money.*

Sit with the minister counseling the young married couple— *money.*

Look at the youth in prison for stealing—*money.*

Listen to the missionary from Africa sharing the needs of his ministry—*money.*

Talk to the weary overworked husband—*money.*

Read the Holy Bible. The teachings of Jesus Christ include this power topic—*money.*

Thousands live unfulfilled and frustrated lives because they do not understand the truth about money.

LIE #1: *Money Is Unimportant.*

Recently, I sat in a coffee shop in the Dallas-Fort Worth airport. I listened as the waitress spoke of her long hours, small apartment and two children.

"Wouldn't you like to be making *more* money?" I asked.

"No, I would not!" She replied indignantly. "That's what is wrong with our world now: greed. I have enough for my bills and support for my two kids, and that's all I want. People place too much emphasis on money. *Money is unimportant.*"

I could hardly believe my ears.

"Have you ever heard of Calcutta, India?"

"Yes," she replied.

"Have you ever seen pictures of the starving children there?"

"Yes."

"Have you ever sent them any money or food?"

"No."

"Why not?" I asked.

"I haven't had enough..." Her voice trailed off.

I could see in her eyes the truth had dawned. Money *does* count. Life hinges on it. *Money is the power part of our world.* With it we bargain, trade and exchange our way through life! Shelter, food, medical care, education, and even self-preservation involve money. Money is a basic method of communication between human beings. In war or peace, love or hate...*money talks.*

LIE #2: *Money Is Evil.*

Many people misquote the Bible verse when the Apostle Paul wrote Timothy: "For the love of money is the root of all evil..." (1 Tim. 6:10). It does not say that money is evil, but that the *love* of, or obsession for money is the root or beginning of evil. Why? Because the love of money is *idolatry.* It is the worship of the creation instead of the Creator. *God is the owner of wealth.*

Haggai 2:8 says: "The silver is Mine, and the gold is Mine, saith the Lord of hosts."

God is the Giver of wealth. Deuteronomy 8:18: "But thou shalt remember the Lord thy God: for it is He that giveth thee power to get wealth..."

When God gives you a gift, it must have value, importance and purpose for your life: "Every good gift and every perfect gift is from above, and cometh down from the Father..." (James 1:17).

God would never give evil gifts to His children.

It is the *misuse* and *abuse* of money that can be destructive. Not money itself. For example, *fire* destroys homes, beautiful forests and kills human beings. Yet, properly controlled, it is a tremendous tool for cooking food, warming houses and running automobile engines. *Flood waters* have drowned many human lives. Yet, water is necessary for human life. Cleanliness and even nature depend on it. So it is with *money.* It can be used *for good!*

As one humorist has said, "Money is not cold, hard cash, but warm, soft blessings!" "Beloved, I wish above all things that thou mayest prosper and be in health, even as thy soul prospereth" (3 Jn. 1:2).

LIE #3: *Money Never Hurt Anyone.*

This truth is undeniable: *Money will affect you.*

Why? What is behind the mysterious magnetism of gold? Men have killed for money. Men have deserted children and wife in search of gold. You see, the basic craving of man is a *sense of worth,* a sense of importance. Money represents *power,* influence, achievements and security. That is why money can be deceptive. Jesus referred to this as the *"deceitfulness of riches"* which arrested spiritual development (see Matt. 13:22). It is a false sense of security.

A wise and wealthy ruler advised, "For riches are not for ever..." and "...riches certainly make themselves wings; they fly away as an eagle toward Heaven" (Prov. 27:24; Prov. 23:5).

Money often produces pride. This is spiritually devastating (see Mk. 10:25). Whatever consumes your time, whatever you think about most is really your "god" (see Matt. 6:24). God refuses to compete and guarantees that "he that trusteth in his riches shall fall..." (Prov. 11:28). Yes, money can hurt you.

LIE #4: *Money Will Cure Your Problems And Guarantee Personal Happiness.*

Unfortunately, the opposite is true in many cases (see Ecc. 5:12). The rich sometimes feel that their friendships are fragile and plastic, based on their possessions and not themselves. Bitter, frustrated and lonely, some have even committed suicide.

Think for a moment. Are you still content with your last salary increase? Probably not. Ecclesiastes 5:10 says: "He that loveth silver shall not be satisfied with silver...." "Neither is his eye satisfied with riches..." (Ecc. 4:8).

It is having a *purpose* in life, not possessions, that is truly satisfying. And that purpose can only be realized in the person Jesus Christ. "He that hath the Son hath life; and he that hath not the Son of God hath not life" (1 Jn. 5:12).

▶ Unbelievers often ignore the *problems of prosperity.*

▶ Believers often ignore the *purpose for prosperity.*

Whether it is the deterioration of a marriage, or the moral fiber of an entire nation, man's basic problem is *spiritual.*

LIE #5: *Some Are Gifted For Wealth And Some Are Destined For Poverty.*

This ridiculous lie has destroyed initiative, drive and motivation in many would-be winners throughout the world. Many capable people have believed, "Whatever *is,* was *meant* to be." *Nonsense!*

The truth is, through development of your God-given *talents* and the principles of *giving,* you determine the financial Harvest of your life.

"Hard work means prosperity; only a fool idles away his time...Work hard and become a leader; be lazy and never succeed" (Prov. 12:11,24 TLB).

"Work brings profit; talk brings poverty!" (Prov. 14:23 TLB).

Jesus said, "Give, and it shall be given unto you..." (Lk. 6:38).

Solomon said, "There are those who [generously] scatter abroad, and yet increase more; there are those who withhold more than is fitting or what is justly due, but it results only in want. The liberal person shall be enriched, and he who waters shall himself be watered" (Prov. 11:24,25 AMP).

God explained that financial curse or financial blessing depended on the *attitude of obedience:* "Blessed shalt thou be..." (read

Deut. 28:1-14) or "cursed shalt thou be..." (read Deut. 28:15-68). Malachi 3:8-11 reveals the reason many are not prosperous: "Will a man rob God? Yet ye have robbed Me. But ye say, Wherein have we robbed Thee? In tithes and offerings. Ye are cursed with a curse: for ye have robbed Me, even this whole nation. Bring ye all the tithes into the storehouse, that there may be meat in Mine house, and prove Me now herewith, saith the Lord of Hosts, if I will not open you the windows of Heaven, and pour you out a blessing, that there shall not be room enough to receive it. And I will rebuke the devourer for your sakes, and he shall not destroy the fruits of your ground; neither shall your vine cast her fruit before the time in the field, saith the Lord of Hosts."

LIE #6: *God Does Not Want You To Be Financially Prosperous.*

This is absurd! The *necessities* of our lives, and the *needs* of others demand financial blessings. Jesus assured us, "...your Heavenly Father knoweth that ye have need of all these things" (Matt. 6:32). The Apostle Paul denounced the man who would not provide for his family: "But if any provide not for his own house, he hath denied the faith, and is worse than an infidel" (1 Tim. 5:8).

God Is Your Source. "If ye then, being evil, know how to give good gifts unto your children, how much more shall your Father which is in Heaven give good things to them that ask Him?" (Matt. 7:11).

God Gives Wealth. "But thou shalt remember the Lord thy God: for it is He that giveth thee power to get wealth..." (Deut. 8:18). He promised Solomon: "...I will give thee riches, and wealth..." (2 Chr. 1:12). God "hath pleasure in the prosperity of His servant" (Ps. 35:27).

Money is a tool. While money may become a *snare* for the unbeliever, it is the Christian's *tool for evangelization.* There are two types of achievers in the Christian world...

1) Those who GO. "He said unto them, "Go ye into all the world, and preach the gospel to every creature" (Mk. 16:15).

2) Those who SEND. "How then shall they call on Him in whom they have not believed? and how shall they believe in Him of whom they have not heard? and how shall they hear without a preacher? And how shall they preach, except they be sent? as it is written, How beautiful are the feet of them that preach the gospel of peace, and bring glad tidings of good things!" (Rom. 10:14,15).

Money in the hands of Christians is a threat to satan. As we spread the gospel, the timing of the return of Christ is even affected.

Satan's period of power can be shortened when believers use prosperity as a tool for God's work! "And this gospel of the kingdom shall be preached in all the world for a witness unto all nations; and then shall the end come" (Matt. 24:14). Through our giving, missionaries are sent, Christian television and radio stations established, churches built, and Bibles printed. Prosperity is much more than Rolls Royce's and palaces. *Prosperity is having enough of God's supply to complete His instructions for your life—enough of His provisions to accomplish His commands.*

<u>LIE #7</u>: *There Is Nothing You Can Do About Your Financial Situation.*

While losers wait for some "magic moment of luck," the Winner works God's Principles of Prosperity.

Your financial circumstances depend on three factors:

Spending—following God's timing for *purchases.*

Saving—the discipline of planning ahead (see Prov. 6:6).

Sharing—releasing offerings into ministries in the work of God for spreading the gospel (see 2 Cor. 9:6).

<u>LIE #8</u>: *Regularity Of Giving And Amount Of Your Seed Does Not Really Matter To God.*

Wrong. Inconsistent, erratic giving does not produce a consistent Harvest. The successful farmer depends on the regularity of evolving seasons, not momentary feelings: "Upon the first day of the week let every one of you lay by him in store, as God hath prospered him..." (1 Cor. 16:2). Whether weekly or monthly, establish the success *pattern* of consistent giving to your home church and various ministries that bless you.

Jesus noted the size of offerings (read Mk. 12:42-44). He respected "sacrificial giving;" doing without temporal things temporarily, to secure the eternal benefits. The attitude is revealed by the amount we keep for ourselves, and that which is given back to God: "Every man according as he purposeth in his heart, so let him give; not grudgingly, or of necessity: for God loveth a cheerful giver" (2 Cor. 9:7).

LIE #9: *Money Is An Unspiritual Subject And Not To Be Discussed In Church.*

Ridiculous! The Bible is filled with warnings and promises regarding riches and wealth.

Money lovers must be *warned.*

The *giver* should be *encouraged.*

Money is a major part of our daily life. The minister is responsible for putting *balance* to its importance.

Offering time in churches is *worship time.*

Offering time is *investment time.*

Offering time is a period of *ministering* unto God and to our own future.

Offering time is a season of thanksgiving and appreciation.

A Personal Word To Ministers

Oh, my minister friend, take time to *inform* your people of the Principles of Blessing in God's Word! How else will they know? Do not let a cynical sinner or critical church member limit or dilute your revelation on financial blessing.

The Bible teaches it. God must assuredly value the *giving system.* Certainly offerings deserve more time than a three-minute "usher-rush" to the back of the church! Take time to *inform* your people. *Information breeds confidence.* And, they have a right to be a part of God's *reward-systems.*

LIE #10: *It Is Selfish And Wrong To Give Expecting To Receive More In Return.*

Though this lie makes little sense, thousands believe it. Wearing the mask of false humility, a man approached me recently with a proud, Pharisee strut. "I think it is selfish to want something in return. When I give, I expect nothing back from God," he snorted. His blatant ignorance and desire to advertise it appalled me! I had to ask him three questions.

"When you gave your *life* to Christ, did you expect *forgiveness* in return?"

"Uh, yes," he replied nervously.

"Aha! Selfish, were you?" I responded.

"When you are *sick,* do you expect *healing?*"

"Yes," his reply was a bit slow.

"I see. Selfish streak there. Then when you became a Christian, you gave God what *you* had, to get what *He* had for you? Peace of mind, inner joy?"

He began to grin sheepishly. "I see what you mean."

Oh, my friend, listen to me today! *Your expectation is faith.*

Nothing pleasures your Father more. You see, the God-man relationship is based on *exchange.* Life itself is based on *exchange.*

God wants your heart. You want *His* peace.

God wants your will. You want *His* plan.

Deuteronomy 28 promises that your *obedience* will bring God's *blessing.* You give God what He wants, and in return He gives you the desires of your heart (read Deut. 28:1,2).

If a father offers $5 to his son to wash the car, he does it to *motivate. It is not wrong for the son to wash the car to receive* $5! While the son acted in obedience to please his father, the money was the incentive.

Selfishness Vs. Self-Care

Self-care is wanting something good for yourself. That is not evil. You want salvation. You want peace, success and victory for your life. *God* wants you to have it.

Selfishness is *depriving another to advantage yourself.* Selfish people willingly hurt others to get ahead. This is an abomination to God.

God placed a desire for *more* inside your heart. When it becomes distorted and magnified, it is destructive. When focused on God and His principles, it is the energy for your progress in life. Dare to reach up! Dare to grow! Dare to *expect* financial blessings as you share the gospel. *Jesus gave it for motivation* in Luke 6:38: "Give, and it shall be given unto you; good measure, pressed down, and shaken together, and running over, shall men give into your bosom..."

Your strongest desire should be to please your Father, *regardless* of the cost. The proof of your faith is in your *expectation* of *Harvest. Your release* determines your *increase.*

Giving is God's cure for greed.

It reveals your faith that He is your Provider.

It shows you care about others.

It is God's investment plan for His children.

And, it works!

Perhaps your greatest problem is not financial, but spiritual or physical. God's laws of giving and receiving are effective in all areas. If you are lacking a relationship with God, *you must give in order to receive.* Give your heart, mind, soul and spirit! Let go of your past failures, sins and guilt. *Receive* Jesus as Lord, eternal life, healing for your disease, financial prosperity and forgiveness! Receive now the mentality of a victorious and successful *Winner!*

Your Credit Cage

Learn to break the bars of the credit cage. "The borrower is servant to the lender" (Prov. 22:7). Impulse buying and pride-motivated purchasing can paralyze your chances for prosperity. Romans 13:8: "Owe no man anything, but to love one another..."

Determine to get debt-free.

Study the methods of others who have already achieved financial success.

100-Fold Return

Activate the principles of tithing and Seed-faith. Even the Pharisees were commended by Jesus for tithing (see Matt. 23:23). The best investment you can make is in God's work. Mark 10:29,30 says: "And Jesus answered and said, Verily I say unto you, There is no man that hath left house, or brethren, or sisters, or father, or mother, or wife, or children, or lands, for My sake, and the gospel's, But he shall receive an hundredfold now in this time, houses, and brethren, and sisters, and mothers, and children, and lands, with persecutions; and in the world to come eternal life."

God guaranteed abundance in Malachi 3, as the resulting rewards for obedience for sowing our finances into His work. Start giving *regularly and liberally, with expectation!* The *amount* and *attitude* determine your Harvest.

"Give, and it shall be given unto you; good measure, pressed down, and shaken together, and running over, shall men give into your bosom. For with the same measure that ye mete withal it shall be measured to you again" (Lk. 6:38).

"But this I say, he which soweth sparingly shall reap also sparingly; and he which soweth bountifully shall reap also bountifully" (2 Cor. 9:6).

RECOMMENDED BOOKS AND TAPES ON THIS TOPIC
B-22   Seeds of Wisdom on Prosperity (Book/$3)
B-99   Secrets of the Richest Man Who Ever Lived (Book/$10)
TS-82   31 Reasons People Do Not Receive Their Financial Harvest
        (Six tapes/$30)

You Have No Right To Anything You Have Not Pursued.

-MIKE MURDOCK

❧ 35 ❧

NEGOTIATION

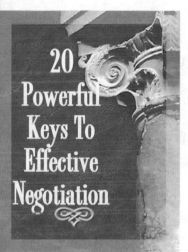

Negotiation Begins At Birth.

When babies cry, they are negotiating for attention. Teenagers constantly negotiate with parents. Husbands and wives negotiate continuously. One dictionary says that negotiation is "to discuss with a view to reaching an agreement."

Negotiation is the ability to change the opinions of others through a climate of favor; instead of force.

The decisions of others affect your circumstances. The city council determines the zoning of your land, whether it is residential or commercial. The salesman decides whether you purchase the car at his price or your price.

Your Assignment will always involve others. They will have different viewpoints, experiences and needs. Their needs will generally matter far more to them than your needs.

You cannot avoid the negotiating table. Almost every decision you make will involve others at some level. It will affect those you love financially, emotionally, physically or even spiritually.

Everyone is pursuing something that really matters to them. Obviously, the levels of desire vary. The integrity of others will vary.

Some *will lie* to achieve their goal.

Some will *steal* to achieve their goal.

Some will *kill* to achieve their goal.

Some will *terminate* your friendship to achieve something else they desire.

Some will *risk their own health* to achieve something they want.

Some will risk their entire *fortune* to achieve something they desire.

Some parents will *forfeit* the love of their children to achieve a goal.

Some children will walk away from their parents forever to achieve a temporary goal.

You will be continuously drawn to the negotiating table throughout your lifetime. It is like a magnet.

You cannot control the *desires* of others.

You cannot control the *behavior* of others.

You cannot *predict the price* another will pay at the negotiating table.

Negotiation gifts will be developed with your family. It starts in your childhood. Your family is the *testing ground* for your future. It may be good or it may be bad. But, your family is a gift from God to help you become qualified for enemy territory.

If you do not learn to negotiate effectively with your family, you will not negotiate effectively with your enemies. If you learn the true secrets of negotiation with those you love, it will inevitably affect your negotiation experiences with others in your future.

That is why the Bible has been given to us. It gives us the secrets, principles and laws of negotiating with others. It reveals how children are to conduct themselves toward their parents. "Children, obey your parents in the Lord: for this is right. Honour thy father and mother; which is the first commandment with promise; That it may be well with thee, and thou mayest live long on the earth" (Eph. 6:1-3). When you address your parent with favor, honor and integrity, God becomes involved. He is committed to your success. He guarantees your well-being and prosperity. An obedient child is always rewarded. *Always.*

Let me say something strong here. I have known of children who borrowed money from loving and caring parents. Years go by and the loans go unpaid. *God notices.* It will never be well with that child. Why? An unpaid bill is not honorable. It may be 20 years before the consequences occur, but they will occur.

The Word of God is Truth.

Parents have shared with me how their children have negotiated and argued with them. Thousands of parents are experiencing mistreatment at the hands of the children they raised. *It will not go well with them.*

It is also true that many parents mistreat their children. The Bible instructs fathers concerning their children, "And ye fathers, provoke not your children to wrath: but bring them up in the nurture and admonition of the Lord" (Eph. 6:4).

The most important truth you will ever learn in negotiating with others is to *listen for the inner voice of the Holy Spirit*. Whether you are in the presence of a serious enemy or your best friend, listen to the voice of the Holy Spirit regarding them. Jesus instructed His disciples to depend on the Holy Spirit in these times: "And when they bring you unto the synagogues, and unto magistrates, and powers, take ye no thought how or what thing ye shall answer, or what ye shall say: For the Holy Ghost shall teach you in the same hour what ye ought to say" (Lk. 12:11,12).

4 Powerful Principles In The Negotiating World Of The Christian

1.   God Anticipated Difficult Situations Where Negotiation Would Be Necessary.

2.   God Wants You To Be Relaxed And Unworried, But Aware That The Holy Spirit Is Present In These Scenarios Of Negotiation.

3.   God Desires That You Become A Learner; One Who Is Willing To Be Taught And Mentored By The Holy Spirit In Such Situations.

4.   God Wants You To Trust Him For The Outcome.

20 Powerful Keys To Effective Negotiation

1.   *Never Fear What Others Can Do To You.* "For God hath not given us the spirit of fear; but of power, and of love, and of a sound mind" (2 Tim. 1:7). "In God have I put my trust: I will not be afraid what man can do unto me" (Ps. 56:11).

2.   *Concentrate On How Much Good You Can Do For The Other Person With Whom You Are Negotiating.* "Withhold not good from them to whom it is due, when it is in the power of thine hand to do it" (Prov. 3:27).

3.   *Expect God To Reward You For The Good You Do, Not The Person With Whom You Are Negotiating.* "Knowing that whatsoever good thing any man doeth, the same shall he receive of the Lord, whether he be bond or free" (Eph. 6:8).

4.   *Speak Nothing That Does Not Edify And Strengthen Those At The Negotiating Table.* "Let no corrupt communication proceed out of your mouth, but that which is good to the use of edifying, that it may minister grace unto the hearers" (Eph. 4:29).

5.   *Stifle Any Anger That Threatens To Enter The Negotiations.* "Let all bitterness, and wrath, and anger, and clamour, and evil speaking, be put away from you, with all malice: And be ye kind one to another, tenderhearted, forgiving one another, even as God for Christ's sake hath forgiven you" (Eph. 4:31,32).

6. *Avoid Any Attempt By Others To Make The Atmosphere Become Foolish, Lighthearted Or Jesting.* "Neither filthiness, nor foolish talking, nor jesting, which are not convenient: but rather giving of thanks" (Eph. 5:4).

7. *Stay Alert To Any Attempt To Deceive You At The Negotiating Table.* "Let no man deceive you with vain words:" (Eph. 5:6).

8. *Do Not Enter Into Any Bond, Covenant Or Contract With The Enemies Of God.* "And have no fellowship with the unfruitful works of darkness, but rather reprove them" (Eph. 5:11).

9. *Permit The Tool Of Time To Sculpture An Acceptable Agreement With Others.* "The Lord is good unto them that wait for Him, to the soul that seeketh Him" (Lam. 3:25).

10. *Expect The Ability And Wisdom Of God To Compensate For Your Personal Weaknesses, Limitations And Fears.* "And I was with you in weakness, and in fear, and in much trembling. And my speech and my preaching was not with enticing words of man's Wisdom, but in demonstration of the Spirit and of power: That your faith should not stand in the Wisdom of men, but in the power of God" (1 Cor. 2:3-5).

11. *Develop The Ability To Listen Carefully To Every Word Spoken.* "A wise man will hear, and will increase learning;" (Prov. 1:5). Listen to what is *not* spoken as well as words spoken. Listen for *attitudes.* Listen for areas of *pain* in others.

12. *Do Not Make Any Decision Without Sufficient Information.* "He that answereth a matter before he heareth it, it is folly and shame unto him" (Prov. 18:13).

13. *Remember The Power Of Silence.* "Even a fool, when he holdeth his peace, is counted wise: and he that shutteth his lips is esteemed a man of understanding" (Prov. 17:28).

14. *Refuse To Accept Any Gift That Could Possibly Influence The Negotiations Unwisely.* "A wicked man taketh a gift out of the bosom to pervert the ways of judgment" (Prov. 17:23).

15. *Stay Cheerful Through The Negotiation.* "A merry heart doeth good like a medicine: but a broken spirit drieth the bones" (Prov. 17:22). God will not let you fail.

16. *Do Not Share Everything You Know At The Negotiation Table.* "He that hath knowledge spareth his words:" (Prov. 17:27).

17. *Keep A Congenial But Focused Attitude Throughout The Negotiations.* "A man that hath friends must shew himself friendly:" (Prov. 18:24).

18. *Define Clearly Everything You Expect During The Negotiations.* "Ask, and it shall be given you; seek, and ye shall find;

knock, and it shall be opened unto you:" (Matt. 7:7). You have nothing to lose by asking. The worst thing that could happen when you ask someone for something is that they could reject you. If you fail to pursue something you really desire, you will live the remainder of your life wondering "what could have been."

19. *Listen Carefully To Hear What Is Loudest In The Mind Of Another.* When Abigail sent her employees to ward off David's assault on Nabal, her husband, she brought him food. Why? It was the focus of David. You must hear what another person is hearing *inside their mind.* You must listen carefully to what is *loudest* inside of them (read 1 Sam. 25).

20. *Make Certain You Understand Completely What Their Expectations Are From The Negotiations.* They have needs. Some may be overwhelming to them. Do you know what these needs are? Do you know what they cannot give up?

Uncommon negotiation occurs when you get what you desire by helping someone else get what they desire.

The Apostle Paul was a master negotiator. Educated in law, skilled in debate, and known for persuasion and logic, his writings are marvelous studies.

Pilate did not intimidate him. Prestige did not intrigue him. Wealth did not beckon to him.

Yet, when he spoke, kings listened and trembled.

Leadership sought him out.

His adversaries listened raptly and with great attentiveness to his viewpoints.

He knew when to be gentle, and when to be firm.

He knew when to listen, and when to speak. He knew what to pursue, and what to avoid. He knew a Master Key, Negotiation. His success was greatly affected by these negotiating skills.

You, too, must not forget this powerful principle: *The Success Of Your Assignment May Require An Ability To Negotiate Effectively With Others.*

RECOMMENDED BOOKS AND TAPES ON THIS TOPIC

B-99   Secrets of the Richest Man Who Ever Lived (Book/$10)
TS-13   Paul's 26 Secrets for Negotiation (Six tapes/$30)
TS-99   Secrets of the Richest Man Who Ever Lived (Six tapes/$30)

The Presence Of God
Is The Only Place
Your Weakness
Will Die.

-MIKE MURDOCK

≈ 36 ≈

PRAYER

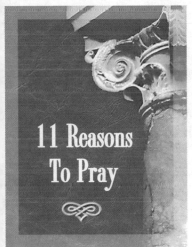

11 Reasons
To Pray

Prayer Is Your Greatest Weapon On Earth.

Champions always use it against satanic pressures. It is a subject talked about... preached about...written about but, usually, it is not really practiced. Few people grasp prayer's incredible potential.

"And when they had prayed, the place was shaken where they were assembled together; and they were all filled with the Holy Ghost, and they spake the word of God with boldness" (Acts 4:31).

"And at midnight Paul and Silas prayed, and sang praises unto God: and the prisoners heard them. And suddenly there was a great earthquake, so that the foundations of the prison were shaken: and immediately all the doors were opened, and every one's bands were loosed" (Acts 16:25,26).

Prayer is visiting with your Father.

Jesus, as your example, often communicated with God through prayer. He knew it was the only way to truly win over sickness or the power of demonic spirits. It built His relationship with His Father. "And He went a little farther, and fell on His face, and prayed, saying, O My Father, if it be possible, let this cup pass from Me: nevertheless not as I will, but as Thou wilt. And He cometh unto the disciples, and findeth them asleep, and saith unto Peter, What, could ye not watch with Me one hour? Watch and pray, that ye enter not into temptation: the spirit indeed is willing, but the flesh is weak. He went away again the second time, and prayed, saying, O My Father, if this cup may not pass away from Me, except I drink it, Thy will be done. And He came and found them asleep again: for their eyes were heavy. And He left them, and went away again, and prayed the third time, saying the same words" (Matt. 26:39-44).

"At that day ye shall ask in My name: and I say not unto you, that

I will pray the Father for you: For the Father Himself loveth you, because ye have loved Me, and have believed that I came out from God" (Jn. 16:26,27).

1. *God Commanded It.* "And He spake a parable unto them to this end, that men ought always to pray, and not to faint;" (Lk. 18:1). In His words, we are to "always" pray. He expects it daily.

2. *Prayer Is Your Key To Power.* Read fully this unforgettable passage in Acts 12.

"Peter therefore was kept in prison: but prayer was made without ceasing of the church unto God for him. And when Herod would have brought him forth, the same night Peter was sleeping between two soldiers, bound with two chains: and the keepers before the door kept the prison. And, behold, the angel of the Lord came upon him, and a light shined in the prison: and he smote Peter on the side, and raised him up, saying, Arise up quickly. And his chains fell off from his hands" (Acts 12:5-7).

Prayer gives you, the believer, *authority* over satan.

3. *Prayer Changes Your "Inner World."* The peace and presence of God fills you. It also changes your *external* circumstances. The hand of God moves people around you and miracles begin to happen.

4. *Prayer Pleasures The Heart Of God.* "And there will I meet with thee, and I will commune with thee from above the mercy seat, from between the two cherubims which are upon the ark of the testimony, of all things which I will give thee in commandment unto the children of Israel" (Ex. 25:22).

God enjoys your companionship.

He seeks communion with you.

5. *Prayer Pleasures You.* "Come unto Me, all ye that labour and are heavy laden, and I will give you rest" (Matt. 11:28). When you pray, your spirit is fed the essential "bread of life." Prayer is as necessary for your spirit as food is for your body.

6. *Prayer Blesses Others.* "I exhort therefore, that, first of all, supplications, prayers, intercessions, and giving of thanks, be made for all men;" (1 Tim. 2:1).

When you lift others and their needs before God, not only will their needs be met, but yours will be satisfied also. "And the Lord turned the captivity of Job, when he prayed for his friends: also the Lord gave Job twice as much as he had before" (Job 42:10).

7. *Prayer Opens The Door For God To Show Us Great And Mighty Things.* "Call unto Me, and I will answer thee, and shew thee

great and mighty things, which thou knowest not" (Jer. 33:3).

8. *Prayer Puts Fear In The Heart Of Satan, Your Adversary.* "Humble yourselves therefore under the mighty hand of God, that He may exalt you in due time: Casting all your care upon Him; for He careth for you. Be sober, be vigilant; because your adversary the devil, as a roaring lion, walketh about, seeking whom he may devour: Whom resist stedfast in the faith, knowing that the same afflictions are accomplished in your brethren that are in the world. But the God of all grace, who hath called us unto His eternal glory by Christ Jesus, after that ye have suffered a while, make you perfect, stablish, strengthen, settle you. To Him be glory and dominion for ever and ever" (1 Pet. 5:6-11).

God expects it.

Angels respect it.

"And another angel came and stood at the altar, having a golden censer; and there was given unto him much incense, that he should offer it with the prayers of all saints upon the golden altar which was before the throne. And the smoke of the incense, which came with the prayers of the saints, ascended up before God out of the angel's hand" (Rev. 8:3,4).

9. *Prayer Is The Most Powerful Way To Change The Destiny Of Your Life.* "If My people, which are called by My name, shall humble themselves, and pray, and seek My face, and turn from their wicked ways; then will I hear from Heaven, and will forgive their sin, and will heal their land" (2 Chr. 7:14).

"Therefore also now, saith the Lord, turn ye even to Me with all your heart, and with fasting, and with weeping, and with mourning: And rend your heart, and not your garments, and turn unto the Lord your God: for He is gracious and merciful, slow to anger, and of great kindness, and repenteth him of the evil. Let the priests, the ministers of the Lord, weep between the porch and the altar, and let them say, Spare thy people, O Lord, and give not Thine heritage to reproach, that the heathen should rule over them: wherefore should they say among the people, Where is their God? Then will the Lord be jealous for His land, and pity His people" (Joel 2:12,13,17,18).

10. *Prayer Is The Only Pathway To True Peace.* "Be careful for nothing; but in every thing by prayer and supplication with thanksgiving let your requests be made known unto God. And the peace of God, which passeth all understanding, shall keep your hearts and minds through Christ Jesus" (Phil. 4:6,7).

11. *Prayer Is The Pathway To Daily Strength.* "But I have prayed for thee, that thy faith fail not: and when thou art converted, strengthen thy brethren" (Lk. 22:32).

"Blessed is the man whose strength is in Thee; in whose heart are the ways of them. Who passing through the valley of Baca make it a well; the rain also filleth the pools. They go from strength to strength, every one of them in Zion appeareth before God. O Lord God of hosts, hear my prayer: give ear, O God of Jacob. Selah. Behold, O God our shield, and look upon the face of thine anointed" (Ps. 84:5-9).

Schedule Your Morning Appointment In The Secret Place, It Is The Secret To Permanent Change.

RECOMMENDED BOOKS AND TAPES ON THIS TOPIC
B-69   Wisdom Keys for a Powerful Prayer Life (Book/$3)
B-100   The Holy Spirit Handbook, Vol. 1 (Book/$10)
B-115   Seeds of Wisdom on The Secret Place (Book/$5)
TS-100 The Holy Spirit Handbook, Vol. 1 (Six tapes/$30)

❧ 37 ❧

PROBLEM SOLVING

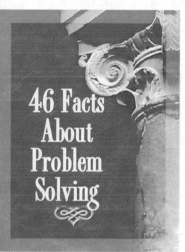

46 Facts About Problem Solving

You Were Created To Solve A Problem.

Doctors solve physical problems. Mothers solve emotional problems. Dentists solve teeth problems. Mechanics solve car problems. Everything God created was created to solve an existing problem.

Millions of problems exist on the earth. Solving those problems provides income, favor and the flow of financial provision for the billions living on the earth.

Thousands remain impoverished because they have not recognized the problem closest to them that needs to be solved. Millions will never receive promotion because they ignore the problem closest to them. *Marriages* have deteriorated because a mate *refused to recognize* the problem closest to them.

The Problem Closest To You Is The Golden Gate Out Of Trouble.

The Problem Closest To You Is Your Secret Code To The Throne.

When Joseph solved the problem nearest him, he moved into his next season of promotion.

1. *You Were Created To Solve A Problem.* "To rejoice in his labour; this is the gift of God" (Ecc. 5:19).

2. *The Problem You Solve Provides The Provision For Your Life.* "And also that every man should eat and drink, and enjoy the good of all his labour, it is the gift of God" (Ecc. 3:13).

3. *The Problem That Infuriates You The Most Is Often The Problem God Has Assigned You To Solve.* When Moses observed an Egyptian beating an Israelite, anger arose. Anger is a clue, a signal that God wants you to *correct* something that grieves Him. Anger is the birthplace for change.

4. *Your Gifts And Skills Are Clues To The Problem You Were Created To Solve.* You may be gifted with numbers, working with children or administration. Your gift is revealed by what you *love.*

The proof of love is the investment of *time*. What you are willing to invest time in learning is a clue to an existing gift within you.

5. *Uncommon Men Often Solve Uncommon Problems.* Those who design skyscrapers have a different creativity than those who build doghouses. The pay differs, too!

6. *Uncommon Men Often Solve Common Problems In An Uncommon Way.* It is the secret of McDonald's, the largest hamburger restaurant chain on earth. Killing a man in battle is common. But, David became known because he did it with an Uncommon Weapon against an Uncommon Enemy.

7. *You Will Only Be Remembered For The Problems You Solve Or The Ones You Create.* Joseph is remembered because he solved the problem of provision during famine.

8. *Uncommon Men Often Distinguish Themselves By The Method They Use To Solve A Problem.* The leprosy of Naaman disappeared because of an illogical instruction from Elisha— "dip in Jordan seven times."

9. *Currents Of Favor Will Flow Into Your Life The Moment You Solve A Problem For Somebody.* When the Apostle Paul brought the healing power of God to the father of Publius, the chief of the island, favor flowed. Others were healed. Then, the Apostle Luke documents, "Who also honoured us with many honours; and when we departed, they laded us with such things as were necessary" (Acts 28:10).

David pursued a knowledge of the reward for killing Goliath. "The king will enrich him with great riches, and will give him his daughter, and make his father's house free in Israel" (1 Sam. 17:25).

10. *The Problem You Solve Determines The Salary You Earn.* Lawyers make $200 an hour while a gardener earns $8 an hour. Both men are worthy. But, the problem they have chosen to solve has a different value.

11. *Problems Should Never Be Discussed With Those Incapable Of Solving Them.* Their answers will incense you.

12. *The Problem You Solve For Others Determines The Problems God Will Solve For You.* "Knowing that whatsoever good thing any man doeth, the same shall he receive of the Lord, whether he be bond or free" (Eph. 6:8).

13. *The Blessing Of The Lord Will Always Be Proportionate To The Problem You Have Chosen To Solve.* "The Lord shall open unto thee His good treasure, the Heaven to give the rain unto thy land in His season, and to bless all the work of thine hand:" (Deut. 28:12).

14. *Those Who Refuse To Solve Problems Should Not Be Supported By Those Who Do.* "For even when we were with you, this we commanded you, that if any would not work, neither should he eat" (2 Thess. 3:10).

15. *Scriptures Forbid Intimacy And Relationship With Those Who Are Unwilling To Work And Solve Problems.* "For we hear that there are some which walk among you disorderly, working not at all, but are busybodies...note that man, and have no company with him, that he may be ashamed" (2 Thess. 3:11,14).

16. *Those Skilled In Solving Problems Are Qualified To Rule Over Others.* "The hand of the diligent shall bear rule: but the slothful shall be under tribute" (Prov. 12:24).

17. *Uncommon Problem Solvers Are Pursued By Uncommon Men Of Greatness.* "Seest thou a man diligent in his business? he shall stand before kings;" (Prov. 22:29).

18. *Solving A Problem Cheerfully Increases Favor.* "A merry heart doeth good like a medicine:" (Prov. 17:22).

19. *Your Flexibility And Willingness To Solve A Problem Affects Your Salary And Respect Received.* Twenty-four hour cafes exist because of *flexibility.*

20. *Many Eventually Hear About The Problem You Solve For Others.* Boaz knew that Ruth treated Naomi better than seven sons would treat their mother.

21. *God Expects You To Observe And Recognize The Problem Nearest You.* "But whoso hath this world's good, and seeth his brother have need, and shutteth up his bowels of compassion from him, how dwelleth the love of God in him?" (1 Jn. 3:17).

22. *God Expects You To Solve The Problem Nearest You.* "Withhold not good from them to whom it is due, when it is in the power of thine hand to do it" (Prov. 3:27). Joseph applied this to the butler.

23. *Your Assignment Determines The Kinds Of Problems You Notice And Desire To Solve.* Tailors notice missing buttons. Hairstylists notice your hair. Mechanics *hear* something wrong in your car engine. Why? That is their Assignment. Your Assignment heightens and *magnifies* the problems you notice and are called to solve.

24. *You Are Not Assigned To Solve Problems For Everybody.* Determine to whom you have been assigned. Jesus told the Pharisees that He was not called to those who were whole, but to those who realized they were sick and needed Him.

25. *You Are Not Assigned To Solve Every Kind Of Problem For Everyone.* Pastors are not necessarily anointed to solve real estate problems, automobile breakdowns and estate planning. Others can do that.

26. *Problems Are Catalysts That Cause Us To Reach For Each Other.* You only call a dentist when your teeth hurt. You only call your lawyer about legal matters. Problems create relationships.

27. *Problems Reveal The Value Of Those Nearest Us.* Someone told me that when they went to the hospital, the love and caring of their loved ones meant more to them than ever.

28. *The Problems Others Are Experiencing Often Cause Them To Recognize Your Value.* Children that ignore parents will often reach during a crisis they encounter.

29. *Your Phone Will Never Ring Unless Someone Has A Problem They Want You To Solve.* It may be emotional reassurance, a piece of information or a question that requires answering. Problems initiate reaching.

30. *Any Problem Created By Rebellion Can Only Be Solved By The Repentance Of The Rebellious.* When non-tithers ask a minister to pray for their prosperity, it is futile and absurd for the minister to do so. Their repentance is the key to their prosperity. Likewise, it is foolish to support a son-in-law who is defying the scriptural command to work.

31. *The Holy Spirit Will Often Forbid You To Solve Problems For Specific People.* Paul experienced this. "Now when they had gone throughout Phrygia and the region of Galatia, and were forbidden of the Holy Ghost to preach the word in Asia, After they were come to Mysia, they assayed to go into Bithynia: but the Spirit suffered them not" (Acts 16:6,7).

32. *Those You Love Often Want You To Solve Their Problems Without Them Tasting The Painful Consequences Of Their Own Rebellion.* I begged one pastor not to take on an unnecessary indebtedness. He was determined to build a palace before the people were present to pay for it. I insisted that he was "missing the will of God." He insisted. Then, when he proceeded, he begged me to come back and bail him out of the problem. The Holy Spirit forbade me.

33. *Small Problems Are Often Signals That A Deeper Problem Exists.* When a young couple stays in debt, it indicates that greed runs deep. Their unwillingness to wait reveals impatience. Impatience has caused more debt than we could ever imagine.

34. *You Cannot Solve Problems For Anyone In Rebellion Against God.* "But if ye refuse and rebel, ye shall be devoured with the sword: for the mouth of the Lord hath spoken it" (Isa. 1:20).

Never breathe life into something God is killing. Never kill something God is resurrecting.

Permit God to complete His plan in others around you.

35. *You Cannot Solve A Problem For Someone Who Distrusts Your Ability To Do So.* "He that cometh to God must believe that He is, and that He is a rewarder of them that diligently seek Him" (Heb. 11:6).

36. *You Can Only Solve A Problem For The Person Who Knows He Has One.* God cannot even save someone who does not realize they are lost. Confession is a necessity. Pharisees refused to acknowledge they had a problem. It cost them eternity.

37. *The Problems Of Others Are Not The Commands Of God To Get Involved.* You must develop the ability to hear The Voice of the Spirit, instead of responding to the expectations of people.

Rebellion creates *crisis.*

Continuous rebellion creates *continuous* crisis.

Unending rebellion creates *unending* crisis.

Many parents want to cushion the fall when their rebellious teenagers defy the Scriptures.

38. *You Can Only Solve Problems For The Humble.* The arrogant will alter your instructions. The rebellious will defy them. The prideful will ignore their problem. Confession indicates humility.

39. *You Cannot Solve A Problem For The Unrepentant.* Pharisees were unrepentant. Rebels are disqualified from receiving help.

40. *You Cannot Help Anyone Who Does Not Trust Your Counsel.* A relative asked me for counsel. I gave it. Then, they informed me that they had made a different decision. They asked me for *more* advice. I declined.

41. *Those Who Disagree With Your Solution For Their Problem Disqualify Themselves For Additional Counsel.* "To him that knoweth to do good, and doeth it not, to him it is sin" (James 4:17).

42. *You Can Predict The Success Of Others By The Problem They Have Chosen To Solve.* Joseph chose to solve a problem for those nearest him. It guaranteed his access to Pharaoh.

43. *Somebody You Do Not Know Is Discussing The Problem You Are Capable Of Solving For Them.* Never panic when you do not see

the results of your efforts. Somewhere, you are being discussed. Boaz listened to his servants regarding Ruth and Naomi. He knew that she was better to a mother-in-law than seven sons would be to their mother.

44. *Someone In Leadership Is Carefully Observing The Attitude With Which You Are Solving Your Present Problems.* Boaz respected Ruth because of her attitude toward Naomi.

45. *Money Is Merely A Reward For Solving A Problem.* When you observe someone who never has any money, they obviously are not solving problems or they are solving them for the wrong person.

46. *Everyone Has Problems They Are Incapable Of Solving.* That is why the banker is necessary, the taxi driver, the brick layer, the truck driver and the psychologist. You are necessary...to someone.

Recognition Of The Problem Closest To You Is The Golden Exit From Your Chaos, The Golden Gate To The Throne And Will Catapult Your Life To Promotion.

RECOMMENDED BOOKS AND TAPES ON THIS TOPIC

B-40	Wisdom for Crisis Times (Book/$9)
B-44	31 Secrets for Career Success (Book/$10)
B-74	The Assignment (The Dream & The Destiny) Vol. 1 (Book/$10)
B-75	The Assignment (The Anointing & The Adversity) Vol. 2 (Book/$10)
B-82	31 Reasons People Do Not Receive Their Financial Harvest (Book/$12)
B-97	The Assignment (The Trials & The Triumphs) Vol. 3 (Book/$10)
B-98	The Assignment (The Pain & The Passion) Vol. 4 (Book/$10)
B-118	Seeds of Wisdom on Problem Solving (Book/$5)
TS-9	Secrets of the Greatest Achievers Who Ever Lived, Vol. 1 (Six tapes/$30)
TS-10	Secrets of the Greatest Achievers Who Ever Lived, Vol. 2 (Six tapes/$30)
TS-23	31 Secrets of the Uncommon Problem Solver (Six tapes/$30)
TS-63	31 Secrets of the Uncommon Mentor (Six tapes/$30)
TS-40	Wisdom for Crisis Times (Six tapes/$30)

❦ 38 ❧

PROTÉGÉ

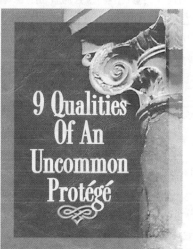

9 Qualities Of An Uncommon Protégé

A Protégé Is An Obedient Learner.
The Wisdom of the Mentor is perpetuated through the Protégé. As I have said for many years, true success will produce a Successor. Jesus took twelve Protégés and revolutionized the earth. It is very important that you recognize those connected to you by the Holy Spirit for the multiplying and perpetuation of your success and life.

You will only remember what you teach another. Our children should become our Protégés.

Passive Protégés only reach when it is convenient or when their personal efforts do not produce their desired result. They subconsciously expect their Mentor to produce success for them.

Parasite Protégés pursue for credibility, not correction. They will use the name and influence of a Mentor to manipulate others into a relationship. They want what the Mentor has *earned,* not what he has learned. They want reputation *without* preparation.

Prodigal Protégés enter and exit the relationship freely. When serious correction occurs, they move toward another Mentor who has not yet discovered their flaws. They distance themselves when their Mentor encounters personal difficulties, loss of credibility or false accusation or persecution. They only return when their pigpen becomes unbearable.

Productive Protégés are Uncommon. They have a servant's heart. They never make a major decision without the counsel and feedback of their Mentor. They view their Mentor as a dominant gift from God. They love their Mentor as much as themselves.

The Uncommon Protégé assigned by God will honor the Mentor. "And we beseech you, brethren, to know them which labour among you, and are over you in the Lord, and admonish you; And to esteem them very highly in love for their work's sake" (1 Thess. 5:12,13).

1. *The Uncommon Protégé Will Invest Everything To Stay In The Presence Of The Uncommon Mentor.* Ruth persisted. "Entreat me not to leave thee, or to return from following after thee: for whither thou goest, I will go;" (Ruth 1:16).

2. *The Uncommon Protégé Follows The Counsel Of The Uncommon Mentor.* God established the punishment of a rebellious Protégé who sneered at the counsel of his covering. "And the man that will do presumptuously, and will not hearken unto the priest that standeth to minister there before the Lord thy God, or unto the judge, even that man shall die: and thou shalt put away the evil from Israel. And all the people shall hear, and fear, and do no more presumptuously" (Deut. 17:12,13).

3. *The Uncommon Protégé Reveals The Secrets And Dreams Of His Heart With The Mentor.* Ruth opened her heart to Naomi. Elisha expressed his longings to Elijah. Vulnerability creates the unbreakable bond between a Mentor and the Protégé.

4. *The Uncommon Protégé Freely Discusses His Mistakes And Pain With The Mentor.* David did. "So David fled, and escaped, and came to Samuel to Ramah, and told him all that Saul had done to him. And he and Samuel went and dwelt in Naioth" (1 Sam. 19:18).

5. *The Uncommon Protégé Defines Clearly His Expectations To The Mentor.* Elisha explained his desire to Elijah. Ruth explained her desire to Naomi.

6. *The Uncommon Protégé Gladly Sows Seeds Of Appreciation Back Into The Life Of The Mentor.* It was the secret of the queen of Sheba. She presented over four million dollars of gifts when she met Solomon for the appointment. "And she came to Jerusalem with a very great train, with camels that bare spices, and very much gold, and precious stones: and when she was come to Solomon, she communed with him of all that was in her heart. And Solomon told her all her questions: there was not any thing hid from the king, which he told her not...And she gave the king an hundred and twenty talents of gold, and of spices very great store, and precious stones: there came no more such abundance of spices as these which the queen of Sheba gave to king Solomon" (1 Kings 10:2,3,10).

The remarkable Mentor, the Apostle Paul, received such gifts. "For even in Thessalonica ye sent once and again unto my necessity" (Phil. 4:16).

7. *The Uncommon Protégé Ultimately Receives The Mantle Of*

The Mentor He Serves. Transference of anointing is a fact, not a fantasy. The Apostle Paul documented it. "Wherefore I put thee in remembrance that thou stir up the gift of God, which is in thee by the putting on of *my hands*" (2 Tim. 1:6).

Joshua received it. "There shall not any man be able to stand before thee all the days of thy life: as I was with Moses, so I will be with thee: I will not fail thee, nor forsake thee" (Josh. 1:5).

8. *The Uncommon Protégé Moves Toward The Shelter Of The Mentor During A Season Of Uncommon Attack And Warfare.* The picture of David and Samuel's relationship is remarkable. "So David fled, and escaped, and came to Samuel to Ramah, and told him all that Saul had done to him. And he and Samuel went and dwelt in Naioth" (1 Sam. 19:18). Think about this seriously. During serious attack, David did not withdraw from Samuel. He pursued him. He invested *time* with him.

9. *The Uncommon Protégé Will Change His Own Schedule To Invest Time In The Presence Of The Mentor.* Paul did. "Neither went I up to Jerusalem to them which were apostles before me; but I went into Arabia, and returned again unto Damascus. Then after three years I went up to Jerusalem to see Peter, and *abode with him* fifteen days" (Gal. 1:17,18).

The Uncommon Protégé Is Someone Who Discerns, Respects And Pursues The Answers God Has Stored In The Mentor For Their Life.

RECOMMENDED BOOKS AND TAPES ON THIS TOPIC

B-14   Seeds of Wisdom on Relationships (Book/$3)

B-44   31 Secrets for Career Success (Book/$10)

B-58   The Mentors Manna On Attitude (Book/$3)

B-71   Wisdom - God's Golden Key to Success (Book/$7)

B-85   Gift of Wisdom for Teenagers (Book/$10)

B-91   The Leadership Secrets of Jesus (Book/$10)

B-99   Secrets of the Richest Man Who Ever Lived (Book/$10)

TS-9   Secrets of the Greatest Achievers Who Ever Lived, Vol. 1 (Six tapes/$30)

TS-10   Secrets of the Greatest Achievers Who Ever Lived, Vol. 2 (Six tapes/$30)

TS-99   Secrets of the Richest Man Who Ever Lived (Six tapes/$30)

Satan's Favorite
Entry Point
Into Your Life
Is Always Through
Someone Close To You.

-MIKE MURDOCK

≈ 39 ≈

SATAN

Always Study An Adversary.

"Submit yourselves therefore to God. Resist the devil, and he will flee from you" (James 4:7).

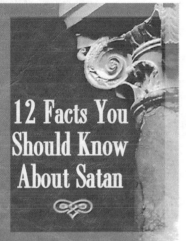

12 Facts You Should Know About Satan

Believe it or not, your enemy is *not* just people! People are often *tools* of your true enemy. Paul wrote, "For we wrestle not against flesh and blood, but against principalities, against powers, against the rulers of the darkness...against spiritual wickedness in high places" (Eph. 6:12).

1. *Your Real Enemy Is The Devil... Satan...Lucifer.* "Be sober, be vigilant; because your adversary the devil, as a roaring lion, walketh about, seeking whom he may devour" (1 Pet. 5:8).

2. *Satan Is An Ex-Employee Of Heaven, A Fallen Angel.* "I beheld satan as lightning fall from Heaven" (Lk. 10:18). "The great dragon was cast out, that old serpent, called the devil, and satan, which deceiveth the whole world: he was cast out into the earth, and his angels were cast out with him" (Rev. 12:9).

3. *Satan's Time Is Limited, So His Efforts Are Intensified.* "For the devil is come down unto you, having great wrath, because he knoweth that he hath but a short time" (Rev. 12:12).

4. *Satan's Power To Tempt You Is Limited.* "God is faithful, Who will not suffer you to be tempted above that ye are able; but will... make a way to escape, that ye may be able to bear it" (1 Cor. 10:13).

5. *Satan Despises God.* And he hates anything that receives God's affection.

6. *Satan Is Quite Aware Of God's Unusual Care And Protection Of You.* Satan reacts with unbridled resentment toward us. His reaction to the blessings upon Job is a prime example (see Job 1:9-12).

7. *Satan Is Deceptive, Cunning, Manipulating, The Father Of All*

Lies. Jesus said, speaking of the devil, "He was a murderer from the beginning...there is no truth in him...for he is a liar, and the father of it" (Jn. 8:44).

8. *Satan Opposes You Because You Are A Potential Source Of Pleasure To God*. "For Thou hast created all things, and for Thy pleasure they are and were created" (Rev. 4:11).

9. *Satan's Real Enemy Is God*. But because he is powerless against God, he attacks that which is *closest* to the heart of God...you and me.

10. *Satan's Main Purpose Of Warfare Is To Pain God's Heart, To Insult Him, To Frustrate His Purposes In Your Life*. "And the Lord said, Simon, Simon, behold, satan hath desired to have you, that he may sift you as wheat: But I have prayed for thee, that thy faith fail not: and when thou art converted, strengthen thy brethren" (Lk. 22:31,32).

11. *Satan Wants You To Grieve God's Heart By Doubting God's Integrity*. "God is not a man, that He should lie; neither the *son* of man, that He should repent: hath He said, and shall He not do it? or hath He spoken, and shall He not make it good?" (Num. 23:19).

12. *Satan Wants To Prevent The Arrival Of Any Miracle That Would Bring Glory To God*. Satan's aim is to:
- ▶ Paralyze your planning
- ▶ Abort your dreams
- ▶ Destroy your hope

"The thief cometh not, but for to steal, and to kill, and to destroy: I am come that they might have life, and that they might have it more abundantly" (Jn. 10:10).

You will never win a spiritual battle *through your own strength or Wisdom*. "Not by might, nor by power, but by My Spirit, saith the Lord of hosts" (Zech. 4:6).

"Submit yourselves therefore to God. Resist the devil, and he will flee from you" (James 4:7).

Expect Your Enemy To Make Mistakes.

Expect Your Advisor, The Holy Spirit, To Aid You.

Expect To Conquer.

RECOMMENDED BOOKS AND TAPES ON THIS TOPIC

B-07   Battle Techniques for War Weary Saints (Book/$3)
B-40   Wisdom for Crisis Times (Book/$9)
TS-5   How to Walk Through Fire (Six tapes/$30)

❧ 40 ❧

SECRET PLACE

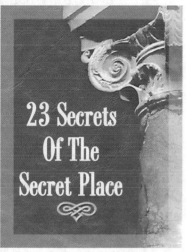

You Must Stay Long Enough In The Secret Place To Create A Memory.

Satan Cannot Steal Your Memories.

That was the secret revealed in the sensational return of the prodigal to his father's house.

His money was stolen.

His friends were gone.

His self-confidence was shattered. *But, his memories remained.*

Memory Is The Miracle Magnet... Attracting You Back To Your Father's House.

Memory Is The Gift Of God Linking You To Your Restoration.

Memory Is The Catalyst For Repentance. You will only return to a Place of Pleasure.

So, you must stay long enough in The Secret Place to create a memory of pleasure, change and strength. If you leave too soon, before the Holy Spirit talks to you, you may become reluctant to return.

How long should you stay?

1. *Stay Long Enough To Receive His Command.* "Therefore Thou shalt keep the commandments of the Lord Thy God, to walk in His ways, and to fear Him" (Deut. 8:6).

2. *Stay Long Enough For Hope To Be Birthed Again.* "My soul fainteth for Thy salvation: but I hope in Thy Word" (Ps. 119:81).

3. *Stay Long Enough To Become Broken.* "The Lord is nigh unto them that are of a broken heart; and saveth such as be of a contrite spirit" (Ps. 34:18).

4. *Stay Long Enough To Recapture Your Motivation.* "I can do all things through Christ which strengtheneth me" (Phil. 4:13).

5. *Stay Long Enough For New Ideas To Be Birthed.* "But my God shall supply all your need according to His riches in glory by

Christ Jesus" (Phil. 4:19).

6. *Stay Long Enough To Be Changed.* "And was transfigured before them: and His face did shine as the sun, and His raiment was white as the light" (Matt. 17:2).

7. *Stay Long Enough To Receive His Wisdom.* "I will instruct thee and teach thee in the way which thou shalt go: I will guide thee with Mine eye" (Ps. 32:8).

8. *Stay Long Enough To Become Stronger.* "But they that wait upon the Lord shall renew their strength; they shall mount up with wings as eagles; they shall run and not be weary; and they shall walk, and not faint" (Isa. 40:31).

9. *Stay Long Enough To Receive His Complete Plan For Achieving Your Goal.* "For I know the thoughts that I think toward you, saith the Lord, thoughts of peace, and not of evil, to give you an expected end" (Jer. 29:11).

10. *Stay Long Enough For Mistakes To Be Exposed.* "He that covereth his sins shall not prosper: But whoso confesseth and forsaketh them shall have mercy" (Prov. 28:13).

11. *Stay Long Enough For Pain To Leave.* "...weeping may endure for a night, but joy cometh in the morning" (Ps. 30:5).

12. *Stay Long Enough For Confusion To Disappear.* "For God is not the author of confusion, but of peace..." (1 Cor. 14:33).

13. *Stay Long Enough For Love To Emerge Again.* "And hope maketh not ashamed; because the love of God is shed abroad in our hearts by the Holy Ghost which is given unto us" (Rom. 5:5).

14. *Stay Long Enough For The Spirit Of Murmuring And Complaining To Dissipate.* "Do all things without murmurings and disputings:" (Phil. 2:14).

15. *Stay Long Enough To Receive Contentment.* "Not that I speak in respect of want: for I have learned, in whatsoever state I am, therewith to be content" (Phil. 4:11).

16. *Stay Long Enough To Lavish Love On Him.* "But whoso keepeth His Word, in him verily is the love of God perfected: hereby know we that we are in Him" (1 Jn. 2:5).

17. *Stay Long Enough To Read His Word Aloud.* "My tongue shall speak of Thy Word: for all Thy commandments are righteousness" (Ps. 119:172).

18. *Stay Long Enough To Listen To His Word.* "So then faith cometh by hearing, and hearing by the Word of God" (Rom. 10:17).

19. *Stay Long Enough To Meditate On Him.* "O how love I Thy

law! it is my meditation all the day" (Ps. 119:97).

20. *Stay Long Enough To Intercede For Your Family Members.* Lay your hands on their pictures in your pictorial prayer book. "Moreover as for me, God forbid that I should sin against the Lord in ceasing to pray for you: but I will teach you the good and the right way:" (1 Sam. 12:23).

21. *Stay Long Enough For Your Anger To Subside.* "He that hath no rule over his own spirit is like a city that is broken down, without walls" (Prov. 25:28).

22. *Stay Long Enough For The Fear Of Man To Dissolve And Leave.* "The fear of man bringeth a snare: but whoso putteth his trust in the Lord shall be safe" (Prov. 29:25).

23. *Stay Long Enough For True Joy To Return.* "Thou wilt shew me the path of life: in Thy presence is fulness of joy; at Thy right hand there are pleasures for evermore" (Ps. 16:11).

Always Exit The Secret Place With Expectation.

Nothing Will Occur Today That You And The Holy Spirit Cannot Handle Together.

Our Prayer Together...

"Holy Spirit, unleash a new passion for Your presence in my dear reader today. Schedule a visitation that will be impossible for them to ever doubt. In Jesus' name. Amen."

RECOMMENDED BOOKS AND TAPES ON THIS TOPIC

B-100   The Holy Spirit Handbook, Vol. 1 (Book/$10)
B-115   Seeds of Wisdom on The Secret Place (Book/$5)
TS-59   Songs from The Secret Place, Vol. 1 (Six music tapes/$30)
TS-100   The Holy Spirit Handbook, Vol. 1 (Six tapes/$30)

Seed-Faith Is Sowing
What You
Have Been Given...
To Create
What You Have Been
Promised.

-MIKE MURDOCK

❧ 41 ❧

SEED-FAITH

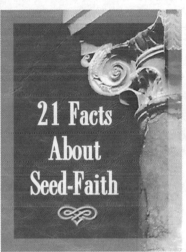

21 Facts About Seed-Faith

You Will Reap What You Sow.

Seed-Faith is when you plant a Seed with *expectation* of a specific Harvest. It is your Seed planted in faith for a specific result or miracle.

Scriptures prove it. "Be not deceived; God is not mocked: for whatsoever a man soweth, that shall he also reap" (Gal. 6:7).

Facts About Seed-Faith

1. *Your Seed Is Anything You Have Received From God That You Can Sow Into Someone Else. Thoughts* are Seeds. *Love* is a Seed. *Time* is a Seed. *Patience* is a Seed. *Mercy* is a Seed. *Kindness* is a Seed. *Money* is a Seed. *Prayers* are Seeds. *Thankfulness* is a Seed.

2. *Seed-Faith Is Sowing What You Have Been Given To Create Something Else You Have Been Promised.*

3. *Your Seed Is The Tool God Has Given You To Create Your Future.* Look at David. He complained about the armor of Saul. But, he had another tool—the slingshot. It was simple. Overlooked. Ignored by other soldiers. But, it was the *Seed* that God had placed in his hand. It was his supernatural tool! God always leaves you with *something.* What is it? *Find it.*

4. *Something You Have Been Given By God Will Create Anything Else You Have Ever Been Promised By God.* Tenacity in the woman who hemorrhaged for twelve years, created the miracle of touching of the hem of Jesus' garment. The loaves and fishes of a small lad created enough for the multitude. Stop looking at what others possess. Instead, start thanking God for something He has already given you.

5. *There Will Never Be A Day In Your Life That You Have Nothing.* You may be impoverished like the widow. Many think she

had nothing. She had something—powerful, incredible and rare.

She had the ability to *discern* a man of God.

She had the ability to *listen* to a man of God.

She had the ability to *obey* a man of God.

6. *God Always Gives You Something To Begin Your Future.* David had a *slingshot* to create a victory. The widow had a *meal* to invest into a man of God. You have *something!* Look for it again!

7. *You Are A Walking Warehouse Of Remarkable Seeds.* Most people have no idea what they contain! They waste thousands of hours studying their losses instead of taking inventory of what they have been given. They look at what they have *not* instead of what they have *got.* Listen carefully. It is rarely destructive or devastating to take an inventory of all the things you need and desire. But, it is tragic beyond words if you *fail to recognize your Seeds*—what you have received from God to plant into the lives of others. Stop focusing on losses. Look longer, closer and thankfully at something you have *already* been given and presently have.

8. *Something You Already Possess Is Your Key To Your Future.* It may be knowledge, money, skills or ideas, insights and concepts. But, you *already* have enough to create your future.

9. *Everything You Have Was Given To You By God.* Don't become cocky over tithing your small amount of ten percent. Your *entire* paycheck came from God! Your *eyesight* came from God! Your *hearing* came from God! Your *health* came from God! Your *intelligence* came from God! Your *favor* from others came from God! You don't have a thing that God did not give you.

10. *If You Keep What You Presently Have, That Is The Most It Will Ever Be.* When you sow it, it is the least it will ever be. This is one of the most vital principles you must understand in unleashing an *Uncommon Harvest.* Releasing what you have is the only evidence of your faith that God will provide for you.

11. *A Seed Of Nothing Guarantees A Season Of Nothing.* Years ago, the Holy Spirit spoke to me to plant a beautiful Mercedes into the life of another. I was upset with this person. I refused. I have wondered about the Harvest I lost...many times. If a Seed of *Something* can create *Something,* it is quite obvious—a Seed of *Nothing* will create a Season of *Nothing* in your life.

12. *Your Seed Sowing Is The Only Proof You Have Mastered Greed.* Men hoard. Satan steals. God has the nature of giving. Giving is the only cure for greed. Your Seed is the proof that you have

mastered hoarding, selfishness and greed.

13. *When You Let Go Of What Is In Your Hand, God Will Let Go Of What Is In His Hand.* When the small lad released the loaves and fishes into the hands of Jesus, the multiplication began. They picked up several baskets later!

14. *Every Seed Contains An Invisible Instruction.* You cannot see it. It is invisible. Yet, a small watermelon seed will follow that instruction and produce more watermelons. The tomato seed will create more tomatoes. Each Seed contains a specific Assignment. The Creator placed it inside.

15. *When You Give Your Seed A Specific Assignment, Faith And Expectation Is Unleashed.* The widow was demoralized. But, the man of God gave her a Portrait of Possibility. She was encouraged to plant a Seed so she would not lack. She did. Faith was born. "And she went and did according to the saying of Elijah: and she, and he, and her house, did eat many days" (1 Kings 17:15).

16. *When You Increase The Size Of Your Seed, You Increase The Size Of Your Harvest.* "But this I say, He which soweth sparingly shall reap also sparingly; and he which soweth bountifully shall reap also bountifully" (2 Cor. 9:6).

17. *When You Get Involved With God's Dream, He Will Get Involved With Your Dream.* That's the power of sowing. You create a Covenant. Think of a tiny Seed that enters into a Covenant with the soil. Within weeks, it has cracked a concrete slab!! That's the power of Two...the Covenant. The widow invested into Elijah. God, then, entered into a Covenant with her that she would never lack in the famine (read 1 Kings 17).

18. *You Can Only Sow What You Have Been Given.* Stop complaining about something you do not have. You lack money? Then, use your Time as a Seed. Work for your boss, the local church, or simply baby-sit for someone overworked! Use your Time as a Seed.

19. *Your Seed Is Always Your Door Out Of Trouble.* It was for the widow. It can be for you. It may be information, motivation or encouragement. Give it an Assignment. It can produce an exit from your present season.

20. *When God Talks To You About A Seed, He Has A Harvest On His Mind.*

21. *An Uncommon Seed Always Creates An Uncommon Harvest.* An Uncommon Seed is one that requires Uncommon Faith...or a Seed you sow during a season of Uncommon Hardship.

Here is one of my miracles I shared in my book, *"7 Keys To 1000 Times More."*

How I Broke The Back Of Poverty In My Life!

I *broke the back of poverty* with an Uncommon Seed. A Seed of $1,000. I will never forget it as long as I live. It happened on a telethon. I had just received an incredible royalty check for my song writing of $5,000. I was ecstatic! You see, I didn't have anything. Sheets were tacked over my windows. I wanted draperies so bad. I needed a kitchen table with chairs. I had *nothing!* So, I really had wonderful plans for my $5,000! It was my Harvest!

Suddenly, the Holy Spirit spoke to me while sitting next to some ministers on the telethon.

"I want you to plant a Seed of $1,000."

Well, I explained to the Holy Spirit, that I was going to buy draperies and a kitchen table with chairs! (It took me over 45 minutes before I fully obeyed Him.)

The next day, He spoke again. I planted a *second* Seed of $1,000. Then the following Sunday morning, the Holy Spirit spoke to me the *third* time to plant a *third* Seed of $1,000 at a church in Dallas. That afternoon cannot be explained or described adequately! I was in torment and ecstasy at the same time. I felt a little sick inside because I felt like I had gotten "carried away." I knelt at the pastor's little office that afternoon before service. My heart was quite troubled.

"Holy Spirit, five days ago I had $5,000. Within the last five days, You have spoken to me to plant three Seeds of $1,000. If this is not You and Your plan, stop me now!"

The Holy Spirit gently conveyed that *when He talked to me about a Seed, He had a Harvest on His mind.* When I opened my hand, He would open His windows. The Seed that would leave my hand would never leave my life—just my hand, and enter into my future where it would multiply!

The miracles began.

That night, a man approached me. He opened a book featuring rare automobiles. He explained one of the cars in it. "There's only 19 of these in the world. I happen to have Serial Number 1—the first one they made. It is my pet car. *God told me to give it to you!"*

The *next* day, a man walked into my office. He said, "I understand you need a van for your ministry. Order the best one you can buy. *I'll pay for it."*

Tuesday morning, the next day, a friend met me for lunch. He explained that he could not sleep that night. The Holy Spirit told him to plant a special Seed of $10,000 into my ministry!

My life has never been the same.

Within a couple of years, over $300,000 came into my pocket and life from song-writing royalties. It was astounding.

Recognition Of Your Seed Can Unlock A Thousand Harvests You Thought Were Impossible.

RECOMMENDED BOOKS AND TAPES ON THIS TOPIC

B-04   Ten Lies People Believe About Money (Book/$3)
B-06   Creating Tomorrow Through Seed-Faith (Book/$3)
B-16   Seeds of Wisdom on Seed-Faith (Book/$3)
B-47   The Covenant of Fifty-Eight Blessings (Book/$8)
B-82   31 Reasons People Do Not Receive Their Financial
        Harvest (Book/$12)
B-91   Leadership Secrets of Jesus (Book/$10)
B-101   The 3 Most Important Things in Your Life (Book/$10)
B-104   7 Keys to 1000 Times More (Book/$10)
TS-62   31 Secrets to Financial Breakthrough (Six tapes/$30)
TS-82   31 Reasons People Do Not Receive Their Financial
        Harvest (Six tapes/$30)
TS-104 7 Keys to 1000 Times More (Six tapes/$30)

Your Significance Is Not
In Your Similarity
To Another,
But In Your
Point Of Difference
From Another.

-MIKE MURDOCK

❧ 42 ❧

SELF-CONFIDENCE

————————✠◦✠————————

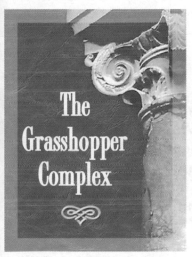

You Will Never Outperform The Self-Portrait You Have Of Yourself.

A few years ago, God gave me one of the most explosive concepts I have ever recognized.

The story is found in the book of Numbers. Moses was the leader of the Israelites. They had left Failure Zone (Egypt) and were headed for their Success Zone (Canaan). Incidentally, Canaan is not really a type of Heaven. It had giants, and Heaven contains none!

Canaan is really a symbol of your dreams, your goals, your places of victories. It is "Success Territory." Every man should have goals of some sort. God intended for you to have them.

Abraham had a dream, Isaac.

Joseph had a dream, prime minister.

Solomon had a dream, the Temple.

The Israelites had a dream, Canaan.

Moses sent twelve spies, or scouts, to review the land before entering. The men saw the land, rich in honey, milk, grapes...and *giants*. When they came back, their reports were contradictory. Ten men had *evil* reports, two had *good* reports. Ignoring the giants was not what made their reports good or evil. All twelve recognized the existence of giants, even the two faith spies, Joshua and Caleb. *Faith living is not ignoring the obvious.* Some people think if you recognize a problem situation, you are admitting doubt. That is incorrect.

Paul recognized once that satan hindered him (see 1 Thess. 2:18). Peter spoke of an adversary (see 1 Pet. 5:8). Jesus, in Matthew 4, did not act as if satan did not exist. Ignoring a cancer or financial bondage or a marriage problem does not dissolve it.

1. *You Must Admit Something Exists Before You Can Confront It Successfully.* The sinner is never converted until he admits his need.

The Baptism of the Holy Spirit comes only to those who realize they are "empty."

All twelve spies had faith.

But, there was a difference. Ten had faith in the giants. Two had faith in God.

Ten were giant-conscious.

Two were God-conscious.

Ten came back moaning, "Did you see the size *of those giants?*" Joshua and Caleb came back licking their lips, saying, "Did you see the size of those *grapes?*"

Ten were "*grasshoppers.*"

Two were "giant-killers."

"*Grape-tasters!*"

2.   *Your Conversation Reveals Whether You Are A Winner Or A Loser.*   Losers major on their problems.   Winners talk about the *possibilities.*   Losers discuss their obstacles.   Winners talk *opportunities.*   Losers talk about disease. Winners talk about *health.* Losers talk about the devil's achievements. Winners talk about God's *victories.* Losers talk like victims. Winners talk like *victors.* Losers have a slaveship mentality. Winners have a *Sonship mentality.*

The Bible is a book of pictures.

It gives you a picture of God, a picture of the devil, and God's photograph of *you.* You will accept one of four possible evaluations of your life.

1.   What *you* think about yourself.

2.   What *others* think about you.

3.   What *satan* thinks about you.

4.   What *God* thinks about you.

The ten spies said, "In our opinion, we are like grasshoppers. Even the giants think we are like grasshoppers."

I have heard many people talk as if they belonged to the First Church of the Grasshopper: "I'm nothing. I'm unworthy." A woman came up to me some time back saying, "Mike, I'm just nothing. I'm so unworthy."

I asked, "Did God create you?"

"Oh yes," she said.   I asked, "Do you think He puts trash together?" She got the point.

God doesn't create cheap merchandise. You are His *creation.* You have *worth.* You have *value. He implanted in you the Seeds of Success, Faith and Power.* Act like it. Live like it. Quit belittling yourself. Quit saying, "I'm stupid, I'm dumb."

3.   *You Must Daily Cultivate The Mind Of Christ.*

Do you have the mind of Christ? Then you are super-brilliant! Say aloud, "I have the mind of Christ. I am amazed at the brilliant mind now in operation in my life." *You are no grasshopper! Quit talking like one! Quit living like one!*

Nineteen years ago, in the midst of a traumatic situation, I began to weep before God. For three hours I sobbed as if my heart would break. Suddenly, the Holy Spirit said, *"Shut up!"* Have you ever had God talk like that to you? It is a bit strong! Even for this Irish lad.

I said, "But God, I'm weeping over what I have lost in my life."

He said, *"Get your mind off what you do not have. Get it on what you do have."*

Something exploded in my system. I had my mind on what I lacked instead of what I already possessed! There is a time to reach for that which you do not have...for that which seems impossible. *Then, there is a time to sit back and create a power climate of thanksgiving for what you possess now!* Quit magnifying your problems. Quit exaggerating the power of the devil. Start emphasizing the power of your *God!* Start testifying about the greatness of God, and what He is planning for *today!* Start planning tomorrow's victories!

4. *Recognize That The Grasshopper Complex Will Destroy Your Faith.* It will stop the faith flow. It will give satan a handle on your life.

Get the giant-killer instinct. You are greater than the enemy because you are a "God-House." He lives inside you. Quit looking at the failure photographs satan shows you of yesterday. God is keeping a photograph album of your victories, your future, your tomorrows! *God is not looking at where you stumbled yesterday, but at your possibilities tomorrow.*

The *grasshopper complex is destroying the power of the local church today.* It is paralyzing the faith flow. It is stopping the praise climate that God intended for us to create in the midst of our homes and our surroundings.

Too many talk like complainers instead of conquerors. *We are not grasshoppers.* The ten spies talked about the size of the *giants*—but Joshua and Caleb talked about the size of the *grapes!*

5. *Focus On Your Opportunities, Not The Obstacles.* Start praising God for what you *already* have—not just what you intend to have! If you are always reaching for that which is beyond your present possession, you will miss out on the joy of the "now" happiness—the "now" victory!

You can tell a *grasshopper* by his reaction to the greeting, "How are you?" He goes into the detailed "pain and hurt" routine. He talks about his health (or I should say his hurt, because few people go about telling how great their ears are hearing, their nose is smelling, their stomach is digesting, their eyes are seeing. They emphasize what is *wrong* instead of what is *right*).

Grasshoppers love talking about the injustices of people toward them. They talk about how they have been mistreated, and how people do not understand them. Have you ever heard a grasshopper stand before a group and say, "I give all the credit to being a failure to myself?" Absolutely not! They have a list of people who caused them to be what they are. (I think I may have a few grasshopper tendencies. Do you?)

Grasshoppers justify their lack of victory. They always give excuses for not conquering the devil. In fact, they sometimes even put down others who are walking and living victoriously.

Grasshoppers constantly talk about their lack of finances. Giant-killers talk about their expectation of God's provision.

Grasshoppers refer to their children's ages as the "terrible two's." Giant-killers call that age the "tremendous two's."

I'm not saying it is easy. But to unleash the Uncommon Life, you must transfer from the *grasshopper complex to the giant-killer mentality.*

6. *You Must Make Up Your Mind To Change.* You can *change.* God has given you the *power of choice:* the power to direct your thinking; your actions!

Make up your mind to *destroy* the "Grasshopper Complex."

Reinforce the giant-killer mentality by choosing friendships that build the faith life in you. You see, if you tolerate any other relationship, it can be damaging to your spiritual growth.

Become choosey.

Become selective.

Become more particular in the friendships you allow.

Discipline your *music,* your *television viewing,* your *reading material.* Use material that will build up your self-confidence as well as your dependency on the Lord and the life of the Spirit.

Dare to become assertive in spiritual things.

Dare to step out in faith.

Dare to believe God for a new *mentality.* Dare to be positive about life.

Dare to step *up...up...up...to a power life in God.*

Enter the Winner's World!

❧ 43 ❧

STRUGGLE

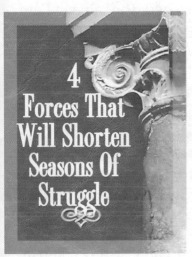

Struggle Is The Proof That You Have Not Yet Been Conquered By Your Enemy.

You may be tired of fighting. Battle may weary you. But, struggle is still the proof that your Enemy has not yet won.

"Fight the good fight of faith, lay hold on eternal life, whereunto thou art also called, and hast professed a good profession before many witnesses" (1 Tim. 6:12).

4 Forces That Will Shorten Your Season Of Struggle

1. *Your Speaking: Words Of Faith Build You Up In The Spirit.* Faith-talk is explosive. "Death and life are in the power of the tongue: and they that love it shall eat the fruit thereof" (Prov. 18:21). *When God wanted the present to end and the future to begin, He spoke.*

2. *Your Singing: Singing Creates A Climate Satan Cannot Tolerate.* Songs of worship and praise dispel demonic spirits as Saul discovered when David played the harp. "And it came to pass, when the evil spirit from God was upon Saul, that David took an harp, and played with his hand: so Saul was refreshed, and was well, and the evil spirit departed from him" (1 Sam. 16:23).

Someone has well said, "Motion creates emotion."

3. *Your Sharing.* 1) Sharing with an intercessor. The prayer of agreement with others is extremely powerful. It is wise for you to initiate the prayer of assistance from intercessors. "Whatsoever ye shall bind on earth shall be bound in Heaven...whatsoever ye shall loose on earth shall be loosed in Heaven...if two of you...agree on earth as touching any thing...it shall done for them of My Father" (Matt. 18:18,19). 2) Sharing with a Mentor. "Two are better than one; because they have a good reward for their labour" (Ecc. 4:9).

4. *Your Seed-Sowing: Sowing Creates Partnership With God*

That Involves Him In Your Adversity. "Bring ye all the tithes into the storehouse, that there may be meat in Mine house, and prove Me now...saith the Lord of hosts, if I will not open...the windows of Heaven, and pour you out a blessing, that there shall not be room enough to receive it. And I will rebuke the devourer for your sakes" (Mal. 3:10,11).

I have always observed significant changes in times of stress, battle and struggle when I have boldly unleashed the above Four Forces.

Never Forget 2 Battle Truths!

1. Your Battle Is Always For A *Reason.*
2. *Your Battle Is Always For A Season.*

Overcomers Are The Only Ones Rewarded In Eternity. "He that overcometh, the same shall be clothed in white raiment; and I will not blot out his name out of the book of life, but I will confess his name before My Father, and before His angels. Him that overcometh will I make a pillar in the temple of My God, and he shall go no more out: and I will write upon him the name of My God, and the name of the city of My God, which is new Jerusalem, which cometh down out of Heaven from My God: and I will write upon him My new name. To him that overcometh will I grant to sit with Me in My throne, even as I also overcame, and am set down with My Father in His throne" (Rev. 3:5,12,21).

Well, go ahead and get back up and going! Something good is en route from the Father to you today!

RECOMMENDED BOOKS AND TAPES ON THIS TOPIC

B-07   Battle Techniques for War Weary Saints (Book/$3)
B-17   Seeds of Wisdom on Overcoming (Book/$3)
B-40   Wisdom for Crisis Times (Book/$9)
B-114   The Law of Recognition (Book/$10)
TS-5   How to Walk Through Fire (Six tapes/$30)
TS-40   Wisdom for Crisis Times (Six tapes/$30)

❧ 44 ❧

SUCCESS

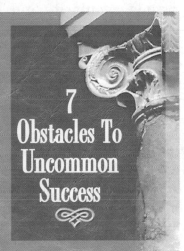

7
Obstacles To
Uncommon
Success

Happiness Is A Now Place.
Yesterday is in the *tomb*.
Tomorrow is in the *womb*.
Your life is *today*.
Today is really the only place you will ever exist. When you get to your future, you will rename it—*Today*. "This is the day which the Lord hath made; we will rejoice and be glad in it" (Ps. 118:24).

What Is Success?

Thousands of people have misunderstood success and prosperity.

Somewhere they have gotten the idea that it is wrong to want to be successful. In fact, some even feel that prosperity is of the devil. Nothing could be further from the truth! Don't be misled. God *does* want you successful! His Word *does* say: "...thou shalt make thy way prosperous, and then thou shalt have good success" (Josh. 1:8).

When you say the word *success,* everybody thinks of yachts, gorgeous homes, big cars, fancy clothes and huge bank accounts. It is quite possible to have all these possessions and be unsuccessful. Unfortunately, merely having these possessions does not necessarily make a person successful. Many who possess all of this have honestly admitted openly that they are still unhappy with their lives.

Some people define success in terms of power, position, prestige and popularity. Again, the successful person may enjoy all these things, but even these attributes are not, in themselves, the foundation stones of success.

Still others say that success is achieving the goals you set for yourself. The question is, does the attainment of those particular goals produce genuine satisfaction in the heart, the *inner world?* The *external* picture of success does not necessarily guarantee *internal* happiness.

I remember reading in history about Alexander the Great. He went out with his armies to conquer the nations of the world. After the last victorious battle had ended, it is said Alexander wept because there were no more worlds left for him to conquer! He achieved all his goals but did not find abiding satisfaction and happiness.

Real Success

If success is not measured in terms of possessions, popularity and performance, how then can it be defined? Perhaps the simplest definition of success for the believer is *knowing and attaining God's goals for your life.* A successful life is one that is happy.

Becoming what God wants you to become.

Doing what God wants you to do.

Possessing what God wants you to own.

As you achieve the goals *God* has set for your life, then you become successful. Someone once said, "Success is not merely getting what you want, but wanting what you got after you get it." Some fellow may throw away all he has to win the heart of a certain girl, only to discover later her greatest talent is making him miserable! *He got what he wanted, but didn't want what he got.*

In their quest for achievement, some people become so greedy and grasping they are *never* satisfied with *any* accomplishment. They never enjoy what God has *already* given them. Real success is not a destination, it is a journey. It is movement. It is the joy created by *progress.* Success is not a city where you will arrive *tomorrow,* it is the enjoyment of today, *the now.* Every person is somewhere on God's maturity schedule, from "A" to "Z." Real success is keeping the schedule God has for you and His Assignment for your life.

Stay On God's Schedule For Success

What does all this mean? Simply that success means different things to different people, depending on where they are on God's maturity schedule. If someone offered a baby the keys to a new car, it would mean very little to him. He wants his bottle of milk! Having the keys to his own automobile would not be success to him. Being given his bottle and a soft pillow for his head is the best thing that could happen to him right now. However, if that baby continued to progress along God's maturity schedule, about 16 years later, if he were offered a baby bottle and a soft pillow, he would be very disappointed. It would not be his idea of the ideal way to spend an evening. That's the time he is interested in the offer of the keys to the car!

That's why I say *true success is achieving the goals God presently has for you.* Some Christians have stopped along God's maturity schedule at about letter "C." Instead of realizing God wants them to prosper and be successful, they sit back with a "baby bottle" and wonder why they find very little satisfaction in life.

On the other hand, it is possible to try to get too far *ahead* of God's schedule. I know some people who are trying to achieve level "S" or "T" when they should be back on about "M." Because of their misdirected attention focus, they are completely dissatisfied with the achievements they are making on their present level.

Remember, *success is different things to different people at different times.* Find out where you are on your journey. Learn to enjoy what you are already receiving instead of being unhappy because you haven't got everything you are wanting.

One man I know thought his "success goal" was a lot of money. You can imagine how he felt when he read in the newspaper about a guy who won a contest and was awarded the prize of $100,000. "Wow, what a lucky guy," the man said. "Nothing could make me unhappy if I could win $100,000 like he did!"

Then my friend read the next paragraph of the news story. He learned that the "winner" was a prisoner on death row, scheduled to be electrocuted in a short time. From the prisoner's point of view, the $100,000 prize didn't spell success. The money wasn't going to do him much good!

Never forget that being successful is achieving the *goals* God has for you in *every* area of your life. What are these areas? God has a success plan for you *spiritually, physically, emotionally, financially, socially* and in your *family life.* And He has provided a Golden Key to help you unlock the Doors of Success in every single area.

Success is the achievement of the goals God has for you!!

Obstacles To Success

People are my life. I have invested over 35 years of global evangelism to increase their success and happiness through conferences, seminars, tapes and books.

Failure angers me. I rebel against unhappiness, sickness and hurt. Most of it could be *avoided* through recognizing and obeying the *Laws of God.* Much could be turned into a stepping stone to greater success if we knew how to *react* to situations.

Obstacle 1: An Unteachable Spirit

An unteachable spirit is an *unwillingness to change.* Millions refuse to implement new and vital information as it becomes available.

Imagine a lawyer who refused to read new laws and *update his understanding.* Would you choose a surgeon who was unfamiliar with the latest medical technology?

The most successful businesses are those which adapt to new policies, produce new products and keep *informed.* They consult with experts. They analyze their own procedures. *Growing means change.* It's a part of prospering.

"My people are destroyed for lack of knowledge:" (Hos. 4:6).

"A wise man will hear, and will increase learning;" (Prov. 1:5).

"If thou criest after knowledge...If thou seekest her as silver, and searchest for her as for hid treasures; then shalt thou understand the fear of the Lord, and find the knowledge of God" (Prov. 2:3-5).

A friend of mine has said, there are *two sources of knowledge:*

Wisdom - learning from the mistakes of *others,* and...

Experience - learning from *your own* mistakes.

Knowledge is exploding all around us. Uncommon men of God are sharing with us their expertise on faith, financial blessings and the power of God. They are teaching us many principles of success for marriage, purity and every part of our lives.

Books are crammed with information from years of research. *Cassette Tapes* are made available for the price of a simple meal. *Magazines* are mailed free of charge.

God placed *Seeds of Greatness* within us at birth. *You* and I are responsible for *growing* those Seeds.

You are what you have decided to be.

If you are unhappy with yourself, *dare to reach* for *new* information, *new* teaching and *new* truths that will elevate you and build your relationship with God. If there is a sin in your life, repent and rededicate your life to Jesus Christ. Allow His precious blood to cleanse you. He will restore that fellowship you need with Him.

Invest in literature and teaching tapes. If your car is worth $30 for gas, surely your mind is worth growing! Don't bankrupt your mind! Don't starve your heart! Feed it what it desperately needs! *Dare to embrace change.* Dare to listen to new ideas and concepts. God may want you on a new job, in a new city. Your best days are just ahead! *You can make it!*

Recognize reasons for any failure. It is crucial that you locate the "bottleneck" in your lives and activate the success and happiness that belongs to you.

Obstacle 2: Unpaid Vows

Unpaid vows are the source of failure for many people. God *holds you responsible for your promises.*

"When thou vowest a vow unto God, defer not to pay it; for He hath no pleasure in fools: pay that which thou hast vowed. Better is it that thou shouldest not vow, than that thou shouldest vow and not pay" (Ecc. 5:4,5).

Sometimes during a crisis you promise God that you will be faithful to attend church, or pay the tithe of your income, or to clear an offense with someone. Then afterwards, when we regain our health, we forget our vow. *This is deadly.*

It is important that you honor God and each other through honesty and the integrity of your words. You can give offerings, attend church and do many beautiful works, but if you allow a vow to go unpaid, it will destroy the *operation of faith* and the miracle God wants to perform.

Do you owe someone money? Make arrangements to pay, regardless how small those payments may have to be. "Bounced" checks are hardly a testimony to the provision of our Lord. What have you promised your *children?* Your *mate?* Your *company?* Are you fulfilling your *vows?* Have you really done your *best* to make things right with your *creditors?*

Dare to step out and take the responsibility for the vows you have made. God will honor you. You will sleep better. *Miracles* become daily events in the life of the obedient.

Obstacle 3: Unforgiven Offenses

Forgiveness is not a suggestion.

It is a requirement. "And when ye stand praying, forgive, if ye have aught against any: that your Father also which is in Heaven may forgive you your trespasses. But if ye do not forgive, neither will your Father which is in Heaven forgive your trespasses" (Mk. 11:25,26).

It is *releasing to God the right to judge* and *penalize another for personal wrong*. Sometimes we feel we have a right to "pay back" a slight or injustice. This is *denying God the right to give mercy or penalty*. It is "playing God." God abhors the human urge to usurp His authority. Quit role playing! Let God judge and schedule punishment.

Visualize your offender as a hurt, damaged, wounded friend lashing out against you as a form of protection. He may be afraid of you and simply want to keep you from "getting the best of him."

Pray for those who have wronged you. Find a way to communicate a personal care and interest. Is it hard to do? Oh, very much so. But the personal *peace* it sets in motion is beyond description.

You have received *mercy*...sow it into others.

You have received *love*...sow it into others.

You have received *kindness*...sow it into others.

Obstacle 4: Unwise Associations

Unwise friendships and associations have destroyed the potential and the abilities of multiplied thousands of could-be winners.

Solomon said it: "He that walketh with wise men shall be wise: but a companion of fools shall be destroyed" (Prov. 13:20).

Paul phrased it: "...evil communications corrupt good manners" (1 Cor. 15:33).

Disconnect from unqualified persons who abuse and misuse your life. Jesus allowed only two kinds of people to absorb His time: first, those who *ministered* to Him and second, those who *received* His ministry to them. He knew that the Pharisees did not deserve His time because they abused it. *When someone does not value your time, neither will they value your Wisdom*.

Re-evaluate your life and friendships.

Do you allow your dreams to be eroded and your goals limited because of relationships with those who laugh at your pursuit of accomplishment? *Disconnect*.

I had an interesting revelation on this Principle of Power. A letter had been placed on my desk by my secretary as one worthy of "special attention." It was from a critical lady who had resented something I said in a meeting in which I was speaking. I spent one full hour trying to write a letter of explanation (really, an appeasement) to this lady.

Suddenly, it dawned on me: I was spending more time on her than I had ever spent writing a letter to my precious mother who had supported and loved me for my entire life! I was actually giving *my time*...the most important commodity of my life...to someone who was completely unappreciative of such investment. I have stopped this practice and have focused instead on helping the thankful, not the critical.

4 Qualities Of Wise Associations

▶ Those who speak words that build your faith and confidence.
▶ Those who see the worthiness of your God-given dreams and goals.
▶ Those who become enthusiastic when you enter their presence.
▶ Those who remind you of your special gifts and abilities.

You must choose the level of mentality you want to live on. If you give time to those unworthy of it, stop complaining. You are the one who gave them the time. They abused it because you allowed them the opportunity. Become more selective. Remember: the same time you waste on losers is that which could have been invested with winners.

Obstacle 5: Unbridled Tongue

"Death and life are in the power of the tongue: and they that love it shall eat the fruit thereof" (Prov. 18:21).

"A fool's lips enter into contention...A fool's mouth is his destruction, and his lips are the snare of his soul. The words of a talebearer are as wounds, and they go down into the innermost parts of the belly" (Prov. 18:6-8).

Words are *forces*. Wrong or right, to build or destroy, words leave a trail of destruction or accomplishment. Words can build confidence or tear faith down.

Words are *tools* God gave you to build up your own spirit and mind. Your *body* responds to *sounds*. Your *spirit* responds to *words*.

Words provide you *mind-pictures* that your entire life reacts to. You *hear* a story. You smile or cry. You *feel*.

What you *hear*, you *think about*.

What you think about, you *feel*.

What you feel, you *do*.

What you do, becomes a *habit*.

Your habits determine your life and eventual destiny.

So, stop talking about shortages and setbacks. Stop talking about defeat and disease. Stop talking about failure and problems. Concentrate on the opportunities at hand. Talk about the blessings you now possess. Take time to taste your triumphs today. *Now* is here.

Reach up. Take in. *Absorb* the beauty of *now.* *Talk* about your *expectations,* not your experiences. *Talk* about your *future,* not your failures.

Help others do the same. *Influence the conversations around you.* Sometimes it is even good to "dominate your turf" with a little "aggressive happiness."

Happy people tend to be a little intimidating to the unhappy. The *Winner* seems *pushy* to a Loser. Dare to do it anyway. Their appreciation will be inevitable. When someone around you becomes ill, *pray* for them. When someone loses their job, *assist them* in stimulating their mind to find a creative alternative.

Control your mouth. "For by thy words thou shalt be justified, and by thy words thou shalt be condemned" (Matt. 12:37).

If you talk about all your losses, setbacks and failures, you are providing others with a photograph album and file of you *as a loser.* They will never see you as a Winner. Remember, every time you talk, you are *programming yourself* and *others.* Start conditioning your mind to accept your successes and triumphs.

A common mistake losers make is sharing their heartbreak stories *during* the period of loss. Winners never do that: they wait until that experience is *past* and share it as a *triumph.*

Instead of discussing people who are takers, *start concentrating on God. Your Giver.* You should memorize Matthew 7:7-11: "Ask, and it shall be given you; seek, and ye shall find; knock, and it shall be opened unto you: For every one that asketh receiveth; and he that seeketh findeth; and to him that knocketh it shall be opened. Or what man is there of you, whom if his son ask bread, will he give him a stone? Or if he ask a fish, will he give him a serpent? If ye then, being evil, know how to give good gifts unto your children, how much more shall your Father which is in Heaven give good things to them that ask Him?"

Your *success future* is set in motion by your *words.* I like the way a friend of mine says it: *"There is a miracle in your mouth."* So, begin talking in the direction you want your life to move.

Obstacle 6: Undeveloped Gifts And Abilities

Winners are people who have discovered their special talents, abilities and *special* God-given gifts. And, seeing their Seeds of Greatness, they have taken the time and energy to *grow* those Seeds into great benefits and advantages.

One secretary watches television all weekend, while another pursues an in-depth seminar study or develops her special shorthand skills. When it comes time for a raise, or promotion, who has placed herself in the *position of advantage?* Certainly, the one secretary may complain that the other "gets all the breaks" or "the boss likes her" but in reality, one cultivated the gift God deposited in her Life-Account.

Our talents and abilities differ. "Having then gifts differing according to the grace that is given to us..." (Rom. 12:6).

Though a man is compensated by other men according to their need for his special gift, God values every man's ability and gift equally. We must do the same.

If you enjoy working, do not play down your role as a secretary. See the greatness of your gift. Take time to find it. Then, invest the time and effort necessary to improve it. The special talents God has given to you will generate everything you will need to be financially successful, but you must grow the Seeds within you.

Important Career Questions

What do you *enjoy* doing?
What would you like to do *better?*
What tasks do you *dread* doing?
What brings you the *greatest* sense of fulfillment?
Find out, and you will be well on your way to the sense of worth thousands have never taken the time to find.

Visit your library. Subscribe to periodicals. Consult the *experts* in the field of your interest. Set up appointments. *Pray* for Divine direction. Respond to the opportunities in your local community for self-improvement and education. God will make the "shovel" available but you must start the "digging."

Obstacle 7: Uncommitted Heart

A committed heart is a decided heart. It is the result of a made-up mind. And it may explain the mystery of "charisma," or *presence*, that powerful people often generate when they walk into a room. "A double minded man is unstable in all his ways" (James 1:8).

Commitment generates an aura of authority. It permeates an atmosphere. The effect is electrifying. Whether you are obsessed with evil as Adolf Hitler, or for righteousness as Billy Graham, *commitment* attracts people, favorable opportunities, and gives power and creativity to your life.

Get involved in something great and give your life to it. Find something bigger than you are. Connect with something you can really believe in. If you are working for somebody you cannot respect, find someone you can admire and attach your Wisdom and energy to them.

Make a commitment to God. He made one to you in the person of His Son, Jesus Christ. *Calvary was commitment.* The blood and cross of Jesus was commitment. Gethsemane was commitment.

Let's do something right now. Before you go any further, pray this prayer with me aloud:

Our Prayer Together...

"Father, I *need* You. I believe You exist. *Forgive* me for every sin I have ever committed. I *commit* my life and heart to Your control. *Cleanse* my mind. *Free* my heart to serve You. I make You Savior and Lord of my life. I accept Your forgiveness, peace and mercy with joy and a thankful heart. Use me to touch another with Your special love. I *love You* with all my mind, my heart and body. In the name of Your Son Jesus, I pray. Amen."

Value the God-Connection. Recognize God as a blessing factor. He is *never* a *disadvantage* to you, *always* an *asset*. He wants you to succeed and "hath pleasure in the prosperity of His servant" (Ps. 35:27). Read the Scriptures on a daily schedule. Practice the power of prayer. Make Jesus Christ Lord of your life. "Acquaint now thyself with Him, and be at peace: thereby good shall come unto thee" (Job 22:21). "...as long as he sought the Lord, God made him to prosper" (2 Chr. 26:5).

RECOMMENDED BOOKS AND TAPES ON THIS TOPIC
B-11   Dream Seeds (Book/$9)
B-44   31 Secrets for Career Success (Book/$10)
B-91   The Leadership Secrets of Jesus (Book/$10)
TS-11   Dream Seeds (Six tapes/$30)
TS-14   How to Stay Motivated (Six tapes/$30)

❦ 45 ❦

TIME MANAGEMENT

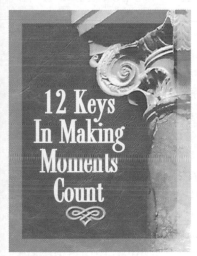

12 Keys In Making Moments Count

One Minute Can Make A Difference.

Time is so precious. It is impossible to save, store or gather Time. You must simply learn the best ways to invest it. *Moments really do matter:* The Apostle Paul treasured time. "See then that ye walk circumspectly, not as fools, but as wise, Redeeming the time, because the days are evil" (Eph. 5:15,16).

12 Keys In Making Moments Count!

1. *View Time As The Currency Of Earth For Success.* Mexico has the peso. France has the franc. Germany has the mark. The United States has the dollar. God has given a currency to us here on earth—the currency called Time.

Think about this. God did not simply give you friends. He gave you *Time.* You accepted Time and invested Time back into people. That produced friendships. God did not simply give you money. He gave you *Time.* You offered your Time to an employer and traded your Time for his money. You took the money and purchased your home. *Time is one of the most precious and valuable gifts God has given to you.*

2. *Study The Success Habits Of Uncommon Achievers.* You will notice one obvious and outstanding quality. All champions and leaders are very conscious of Time. They wear watches. They continually consult them. When you have an appointment with them, they establish the perimeters of the appointment. Boundaries are set. You simply do not meet someone at 3:00 p.m. You will meet with them from 3:00 p.m. until 3:30 p.m.

Why is this? Their Time is the most precious commodity in their life. It is the currency of Time that helps them strengthen their families, birth ideas, and achieve their dreams and goals.

I must make something very clear to you if I am to help you achieve your Assignment. There are people who are poor by the standards of today. Many of those who are struggling seem to have a common thread among them—an obvious disrespect for time. They are late for appointments. They do not have a written plan for each day. Conversations are vague instead of concise.

I can predict your success by your respect for Time. I read an interesting illustration many years ago. If you have 10 pounds of iron, you can use it three different ways:

1) It can be used to make *horseshoes*. If so, it may be worth approximately $30.

2) You can use the 10 pounds of iron to make *needles*. In this form, it would be worth approximately $300.

3) You can use the iron to make *watch springs*. In that form, it may be worth $3,000. The same amount of iron, used three different ways, will produce three different levels of financial income.

Your Time is much like this bar of iron. You can watch a television movie for two hours. Or, you can read and absorb the financial success secrets from the biography of a billionaire. You can sit at your table and eat a meal for ninety minutes and talk with your friends. Or, you can eat for 30 minutes and go walk four miles in the following 60 minutes. You decide.

Champions Make Decisions That Create The Future They Desire.
Losers Make Decisions That Create The Present They Desire.

3. *Cultivate A Total Focus On Your Assignment.* Remember, you will only succeed with something that is an obsession. Last night, I was reading the biography of the fascinating entrepreneur of our generation, the late Sam Walton, head of the Wal-Mart stores. Throughout the book, he continuously referred to the fact that he was obsessed with retailing. He spent *every available moment* studying retail sales. Those moments paid off.

4. *Keep A Calendar Or Day Planner With You At All Times.* What You See Determines What You Desire. Someone has well said, "A short pencil is better than a long memory." God instructed us, "Write the vision, and make it plain upon tables, that he may run that readeth it" (Hab. 2:2).

Your day planner should be handy and kept with you always. If it is too large, you will use its size as an excuse to leave it at home, or in the car. At first, carrying *anything* will become uncomfortable. However, remember that it is your blueprint for the dreams and goals of your life. Others may sit around and discuss the weather, the wind or current news.

You are on an Assignment. You are focused.

5. *Stay Aware Of Each Hour As It Occurs.* Develop precision with each appointment. "For the vision is yet for an appointed time, but at the end it shall speak, and not lie: though it tarry, wait for it; because it will surely come, it will not tarry" (Hab. 2:3).

6. *Review The Appointments And Plans Of Each Day Continually.* Visualize them as links to your eventual goal and dream.

7. *Read Continuously.* When I am in an airplane, waiting at the airport or sitting in a taxi, I *read.* I read newspapers, magazines, books, or my Bible. I try to absorb everything related to my Assignment. Occasionally, I will read a novel for relaxation. When I do, I have a pen in hand to circle anything in that novel linked to something I want to do with my life. I am continuously *extracting an education* from events, people, and reading material around me. You can *cultivate* that kind of appetite, even if you are not born with it.

Clip articles out of newspapers. Tear pages out of magazines, and build files—anything to strengthen your resolve and focus on the Assignment God is burning into your life.

8. *Listen. Listen. Listen.* Listen to happy people for encouragement. Listen to unhappy voices for ideas. While listening, ask questions. When you are with a lawyer, ask him which three most important things he feels you should know. When you are with your pastor, ask him the three most important daily habits necessary for birthing a powerful relationship with God.

9. *Ask Questions That Control The Focus Of Every Conversation.* Keep a legal pad and a pen or a microcassette with you at all times. There is probably never a moment I do not have a microcassette in my hand or pocket, or a legal pad. Why? *One idea could birth a million miracles.*

I cannot afford to waste a minute of my time doing something unrelated to my Assignment. You, too, must make every moment count in your life.

10. *Enter Into Conversations For The Purpose Of Advancing Toward Your Assignment.* Keep focused. Occasionally, I have people approach me and want to talk about things unrelated to my calling. I simply refuse. Why? I am ruthless in protecting my focus on the Assignment God has placed in my life.

If I returned every telephone call, answered every single question asked of me, flew to every city where someone had requested me, listened to every cassette mailed to me, or read every book handed to me, I would not have time to live one single day of my life properly.

Every moment is valuable to me. I have nothing to give to those who treat my time lightly.

Access to God was His first gift to me.

Time was His second gift to me.

I dare not squander it in any way. It is the precious gift of Time that enables me to enter into The Secret Place, read the Word of God, and do what life has assigned me to do.

When a young lady met me at a restaurant for our date, she was 45 minutes late. She laughed it off. I could hardly believe how lightly she considered time. Obviously, the relationship did not work out. We differed regarding time.

11. *Disconnect From People Who Do Not Appreciate Your Time.* Several years ago, I flew 1,500 miles to a crusade. It was a Saturday evening. I was speaking Sunday, both morning and night. Then, I would fly back home Monday afternoon. It involved three days of my life in a strange motel room, away from my home and family. The pastor leaned over to me Sunday morning and whispered, "Could you dismiss us within 45 minutes?"

"I can dismiss you right now," I replied. "If you have flown me 3,000 miles for three days and do not desire me in your presence more than 45 minutes, I am in the wrong place anyway." I have refused to return to that church.

When you see somebody who is flippant and careless with their time, know they will be flippant and careless with your time. I have seen people come and sit around my offices and ministry doing very little, then ask me for a job. If they are careless with their own hours, imagine what they would do working for me.

I replied to a resumé once. Nobody answered the telephone. I was surprised that an answering machine did not accommodate me. When I finally talked to the job applicant, I asked, "Why do you not have a telephone answering machine?" "I do not like answering machines," was her reply.

Obviously, I would not even consider hiring someone who was that insensitive to time. What did that tell me? Her friend's time did not matter. She forced everyone to keep returning phone calls to reach her. When someone telephoned her, they were unable to leave any messages, and consequently they wasted their entire effort, time, energy and finances. I could not afford to have someone so thoughtless on my payroll.

I would be reluctant to hire anyone who wrote me long 15 page letters. Why? Their time does not matter. They refuse conciseness. They force their friends to read trivia and absorb nonessential information—simply because they do not want to think before writing.

I have sat for several hours in the presence of young preachers who are launching their ministries. Few have ever asked me one serious, thoughtful and important question. Oh, how we waste the time God has given to us!

12. *View Time As A Wonderful And Glorious Tool God Has Given You To Build Your Dream, Your Goals And Your Assignment.* Do not throw it away.

"To every thing there is a season, and a time to every purpose under the Heaven: A time to be born, and a time to die; a time to plant, and a time to pluck up that which is planted; A time to kill, and a time to heal; a time to break down, and a time to build up; A time to weep, and a time to laugh; a time to mourn, and a time to dance; A time to cast away stones, and a time to gather stones together; a time to embrace, and a time to refrain from embracing; A time to get, and a time to lose; a time to keep, and a time to cast away; A time to rend, and a time to sew; a time to keep silence, and a time to speak; A time to love, and a time to hate; a time of war, and a time of peace" (Ecc. 3:1-8).

Each *Moment Of Today Is An Opportunity To Advance In Your Assignment.*

Your Assignment is an hourly event with a future result.

RECOMMENDED BOOKS AND TAPES ON THIS TOPIC

B-44   31 Secrets for Career Success (Book/$10)

B-91   The Leadership Secrets of Jesus (Book/$10)

TS-83   School of Wisdom, Vol. 3 - What I'd Do Differently If I Could Begin My Life Over Again (Six tapes/$30)

Whatever You Possess Reveals What You Have Pursued.

-MIKE MURDOCK

～ 46 ～

UNDERSTANDING

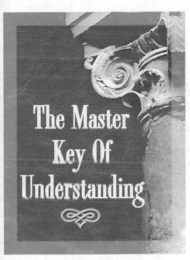

Understanding Is God's Golden Key To Your Success.

"Get Wisdom, get understanding: forget it not; neither decline from the words of My mouth" (Prov. 4:5).

By using the Golden Key to Understanding, we can unlock the doors of opportunity in every part of our life, even in our finances, and walk through them confidently to gain success.

When I was growing up, all the kids in the neighborhood would gather around to talk. One of our favorite topics was the "one-wish game." Someone would say, "If you could have anything in the whole world, what one thing would you wish for?"

The girls usually wanted a date with some popular guy at school. The fellow down the block wished for a motorcycle. A teenager who was having problems at home might say he wished he had no parents! One girl wished she had $1,000 to spend on new clothes.

Everyone in the group always had one or two things to wish for. Every time we played the game there was always something each youngster either wanted to have or wished to avoid. Of course, there was no one listening to our wishes who had the power to grant them. One day a new boy in our neighborhood stunned us all by his statement of his one wish, "I wish for one thing—the *wishing ability* that anything I wish for would come true." Naturally, for such clever thinking he became our leading local genius!

There is a story in the Bible, though, of a man who was actually guaranteed that he would be given anything he asked for: "...the Lord appeared to Solomon in a dream by night: and God said, Ask what I shall give thee" (1 Kings 3:5).

What a dramatic situation! It was as if God had led Solomon to the front of a great hotel and said, "Choose any room you want, and you can have it. One room has *riches* inside. One room has *long life*. One room has *power and authority*. Each room contains something desirable—something you would like to have. Just tell Me which room you want most and I will give you the key to it."

Solomon thought about God's offer for a moment. Then he said quietly, "Give me the key to the room which contains Wisdom and Understanding."

God smiled, and opened up the ring of keys in His hand. He took off a golden key and handed it to Solomon. "You have made a wise choice," He said.

Solomon asked, "Why is this key different from all the rest?"

"Because this is the *Master Key* it will unlock *all the rooms* in the entire building!"

Yes, *understanding is God's Golden Key to your success. Understanding!* At first it sounds like nothing. It seems trite and meaningless. But *Understanding* is the *Master Key* that opens the doors of opportunity to you and gives you free access to every resource. *Understanding* unlocks the doors to all your goals, ambitions and desires. *Understanding* will smash the locks on your prison of prejudices, fears and unhappiness!

Understanding is the sum total of both knowledge and Wisdom. *It is the ability to interpret life as God sees it—the ability to see the total picture that God sees of a person or a situation.* Understanding is the ability:

To *see* through His eyes,
To *hear* through His ears,
To *feel* as with His heart,
To *walk* in His steps,
To *think* with His mind.

No marriage would ever be destroyed by divorce if the husband saw his wife *through the eyes of God,* and the wife could see her husband *as God sees him.*

A man would be able to become wealthy almost overnight if he knew the hearts of people and all the details of business propositions as God knows them.

Parents and children would have no crushing conflicts if they dealt with each other from the standpoint of understanding. How many teenagers look at their parents and wish they could go pack their bags and leave home because nobody understands them? While they are thinking that, the parents' hearts are just aching: "Oh honey, if you could just see how we love you. If you could just know how we think and feel about you!"

The Golden Key of Understanding makes it possible for parents and children to communicate—to hear what the other is saying *with their heart.* Understanding will open the door to harmony and happiness in the home.

Understanding is also seeing God's purpose in some of life's more unpleasant events. The Bible tells how Joseph was sold into slavery by his brothers. As a slave, he tried to do what was right and was the target of vicious lies as a result. He ended up in a dungeon. Through all this pain and persecution, Joseph maintained his faith in God. How? By being aware of God's hand at work in his behalf. Because he was in the dungeon *at the right time,* he was given the *opportunity to minister* by interpreting Pharaoh's troubling dreams. *This catapulted him to power.* In a short time he had become Pharaoh's chief officer of the entire land. With God's direction he was able to prepare for a time of great famine in the land.

When the famine came, Joseph was able to save an entire nation. Plus, he was in a position to save the lives of his own family— including the brothers who had betrayed him. Understanding helped him to see *God's purpose* in his problems and make him successful.

When you ask God for the Golden Key of Understanding, He says to you: "I am the Lord thy God which teacheth thee to profit, which leadeth thee by the way that thou shouldest go" (Isa. 48: 17).

$124,000 Profit In 30 Days!

A friend of mine was driving by a piece of property and suddenly he felt a strong impression that he should buy it. The selling price was $75,000, and my friend didn't have that kind of money. He couldn't see why he should buy such an expensive piece of ground that he didn't even need. But the voice of God kept speaking to him. *God knew something he didn't know and wanted to share it with him.*

My friend felt this leading of the Lord so strongly that he began scraping together what money he could. He took all of his savings out of the bank. He sold some items. He took all the cash he could get together and made a down payment on that piece of property.

Thirty days later he was on that lot, burning some trash and generally cleaning up a bit. A car drove up and a lady got out, walked over and asked if he was the owner. Then she wanted to know if the property was for sale.

When my friend assured her he was the owner, she said, "My husband is a doctor. He has been wanting to buy this land for four years. We're prepared to offer you $199,000 for this property."

In 30 days time, my friend was offered a $124,000 profit! He was able to achieve this remarkable success—not in his own Wisdom, but through the divine Understanding of God—*the ability to see the picture of that property as God saw it. His obedience created the miracle.*

What God did for this man, He will do for *you.*

God is no respecter of persons. His promises are for everybody.

He has a Golden Key of Understanding waiting for you.

Where Does Understanding Come From?

"My son, if thou wilt receive My words, and hide My commandments with thee; So that thou incline thine ear unto Wisdom, and apply thine heart to understanding; Yea, if thou criest after knowledge, and liftest up thy voice for understanding; If thou seekest her as silver, and searchest for her as for hid treasures; Then shalt thou understand the fear of the Lord, and find the knowledge of God. For the Lord giveth Wisdom: out of His mouth cometh knowledge and Understanding" (Prov. 2:1-6).

All Understanding comes from God. It is a gift *only God can give.* That is why Solomon had to ask for Understanding instead of trying to rely upon himself. God bestows Understanding upon us through His Word: "For the Lord giveth Wisdom: out of His mouth cometh knowledge and understanding" (Prov. 2:6). The Psalmist said of God: "Through Thy precepts I get understanding..." (Ps. 119:104).

So the Word of God opens up Understanding to us. The entire Bible was written that you and I would have Understanding—that we would be able to interpret life as God does. Paul, one of the prolific writers of the New Testament, said: "Consider what I say; and the Lord give thee understanding in all things" (2 Tim. 2:7).

By carefully reading the Word of God, we learn to use the Golden Key of Understanding in unlocking the Doors of Success. As we immerse ourselves in the Bible, God speaks to us from His Word and says, "This is what I *think.* This is what I *know.* This is what I *see.* This is what I *hear.*"

God has breathed His divine knowledge into the Word. *Between the covers of your Bible are the treasures you need to be truly successful.* You will find the answer to financial troubles, how to cure worry, even how to solve friendship problems. The Word will direct you in your *family* relationships—the chain of authority in the home, including the position of the husband, the wife, and the children.

The Bible contains a cure for nervousness and depression. The Word is even the purging tool for removing immorality from our minds and lives: "Wherewithal shall a young man cleanse his way? by taking heed thereto according to Thy Word:" (Ps. 119:9).

So, *the Bible is the success book of the world!* It is the source of God's Golden Key for Success: "The entrance of Thy Words giveth light; it giveth Understanding unto the simple" (Ps. 119:130).

An interesting note is that one of the important functions of the Holy Spirit is to interpret the Word of God to believers and produce Understanding. This means when we come to a passage of scripture that is not clear to us, the Holy Spirit enlightens our minds and makes every detail sharp and meaningful: "Howbeit when He, the Spirit of truth, is come, He will guide you into all truth..." (Jn. 16:13).

It was this Spirit that rested upon Jesus as Isaiah prophesied: "And the Spirit of the Lord shall rest upon him, the Spirit of Wisdom and Understanding..." (Isa. 11:2).

But we must desire and ask for this Wisdom. If we will do that, God will give it to us liberally according to James 1:5, "If any of you lack Wisdom, let him ask of God, that giveth to all men liberally, and upbraideth not; and it shall be given him."

What You Pursue, You Will Possess.

RECOMMENDED BOOKS AND TAPES ON THIS TOPIC

B-01   Wisdom for Winning (Book/$10)
B-71   Wisdom - God's Golden Key To Success (Book/$7)
TS-85   School of Wisdom, Vol. 1 - The Uncommon Life (Six
        tapes/$30)

You Can Only Conquer Something You Hate.

-MIKE MURDOCK

☞ 47 ☜

VICTORY

You Decide Your Victories.

6 Keys To A Victorious Life Are:

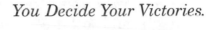

1. *God-Consciousness.* Continuously center your thoughts on God and Scriptural truth. This will crowd out wrong thinking, empower you during temptation and develop Wisdom for important decisions.

"What shall we then say to these things? If God be for us, who can be against us? He that spared not His own Son, but delivered Him up for us all, how shall He not with Him also freely give us all things? Who shall lay any thing to the charge of God's elect? It is God that justifieth. Who is he that condemneth? It is Christ that died, yea rather, that is risen again, Who is even at the right hand of God, Who also maketh intercession for us. Who shall separate us from the love of Christ? shall tribulation, or distress, or persecution, or famine, or nakedness, or peril, or sword? As it is written, For Thy sake we are killed all the day long; we are accounted as sheep for the slaughter. Nay, in all these things we are more than conquerors through Him that loved us" (Rom. 8:31-37).

2. *Your Personal Prayer Life.* Set up a *place* and a daily *time* for visiting with the Holy Spirit. Keep a list of names of those you pray for. Don't stay in an "asking posture"—learn to praise and thank Him for past answers!

3 *Your Daily Bible Reading Habit.* Establish a *place, time* and *system.* Early morning is usually the best time because you have placed *mind-pictures* of truth into your spirit for the rest of the day. *Mark* your Bible. Take notes. Don't miss a single day.

4. *Godly Friendships.* "He that walketh with wise men shall be wise: but a companion of fools shall be destroyed" (Prov. 13:20). Be

selective. Friends will *add to* or *take away* from your life.

5. *A Teachable Spirit.* Several years ago a young lady approached me about a questionable activity in her life. She accepted my counsel. Today, she is a victorious and successful Christian: "A wise man will *hear*..." (Prov. 1:5). Through instruction and even criticism, we grow in grace and humility.

6. *A Winner's Mentality.* Stop thinking about obstacles and start thinking about your *opportunities.* Talk *positive* words. Think good things about yourself and others. Stop complaining! Project enthusiasm! Avoid negative and depressing conversations.

Dominate your turf!

Be aggressively happy!

Recently, I was in a garden of beautiful flowers. While admiring their beauty, I noticed the gardener pulling up weeds that had grown up around them. As weeds choke out the life of a beautiful flower, there are things that we must remove in order to grow. To guarantee maturity and a winning life, you must eliminate the weeds.

Every Victory Is Worth The Price.

Never forget it.

RECOMMENDED BOOKS AND TAPES ON THIS TOPIC

B-07   Battle Techniques for War Weary Saints (Book/$3)

B-17   Seeds of Wisdom on Overcoming (Book/$3)

B-19   Seeds of Wisdom on Warfare (Book/$3)

TS-85   School of Wisdom, Vol. 1 - The Uncommon Life (Six tapes/$30)

≈ 48 ≈

WEAKNESSES

Every Human Contains Weaknesses.

Here Are 21 Facts You Must Recognize About Your Weaknesses

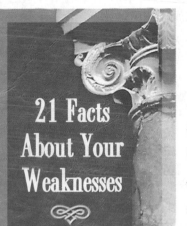

21 Facts About Your Weaknesses

1. *God Has Anticipated Every Weakness.* "For He remembered that they were but flesh; a wind that passeth away, and cometh not again" (Ps. 78:39).

2. *One Weakness Can Destroy You.* Your refusal to recognize it guarantees your destruction.

3. *Recognition Of Your Dominant Weakness Can Prevent A Thousand Nights Of Tears, Failure And Devastation.* Brilliant, articulate and powerful people have permitted a tiny weakness to eat away like a small cancer. *Things that begin small can become huge.* Greed, lust, lying, prayerlessness and even gossip can grow until that weakness becomes a raging inferno.

4. *Ignoring Your Dominant Weakness Schedules Your Tragedy.* Your weakness is like a living person within you, a living organism. It is a force, silent and deadly, that moves your life toward destruction. If ignored, it will wreck every dream, sabotage every worthy relationship and ultimately make you a monument of disgrace on the earth.

"But if we walk in the light, as He is in the light, we have fellowship one with another, and the blood of Jesus Christ His Son cleanseth us from all sin. If we say that we have no sin, we deceive ourselves, and the truth is not in us. If we confess our sins, He is faithful and just to forgive us our sins, and to cleanse us from all unrighteousness. If we say that we have not sinned, we make Him a liar, and His word is not in us. My little children, these things write I unto you, that ye sin not. And if any man sin, we have an advocate with the Father, Jesus Christ the righteous: And He is the propitiation for our sins: and not for ours only, but also for the sins of the whole world" (1 Jn. 1:7-2:2).

5. *Everyone Has A Weakness.* "All have sinned," (Rom. 3:23). Many camouflage their weakness. But, always remember that those around you contain a weakness, too. Failure to discern theirs can destroy you as well.

6. *Your Heavenly Father Is Not Afraid To Deal With Your Personal Weakness.* It matters to Him. He cares. He longs to give you the strength to destroy it. "For He remembered that they were but flesh;" (Ps. 78:39). "He remembereth that we are dust" (Ps. 103:14).

7. *Your Weakness Is The Entry Point For Demonic Spirits.* Satan *entered* Judas (see Jn. 13:26).

"But one of His disciples, Judas Iscariot, who was later to betray Him, objected, 'Why wasn't this perfume sold and the money given to the poor? It was worth a year's wages.' He did not say this because he cared about the poor but because he was a thief; as keeper of the money bag, he used to help himself to what was put into it" (Jn. 12:4-6 NIV).

"Then entered Satan into Judas surnamed Iscariot, being of the number of the twelve. And he went his way, and communed with the chief priests and captains, how he might betray Him unto them. And they were glad, and covenanted to give him money. And he promised, and sought opportunity to betray Him unto them in the absence of the multitude" (Lk. 22:3-6).

8. *God Will Make Every Effort To Reveal Your Weakness To You Before It Destroys You.* "And the Lord said, Simon, Simon, behold, Satan hath desired to have you, that he may sift you as wheat:" (Lk. 22:31).

"For I am not ashamed of the gospel of Christ: for it is the power of God unto salvation to every one that believeth;...Who changed the truth of God into a lie, and worshipped and served the creature more than the Creator, who is blessed for ever. Amen. For this cause God gave them up unto vile affections: for even their women did change the natural use into that which is against nature: And likewise also the men, leaving the natural use of the woman, burned in their lust one toward another; men with men working that which is unseemly, and receiving in themselves that recompence of their error which was meet. And even as they did not like to retain God in their knowledge, God gave them over to a reprobate mind, to do those things which are not convenient; Being filled with all unrighteousness, fornication, wickedness, covetousness, maliciousness; full of envy, murder, debate, deceit, malignity; whisperers, Backbiters, haters of God, despiteful, proud, boasters, inventors of evil things, disobedient to parents, Without understanding, covenant breakers, without natural affection, implacable, unmerciful: Who knowing the judgment of God, that they which commit such things are worthy of death, not only do the same, but have pleasure in them that do them" (Rom. 1:16,25-32).

9. *Somebody Will Be Assigned By Hell To Feed And Strengthen Your Weakness.* Delilah was sent by satan to destroy Samson (see Judges 16:4,5).

"She said unto him, How canst thou say, I love thee, when thine heart is not with me? thou hast mocked me these three times, and hast not told me wherein thy great strength lieth. And it came to pass, when she pressed him daily with her words, and urged him, so that his soul was vexed unto death; That he told her all his heart,...And she made him sleep upon her knees; and she called for a man, and she caused him to shave off the seven locks of his head; and she began to afflict him, and his strength went from him. And she said, The Philistines be upon thee, Samson. And he awoke out of his sleep, and said, I will go out as at other times before, and shake myself. And he wist not that the Lord was departed from him. But the Philistines took him, and put out his eyes, and brought him down to Gaza, and bound him with fetters of brass; and he did grind in the prison house" (Judges 16:15-21).

10. *Your Weakness Will Pursue, Embrace And Seize Any Friendship That Permits It, Feeds On It Or Enjoys It.* The contentious spirit in one person can infiltrate an entire church through those who allow it to exist unrebuked, unchecked or uncorrected.

11. *Your Weakness Has An Agenda, A Plan To Take Over Your Life And Sabotage It.* "When lust hath conceived, it bringeth forth sin: and sin, when it is finished, bringeth forth death" (James 1:15).

12. *Your Weakness Will Bond You With Wrong People.* Remember Samson and Delilah! (see Judges 16:4-20).

13. *Your Weakness Will Separate You From Right People.* Adam withdrew from God in the garden after he sinned. Your weakness makes you uncomfortable in the presence of those who refuse to justify it. "And they heard the voice of the Lord God walking in the garden in the cool of the day: and Adam and his wife hid themselves from the presence of the Lord God amongst the trees of the garden. And the Lord God called unto Adam, and said unto him, Where art thou? And he said, I heard Thy voice in the garden, and I was afraid, because I was naked; and I hid myself" (Gen. 3:8-10).

14. *Your Weakness Can Emerge At Any Time In Your Life, Including Your Closing Years.* "Cast me not off in the time of old age;

forsake me not when my strength faileth" (Ps. 71:9).

I think it was Dr. Lester Summrall who once said, *"What you fail to master in your early years will master you in your later years."* It is true—what you fail to conquer in your early youth will destroy you in the closing years of your life.

15. *Your Weakness Cannot Be Overcome With Humanism, Human Philosophy, Explanations, Or Self-Will Power.* If your weakness could be overcome by yourself, the blood of Jesus is powerless and the Holy Spirit is unnecessary. "Ye shall receive power, after that the Holy Ghost is come upon you:" (Acts 1:8).

"For the good that I would I do not: but the evil which I would not, that I do. Now if I do that I would not, it is no more I that do it, but sin that dwelleth in me. I find then a law, that, when I would do good, evil is present with me. For I delight in the law of God after the inward man: But I see another law in my members, warring against the law of my mind, and bringing me into captivity to the law of sin which is in my members. O wretched man that I am! who shall deliver me from the body of this death? I thank God through Jesus Christ our Lord" (Rom. 7:19-25).

16. *Your Weakness Does Not Necessarily Require A Personal Confession To Everybody, But Recognition Of It In The Presence Of God.* "The Lord is nigh unto them that are of a broken heart; and saveth such as be of a contrite spirit" (Ps. 34:18).

"Blessed is he whose transgressions are forgiven, whose sins are covered. Blessed is the man whose sin the Lord does not count against him and in whose spirit is no deceit. When I kept silent, my bones wasted away through my groaning all day long. For day and night Your hand was heavy upon me; my strength was sapped as in the heat of summer. Selah. Then I acknowledged my sin *to You* and did not cover up my iniquity. I said, 'I will confess my transgressions *to the Lord*'—and You forgave the guilt of my sin" (Ps. 32:1-5 NIV).

"Confess your faults one to another, and pray one for another, that ye may be healed. The effectual fervent prayer of a righteous man availeth much" (James 5:16).

17. *The Easiest Time To Destroy Your Weakness Is At Its Beginning Stages.* Time weaves a steel thread that *becomes* an unbreakable chain. Thousands today hate the very cigarettes they are smoking. But, time has enslaved them.

18. *God Will Permit You To Enjoy Many Victories Even While Your Weakness Is Operating Within You.* He is long-suffering. He is merciful. He provides opportunity after opportunity to reach for deliverance (see Matt. 23:37).

19. *Those You Love Are Waiting In The Shadows For You To Overcome And Triumph Over Your Weakness.* Your victory sends a message to them. When David killed Goliath, the entire nation of Israel changed its season. Your family may be sitting in constant fear that your weakness will destroy you and them. They may be fearful that their own weakness will be exposed. But, when you become victorious, their hearts rejoice and will become strengthened because of it.

20. *Your Weakness Can Only Be Overcome By The Word Of God.* Satan reacts to the Word of God. That is why Jesus used the weapon of the Word during His temptation (read Matt. 4:1-11).

"And when he had fasted forty days and forty nights, he was afterward an hungred. And when the tempter came to Him, he said, If Thou be the Son of God, command that these stones be made bread. But He answered and said, *It is written*, Man shall not live by bread alone, but by every word that proceedeth out of the mouth of God" (Matt. 4:2-4).

21. *Overcoming Your Weakness Will Bring You An Incredible Reward For Eternity.* "As many as I love, I rebuke and chasten: be zealous therefore, and repent. Behold, I stand at the door, and knock: if any man hear My voice, and open the door, I will come in to him, and will sup with him, and he with Me. To him that overcometh will I grant to sit with Me in My throne, even as I also overcame, and am set down with My Father in His throne. He that hath an ear, let him hear what the Spirit saith unto the churches" (Rev. 3:19-22).

What is the most dominant weakness in your life that satan has consistently used to dilute your testimony, break your focus and create depression? You may hide it for a season, but time exposes all things. Address your weakness. *Become an enemy to it.* Trust the Holy Spirit to empower you.

Confession is evidence of trust.

Confession To The Holy Spirit Is Your First Step To Turning Your Worst Weakness Into Your Greatest Weapon.

RECOMMENDED BOOKS AND TAPES ON THIS TOPIC

B-17   Seeds of Wisdom on Overcoming (Book/$3)

TS-5   How to Walk Through Fire (Six tapes/$30)

TS-83   School of Wisdom, Vol. 3 - What I'd Do Differently If I Could Begin My Life Over Again (Six tapes/$30)

The Only Problem
You Will Ever Have
Is A Wisdom Problem.

-MIKE MURDOCK

❧ 49 ❧

WISDOM

12 Rewards Of Wisdom

Wisdom Is The Principal Thing.

"Wisdom is the principal thing; therefore get Wisdom: and with all thy getting get understanding" (Prov. 4:7).

1. *Wisdom Is The Master Key To All The Treasures Of Life.* "And God said to Solomon, Because this was in thine heart, and thou hast not asked riches, wealth, or honour, nor the life of thine enemies, neither yet hast asked long life...Wisdom and knowledge is granted unto thee; and I will give thee riches, and wealth, and honour, such as none of the kings have had that have been before thee" (2 Chr. 1:11,12).

"In Whom are hid all the treasures of Wisdom and knowledge" (Col. 2:3).

2. *The Fear Of God Is The Beginning Of Wisdom.* "The fear of the Lord is the beginning of Wisdom: and the knowledge of the holy is understanding" (Prov. 9:10).

"The fear of the Lord is the beginning of Wisdom:" (Ps. 111:10).

"And unto man He said, Behold, the fear of the Lord, that is Wisdom; and to depart from evil is understanding" (Job 28:28).

3. *Wisdom Is More Powerful Than Weapons Of War.* "Wisdom is better than weapons of war:" (Ecc. 9:18). "And Wisdom and knowledge shall be the stability of thy times, and strength of salvation: the fear of the Lord is His treasure" (Isa. 33:6).

"...But the mouth of the upright shall deliver them" (Prov. 12:6).

4. *Right Relationships Increase Your Wisdom.* "He that walketh with wise men shall be wise: but a companion of fools shall be destroyed" (Prov. 13:20).

"Be not deceived: evil communications corrupt good manners" (1 Cor. 15:33).

"Perverse disputings of men of corrupt minds, and destitute of the truth, supposing that gain is godliness: from such withdraw thyself" (1 Tim. 6:5).

5. *Wisdom Is Better Than Jewels Or Money.* "For Wisdom is better than rubies; and all the things that may be desired are not to be compared to it" (Prov. 8:11).

"Happy is the man that findeth Wisdom, and the man that getteth understanding. For the merchandise of it is better than the merchandise of silver, and the gain thereof than fine gold. She is more precious than rubies; and all the things thou canst desire are not to be compared unto her" (Prov. 3:13-15).

"For the price of Wisdom is above rubies" (Job 28:18).

"How much better is it to get Wisdom than gold! and to get understanding rather to be chosen than silver!" (Prov. 16:16).

6. *The Wise Welcome Correction.* "Reprove not a scorner, lest he hate thee: rebuke a wise man, and he will love thee. Give instruction to a wise man, and he will be yet wiser: teach a just man, and he will increase in learning" (Prov. 9:8,9).

"The ear that heareth the reproof of life abideth among the wise. He that refuseth instruction despiseth his own soul: but he that heareth reproof getteth understanding" (Prov. 15:31,32).

"My son, despise not the chastening of the Lord; neither be weary of His correction. For whom the Lord loveth He correcteth; even as a father the son in whom he delighteth" (Prov. 3:11,12).

7. *Wisdom Creates Currents Of Favor And Recognition Toward You.* "Exalt her, and she shall promote thee: she shall bring thee to honour, when thou dost embrace her" (Prov. 4:8).

"Blessed is the man that heareth Me, watching daily at My gates, waiting at the posts of My doors. For whoso findeth Me findeth life, and shall obtain favour of the Lord" (Prov. 8:34,35).

"My son, forget not My law; So shalt thou find favour and good understanding in the sight of God and man" (Prov. 3:1,4).

8. *Wisdom Guarantees Promotion.* "By Me kings reign, and princes decree justice. By Me princes rule, and nobles, even all the judges of the earth" (Prov. 8:15,16).

"And thou, Ezra, after the Wisdom of thy God, that is in thine hand, set magistrates and judges, which may judge all the people that are beyond the river, all such as know the laws of thy God; and teach ye them that know them not" (Ezra 7:25).

"Exalt her, and she shall promote thee: she shall bring thee to honour, when thou dost embrace her. She shall give to thine head an ornament of grace: a crown of glory shall she deliver to thee" (Prov. 4:8,9).

9. *When You Increase Your Wisdom You Will Increase Your Wealth.*   "Riches and honour are with Me; yea, durable riches and righteousness. That I may cause those that love Me to inherit substance; and I will fill their treasures" (Prov. 8:18,21).

"Length of days is in her right hand; and in her left hand riches and honour" (Prov. 3:16).

"Blessed is the man that feareth the Lord, that delighteth greatly in His commandments. Wealth and riches shall be in his house:" (Ps. 112:1,3).

"The crown of the wise is their riches" (Prov. 14:24).

10. *Wisdom Makes Your Enemies Helpless Against You.* "For I will give you a mouth and Wisdom, which all your adversaries shall not be able to gainsay nor resist" (Lk. 21:15).

"When a man's ways please the Lord, He maketh even his enemies to be at peace with him" (Prov. 16:7).

"For Wisdom is a defence, and money is a defence" (Ecc. 7:12).

"For the Lord giveth Wisdom: To deliver thee from the way of the evil man, To deliver thee from the strange woman" (Prov. 2:6,12,16).

11.   *Wisdom Can Be Imparted By The Laying On Of Hands Of A Man Of God.* "Wherefore I put thee in remembrance that thou stir up the gift of God, which is in thee by the putting on of my hands. That good thing which was committed unto thee keep by the Holy Ghost which dwelleth in us" (2 Tim. 1:6,14).

"And Joshua the son of Nun was full of the Spirit of Wisdom; *for Moses had laid his hands upon him*" (Deut. 34:9).

"Whom they set before the apostles: and when they had prayed, they laid their hands on them. And Stephen, full of faith and power, did great wonders and miracles among the people. And they were not able to resist *the Wisdom* and the Spirit by which he spake" (Acts 6:6,8,10).

12. *The Word Of God Is Your Source Of Wisdom.* "Behold I have taught you statutes and judgments, even as the Lord my God commanded me, that ye should do so in the land whither ye go to possess it. *For this is your Wisdom* and your understanding in the sight of the nations..." (Deut. 4:5,6).

"Thou *through Thy commandments* hast made me wiser than mine enemies: for they are ever with me. I have more understanding than all my teachers: for Thy testimonies are my meditation. I understand more than the ancients, because I keep Thy precepts" (Ps. 119:98-100).

"For the Lord giveth *Wisdom:* out of His mouth cometh knowledge and understanding" (Prov. 2:6).

Sometimes The Smallest Key Unlocks The Greatest Treasures. A simple statement can answer a hundred questions. Words of others bring answers to me. Words have often brought healing to me. Words unlock a flood of blessings.

Here are some Wisdom Keys God has given me in the first half century of my life. These keys could make your life easier than it has ever been before.

It is possible that one of these keys could stop a hundred heartaches in your life and bring a thousand days of joy!

101 Wisdom Keys

1. Never Complain About What You Permit.
2. The Problem That Infuriates You The Most Is The Problem God Has Assigned You To Solve.
3. Those Who Unlock Your Compassion Are Those To Whom You Have Been Assigned.
4. What You Are Willing To Walk Away From Determines What God Will Bring To You.
5. The Secret Of Your Future Is Hidden In Your Daily Routine.
6. Your Rewards In Life Are Determined By The Kind Of Problems You Are Willing To Solve For Others.
7. When You Want Something You Have Never Had, You Have Got To Do Something You Have Never Done.
8. All Men Fall, The Great Ones Get Back Up.
9. Intolerance Of Your Present Creates Your Future.
10. Those Who Cannot Increase You Will Inevitably Decrease You.
11. You Will Never Leave Where You Are Until You Decide Where You Would Rather Be.
12. You Will Only Have Significant Success With Something That Is An Obsession.
13. Give Another What He Cannot Find Anywhere Else And He Will Keep Returning.
14. Your Assignment Is Not Your Decision But Your Discovery.
15. When Fatigue Walks In, Faith Walks Out.
16. If What You Hold In Your Hand Is Not Enough To Be Your Harvest, Make It Your Seed.

17. You Will Never Change What You Believe Until Your Belief System Cannot Produce Something You Want.
18. You Will Only Be Pursued For The Problems You Solve.
19. Champions Are Willing To Do Things They Hate To Create Something They Love.
20. You Will Never Possess What You Are Unwilling To Pursue.
21. The Only Reason Men Fail Is Broken Focus.
22. Stop Looking At Where You Have Been And Start Looking At Where You Can Be.
23. You Will Only Be Remembered For Two Things, The Problems You Solve Or The Ones You Create.
24. Those Who Transfer Knowledge Are Also Capable Of Transferring Error.
25. Your Seed Is The Only Influence You Have Over Your Future.
26. Loneliness Is Not The Absence Of Affection, But The Absence Of Direction.
27. You Cannot Be What You Are Not, But You Can Become What You Are Not.
28. False Accusation Is The Last Stage Before Supernatural Promotion.
29. Your Seed Is A Photograph Of Your Faith.
30. What You Repeatedly Hear, You Will Eventually Believe.
31. God Never Consults Your Past To Determine Your Future.
32. Satan Always Attacks Those Next In Line For A Promotion.
33. Power Is The Ability To Walk Away From Something You Desire To Protect Something Else You Love.
34. Anything That Does Not Change You Is Unnecessary In Your Life.
35. When You Discover Your Assignment, You Will Discover Your Enemy.
36. What You Respect You Will Attract.
37. Men Decide Their Habits; Their Habits Decide Their Future.
38. You Cannot Correct What You Are Unwilling To Confront.
39. The Proof Of Desire Is Pursuit.
40. Crisis Always Occurs At The Curve Of Change.
41. If Time Heals, God Is Unnecessary.
42. Your Seed Is Anything That Benefits Another While Your Harvest Is Anything That Benefits You.
43. Satan's Favorite Entry Point Into Your Life Is Always Through Someone Close To You.

44. What You Hate Reveals What You Were Created To Correct.
45. Losers Focus On What They Are Going Through, While Champions Focus On What They Are Going To.
46. When You Let Go Of What Is In Your Hand, God Will Let Go Of What Is In His Hand.
47. Pain Is Not An Enemy, Merely The Proof That One Exists.
48. When God Wants To Bless You, He Puts A Person In Your Life. When Satan Wants To Destroy You, He Puts A Person In Your Life.
49. Currents Of Favor Begin To Flow The Moment That You Solve A Problem For Someone.
50. The Seed That Leaves Your Hand Never Leaves Your Life, But Enters Your Future Where It Multiplies.
51. Each Act Of Obedience Shortens The Distance To Any Miracle You Are Pursuing.
52. The Quality Of Your Preparation Determines The Quality Of Your Performance.
53. Champions Make Decisions That Create The Future They Desire; Losers Make The Decisions That Create The Present They Desire.
54. Creativity Is The Search For Options. Concentration Is The Elimination Of Them.
55. Seed-Faith Is Sowing What You Have Been Given To Create What You Have Been Promised.
56. The Seasons Of Your Life Will Change Every Time You Decide To Use Your Faith.
57. Someone Is Always Observing You Who Is Capable Of Greatly Blessing You.
58. Giving Is The Proof You Have Conquered Greed.
59. The Season For Research Is Not The Season For Marketing.
60. What You Fail To Master In Your Life Will Eventually Master You.
61. Go Where You Are Celebrated Instead Of Where You Are Tolerated.
62. The Broken Become Masters At Mending.
63. Your Significance Is Not In Your Similarity To Another, But In Your Point Of Difference From Another.
64. You Will Always Pursue The Friendship That Solves Your Most Immediate Problem.
65. The Worth Of Any Relationship Can Be Measured By Its Contributions To Your Priorities.

66. You Will Never Conquer What You Refuse To Hate.
67. Injustice Is Only As Powerful As Your Memory Of It.
68. Every Relationship In Your Life Is A Current Moving You Toward Your Dreams Or Away From Them.
69. You Will Never Be Promoted Until You Have Become Over-Qualified For Your Present Assignment.
70. Money Is Merely A Reward For Solving Problems.
71. Your Reaction To Someone In Trouble Will Determine God's Reaction To You The Next Time You Get In Trouble.
72. What You Can Tolerate, You Cannot Change.
73. The Waves Of Yesterday's Disobedience Will Splash On The Shores Of Today For A Season.
74. You Will Never Outgrow Warfare, You Must Simply Learn To Fight.
75. Nothing Is Ever As Bad As It First Appears.
76. The Evidence Of God's Presence Far Outweighs The Proof Of His Absence.
77. Patience Is The Weapon That Forces Deception To Reveal Itself.
78. One Hour In The Presence Of God Will Reveal Any Flaw In Your Most Carefully Laid Plan.
79. Never Spend More Time On A Critic Than You Would Give To A Friend.
80. Those Who Do Not Respect Your Assignment, Disqualify Themselves For A Relationship.
81. You Will Never Reach The Palace Talking Like A Peasant.
82. Struggle Is The Proof You Have Not Yet Been Conquered.
83. Never Discuss Your Problem With Someone Incapable Of Solving It.
84. Greatness Is Not The Pursuit Of Perfection, But The Pursuit Of Completion.
85. Never Rewrite Your Theology To Accommodate A Tragedy.
86. The Greatest Quality Of Success On Earth Is The Willingness To Become.
87. Warfare Always Surrounds The Birth Of A Miracle.
88. Failure Is Not An Event But An Opinion.
89. You Are Never As Far From A Miracle As It First Appears.
90. What You See Determines What You Desire.
91. The Atmosphere You Permit Determines The Product You Produce.

92. Prosperity Is Simply Having Enough Of God's Provisions To Complete His Instructions For Your Life.
93. God Will Never Advance Your Instructions Beyond Your Last Act Of Disobedience.
94. Anger Is The Birthplace For Solutions.
95. Those Who Do Not Respect Your Time Will Not Respect Your Wisdom Either.
96. Discontent Is The Catalyst For Change.
97. Crisis Is Merely Concentrated Information.
98. Silence Cannot Be Misquoted.
99. Those Who Created The Pain Of Yesterday Do Not Control The Pleasure Of Tomorrow.
100. When You Change Your Focus, You Will Change Your Feelings.
101. What You Make Happen For Others, God Will Make Happen For You.

► Wisdom Is The Law Of God Applied. "Keep therefore and do them: for this is your Wisdom and your understanding in the sight of the nations, which shall hear all these statutes, and say, Surely this great nation is a wise and understanding people" (Deut. 4:6).

► Wisdom Is The Scriptural Solution To Any Problem You Are Facing. "Wisdom is the principal thing: therefore get Wisdom: and with all thy getting get understanding" (Prov. 4:7).

Pursue it...today.

RECOMMENDED BOOKS AND TAPES ON THIS TOPIC

B-01   Wisdom for Winning (Book/$10)
B-40   Wisdom for Crisis Times (Book/$9)
B-45   101 Wisdom Keys (Book/$5)
B-71   Wisdom - God's Golden Key to Success (Book/$7)
TS-01   Wisdom for Winning (Six tapes/$30)
TS-40   Wisdom for Crisis Times (Six tapes/$30)
TS-90   School of Wisdom, Vol. 2 - 101 Wisdom Keys That Have Most Changed My Life (Six tapes/$30)

❧ 50 ❧

WORD OF GOD

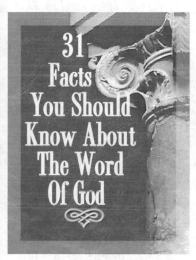

My Greatest Mind Battle Was Over The Word Of God.

When I entered my late teens, intense warfare emerged in my mind. It seemed that contradictions in the Scriptures existed. Then, I began to doubt the validity of the Bible when I saw hypocrisy in believers, inconsistencies in ministers and my own difficulty to live "the Biblical standard."

Two years of erratic and emotional turmoil occurred. I loved the presence of God and *received* from the Word of God. However, it seemed that the logic of my mind and the faith in my heart were in constant opposition.

One day, in honest desperation, I asked the Lord to provide confidence and inner peace that the Bible was truly His infallible Word, not merely the compilation of human thoughts and ideas.

The first three powerful truths that emerged changed me forever. Here are facts you should know about the Word of God:

1. *No Human Would Have Written A Standard As High As The Scriptures Teach.* No husband would have written to treat your wife like Christ treats the church. No wife would have written to obey your husband. No teenager would have written that foolishness is bound in the heart of a child, but the rod of correction will drive it far from him. No rich man would have admitted that he that trusts in his riches shall fall.

2. *The Changes That Occur In Those Who Embrace The Word Of God Are Supernatural.* Drug addiction has been broken. Alcoholics have been set free and delivered. Those who are violent have become meek and submitted.

3. *The Very Presence Of A Bible Often Produces An Aura And Change In The Atmosphere.* I have been on planes and noted an entire group of people become instantly silent when I pulled out my Bible.

No novel of fiction affects men like this. Encyclopedias do not affect men like this. Lay a dictionary on a restaurant table. Nobody looks at you twice. But, lay a Bible on a restaurant table in visible view, and they will stare at you the entire meal. The magnetism of the Word of God is indescribable, irrefutable and unforgettable. Yet, it is the *Unused Weapon*, the *Undiscovered Map*, the *Untapped Well of Wisdom* on earth.

4. *The Word Of God Is The Master Weapon Provided To Us By The Father To Escape Satanic Deception And Snares.* The Word Of God Will Solve Every Problem On Earth.

5. *The Word Of God Is Your Success Handbook.* Encyclopedias impart knowledge of people, places and events. Dictionaries impart knowledge of words. But, nothing is as important as the Wisdom of God for communicating Laws of Success for your life.

6. *The Word Of God Is The Wisdom Of God.* What is Wisdom? Wisdom is simply the Law of God applied accurately to solve your problem. Wisdom is the *scriptural solution* to any problem you are facing. "...for this is your Wisdom and your understanding..." (Deut. 4:6; see also 2 Pet. 3:15, Prov. 2:6).

7. *The Word Of God Is The Love Book Of The Universe.* The Word explains the love of God. "For God so loved the world, that He gave His only begotten Son, that whosoever believeth in Him should not perish, but have everlasting life" (Jn. 3:16; see also 1 Jn. 3:16, 1 Jn. 4:8, Jude 21).

8. *The Word Of God Is A Book On Order.* Order is the accurate arrangement of things (see 1 Chr. 12:33). It shows the rewards of honoring authority, parental authority and even spiritual authority.

9. *The Word Of God Reveals The Laws Of The Universe.* It explains the Law of the Seed, the Law of the Harvest, the Law of Love, the Law of Process, the Law of Eventuality, and even the Law of Truth. "The Law of Truth was in his mouth..." (Mal. 2:6; see also Ezek. 44:4,5).

10. *The Word Of God Is A Relationship Handbook.* It reveals the conduct necessary to maintain worthy relationships. It exposes fools and how to recognize those who do not qualify for relationship in your life.

11. *The Word Of God Is A Worship Encyclopedia.* "God is a Spirit: and they that worship Him must worship Him in Spirit and in truth" (Jn. 4:24). The Word of God explains worship and its value and importance in your daily life. God inhabits the praises of His people. So, the Word of God shows you how to conduct yourself in His presence

and how to attract His presence (see Ps. 100:2).

12. *The Word Of God Teaches Spiritual Protocol.* It reveals the appropriate conduct necessary in...

▶ approaching God effectively;

▶ approaching leaders and those in authority;

▶ your relationship with your parents and children.

13. *The Word Of God Is A Problem-Solving Handbook.* It reveals how to solve financial problems, sin problems, marriage problems and even how to solve church problems when strife arises.

14. *The Word Of God Is A Deliverance Handbook For Captives.* It contains the biography of Uncommon Deliverers of nations, of people and of the sick and afflicted. Gideon, Abraham, David, Paul and Jesus were *Deliverers.* The Word reveals how people become captives...and even explains the Assignment of every minister (see Isa. 61:1).

15. *The Word Of God Creates Conviction That Causes Change.* Without conviction, you could live a lifetime in error and die without even moving toward God.

16. *The Word Of God Is The Book Of Divine Secrets.* "The *secret* of the Lord is with them that fear Him; and *He will shew them His covenant*" (Ps. 25:14; see also Gen. 18:17,18). It reveals the Secrets of Uncommon Achievers, the secrets of financial increase, victorious living and even uncommon promotion (see Prov. 22:29).

Yes, The Word Of God Is The Most Important Book On Earth.

17. *When You Get Into the Word...The Word Will Get Into You.* "Thy word is a lamp unto my feet, and a light unto my path" (Ps. 119:105).

18. *The Greatest Success Habit On The Earth Is The Habit Of Receiving The Word Into Your Spirit Daily.* Hourly...thinking and meditating on the Word. The Word of God solves every problem in your life. The Bible is literally a success handbook.

The essence of the entire 1,189 chapters in the Bible is in Numbers 23:19, "God is not a man, that He should lie; neither the Son of Man that He should repent: hath He said, and shall He not do it? or hath He spoken, and shall He not make it good?"

19. *The Word Of God Solves The Problem Of Depression.* Jesus Himself stated, "These things have I spoken unto you, that My joy might remain in you, and that your joy might be full" (Jn. 15:11).

In Nehemiah, when the people *understood* the law of God, they *rejoiced.* "...to celebrate with great joy, because they now understood the words that had been made known to them" (Neh. 8:12 NIV).

20. *The Word Of God Exposes Any Seeds Of Falsehood That Have Entered Your Life.* "Thy Law is the Truth..." (Ps. 119:142). "Thy Word is truth" (Jn. 17:17).

21. *The Word Of God Births The Fear Of God Within You.* "And it shall be with him, and *he shall read* therein all the days of his life: *that he may learn to fear the Lord* his God, to keep all the words of this Law and these statutes, to do them..." (Deut. 17:19; see also Prov. 1:1-5).

22. *The Word Of God Destroys Pain, Sickness And Disease.* "He sent His Word and healed them" (Ps. 107:20).

"And said, If thou wilt diligently hearken to the Voice of the Lord thy God, and wilt do that which is right in His sight, and wilt give ear to His commandments, and keep all His Statutes, I will put none of these diseases upon thee, which I have brought upon the Egyptians: for I am the Lord that healeth thee" (Ex. 15:26).

"My son, attend to My words;...for they are life...and health to all their flesh" (Prov. 4:20,22).

23. *The Word Of God Births Hope.* "I have *hoped* in Thy Judgments" (Ps. 119:43).

"Remember the Word unto Thy servant, *upon which Thou hast caused me to hope*" (Ps. 119:49).

24. *The Word Of God Produces True Peace.* "O that thou hadst hearkened to My commandments! then had thy peace been as a river and thy righteousness as the waves of the sea" (Isa. 48:18).

"I will hear what God the Lord will speak: for He will speak peace unto His people," (Ps. 85:8).

25. *The Word Of God Solves Emotional Problems.* "Great peace have they which love Thy Law: and *nothing shall offend them*" (Ps. 119:165). Emotional wounds occur through offenses from others. The Word of God is a shield and enables you to see the attacks of others as opportunities rather than obstacles. Joseph saw this. He told his brothers that though they meant to destroy him, he was in the "place of God."

26. *The Word Of God Unleashes Uncommon Faith.* Faith is confidence in God. Faith comes when the words of God enter your heart. "So then faith cometh by hearing, and hearing by the Word of God" (Rom. 10:17).

27. *The Word Of God Enables You To Make Wise Decisions.*

"Keep sound Wisdom...Then shalt thou walk in thy way safely, and *thy* foot shall not stumble" (Prov. 3:21,23).

28. *The Word Of God Solves Financial Problems.* "Wherefore ye shall do My statutes...ye shall dwell in the land in safety. And the land shall yield her fruit, and ye shall eat your fill, and dwell therein in safety" (Lev. 25:18,19).

Prosperity is always the result of obedience to a principle of God. "If ye walk in My statutes, and keep My commandments, and do them; Then I will give you rain in due season, and the land shall yield her increase, and the trees of the field shall yield their fruit" (Lev. 26:3,4).

"Blessed is the man that feareth the Lord, that delighteth greatly in His commandments...Wealth and riches shall be in his house..." (Ps. 112:1,3).

29. *The Word Of God Enables You To Withstand Temptation.* "Thy Word have I hid in mine heart, that I might not sin against Thee" (Ps. 119:11; see also Lk. 4; Matt. 4).

30. *The Word Of God Increases Favor With God And Man.* "Let not mercy and truth forsake thee: bind them about thy neck; write them upon the table thine heart: So shalt thou find favour and good understanding in the sight of God and man" (Prov. 3:3,4).

31. *Your Passion For The Word Of God Is Your Greatest Asset In Your Pursuit For Success.*

The Word Of God Contains The Solution For Every Problem You Are Facing Today.

RECOMMENDED BOOKS AND TAPES ON THIS TOPIC

B-28   The Blessing Bible (Book/$10)
B-29   The Survival Bible (Book/$10)
B-80   The Greatest Success Habit on Earth (Book/$3)
B-117   Seeds of Wisdom on The Word Of God (Book/$5)

What You *Say* Determines What Another *Sees.*

-MIKE MURDOCK

☞ 51 ☜

WORDS

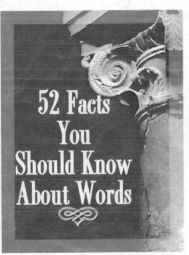

52 Facts
You
Should Know
About Words

Words Are Bridges, Doors, Walls, Or Windows.

Your daily words affect your success. Uncommon achievers place great importance on your ability to speak right words. "By thy words thou shalt be justified, and by thy words thou shalt be condemned" (Matt. 12:37).

1. *Words Can Poison And Destroy A Young Man's Entire Life* (read Prov. 7).

2. *Right Advice Guaranteed Safety And Protection.* "In the multitude of counsellors, there is safety" (Prov. 11:14).

3. *Any Man Who Controls His Mouth Is Literally Protecting His Own Life.* "He that keepeth his mouth keepeth his life" (Prov. 13:3).

4. *Those Who Talk Too Much Will Eventually Be Destroyed.* "...he that openeth wide his lips shall have destruction" (Prov. 13:3).

5. *Right Words Can Turn An Angry Man Into A Friend, And Wrong Words Can Turn A Friend Into An Enemy.* "A soft answer turneth away wrath: but grievous words stir up anger" (Prov. 15:1).

6. *Your Words Reveal Whether You Are Wise Or A Fool.* "The tongue of the wise useth knowledge aright: but the mouth of fools poureth out foolishness" (Prov. 15:2).

7. *Right Words Breathe Life Into Everything Around You.* "A wholesome tongue is a tree of life" (Prov. 15:4).

8. *The Purpose Of Words Is To Educate, Enthuse And Enlarge Those Around You.* "The lips of the wise disperse knowledge" (Prov. 15:7).

9. *Your Personal Happiness Is Influenced By The Words That Come Out Of Your Own Mouth.* "A man hath joy by the answer of his mouth: and a word spoken in due season, how good is it!" (Prov. 15:23).

10. *The Wise Are Cautious With Their Words.* "He that hath knowledge spareth his words" (Prov. 17:27).

11. *Right Words Are As Important As Water On Earth And The Sustaining Of Human Life.* "The words of a man's mouth are as deep waters, and the wellspring of Wisdom as a flowing brook" (Prov. 18:4).

12. *Men Fail Because Of The Words They Speak.* "A fool's mouth is his destruction, and his lips are the snare of his soul" (Prov. 18:7).

13. *Wrong Words Wound Others And Destroy People And Friendships Forever.* "The words of a talebearer are as wounds, and they go down into the innermost parts of the belly" (Prov. 18:8).

14. *Words Determine Which Dreams Live Or Die.* "Death and life are in the power of the tongue: and they that love it shall eat the fruit thereof" (Prov. 18:21).

15. *The Words You Allow Others To Speak Into You Is Deciding The Wisdom You Contain.* "Hear counsel, and receive instruction, that thou mayest be wise in thy latter end" (Prov. 19:20). Solomon knew that words were the difference between his present season and his future season.

16. *Wrong Words Are The Reason Men Fall Into Error.* "Cease, my son, to hear the instruction that causeth to err from the words of knowledge" (Prov. 19:27).

17. *Good Men Study Their Words Before They Speak Them.* "The heart of the righteous studieth to answer" (Prov. 15:28).

18. *The Tongue Is The Major Cause Of All Troubles.* "Whoso keepeth his mouth and his tongue keepeth his soul from troubles" (Prov. 21:23).

19. *Fools Seldom Understand The Power Of Words.* "Speak not in the ears of a fool: for he will despise the Wisdom of thy words" (Prov. 23:9).

20. *Talking To Fools Is A Waste Of Time.* "Speak not in the ears of a fool: for he will despise the Wisdom of thy words" (Prov. 23:9).

21. *Wisdom Is A Result Of The Words You Hear.* "Hear thou, my son, and be wise" (Prov. 23:19).

22. *The Timing Of Your Words Often Decides Your Success Or Failure In A Situation.* "A fool uttereth all his mind: but a wise man keepeth it in till afterwards" (Prov. 29:11).

23. *Influential People Should Use Their Words And Influence To Help The Poor And Needy.* "Open thy mouth, judge righteously, and plead the cause of the poor and needy" (Prov. 31:9).

24. *The Words Of Wise Women Are Consistently Kind.* "She openeth her mouth with Wisdom; and in her tongue is the law of kindness" (Prov. 31:26).

25. *Your Words Can Become The Trap That Destroys You.* "Thou art snared with the words of thy mouth" (Prov. 6:2).

26. *Right Words Feed And Sustain Those Around You.* "The lips of the righteous feed many: but fools die for want of Wisdom" (Prov. 10:21).

27. *Right Words Are As Important As Silver And Gold.* "The tongue of the just is as choice silver" (Prov. 10:20).

28. *Right Words Can Get You Out Of Any Difficulty And Trouble.* "The mouth of the upright shall deliver them" (Prov. 12:6).

29. *Right Words Bring Health And Healing.* "The tongue of the wise is health" (Prov. 12:18).

30. *The Wise Avoid The Presence Of Those Who Consistently Speak Wrong Words.* "Go from the presence of a foolish man, when thou perceivest not in him the lips of knowledge" (Prov. 14:7).

31. *Only The Simple And Fools Believe Everything Others Say.* "The simple believeth every word: but the prudent man looketh well to his going" (Prov. 14:15).

32. *Right Words Give You Access To Powerful And Important People.* "Righteous lips are the delight of kings; and they love him that speaketh right" (Prov. 16:13).

33. *Wisdom Is Necessary In Order To Speak The Right Words.* "The heart of the wise teacheth his mouth, and addeth learning to his lips" (Prov. 16:23).

34. *Pleasant Words Are The Sweetest Sounds On Earth.* "Pleasant words are as an honeycomb, sweet to the soul, and health to the bones" (Prov. 16:24).

35. *The Sweetness Of Right Words Could Help To Cure Any Bitterness Existent In The Human Soul.* "Pleasant words are as an honeycomb, sweet to the soul, and health to the bones" (Prov. 16:24).

36. *The Quality Of Your Words Reveals The Quality Of Your Heart.* "An ungodly man diggeth up evil: and in his lips there is as a burning fire" (Prov. 16:27). You can read the heart of any person by listening to the words they are speaking about others.

37. *Words Will Quickly Expose Envy And Jealousy Or Admiration And Respect.* "An ungodly man diggeth up evil: and in his lips there is as a burning fire" (Prov. 16:27).

38. *The Greatest Friendships On Earth Are Broken Because Of Wrong Words.* "A whisperer separateth chief friends" (Prov. 16:28).

39. *Strife Can Always Be Traced To Someone's Words.* "A froward man soweth strife" (Prov. 16:28).

40. *Evil Is Released Through The Lips.* "Moving his lips he bringeth evil to pass" (Prov. 16:30).

41. *You Should Not Answer Anything Until You Have Heard All The Details.* "He that answereth a matter before he heareth it, it is folly and shame unto him" (Prov. 18:13). Accuracy is only possible when adequate information is available.

42. *Words Influence And Affect The Accumulation Of Your Wealth.* "A man's belly shall be satisfied with the fruit of his mouth; and with the increase of his lips shall he be filled" (Prov. 18:20). This is almost never mentioned in prosperity teaching today. Yet using the wrong words can get you fired or prevent you from getting promoted.

I remember times I was going to give someone a raise until I brought them in and heard the words they were speaking. Complaining, blaming, fault-finding words can stop a boss from promoting you.

43. *Right Words Can Release A Boss To Promote You Or Give You A Raise.* "A man's belly shall be satisfied with the fruit of his mouth; and with the increase of his lips shall he be filled" (Prov. 18:20).

44. *One Conversation With The Wrong Woman Can Destroy Your Life.* "The mouth of strange women is a deep pit: he that is abhorred of the Lord shall fall therein" (Prov. 22:14).

45. *Never Enter Into Battle Without Sufficient Counsel.* "For by wise counsel thou shalt make thy war: and in multitude of counsellors there is safety" (Prov. 24:6).

46. *The Wise Avoid "Self-Praise."* "Let another man praise thee, and not thine own mouth; a stranger, and not thine own lips" (Prov. 27:2).

47. *Lying Words Can Poison The Attitude Of A Boss Toward An Employee.* "If a ruler hearken to lies, all his servants are wicked" (Prov. 29:12).

48. *Right Words Can Energize And Motivate Your Own Life.* "A man hath joy by the answer of his mouth: and a word spoken in due season, how good is it!" (Prov. 15:23).

49. *Words Reveal What Kind Of Heart You Possess.* "For of the abundance of the heart his mouth speaketh" (Lk. 6:45).

50. *Words Can Move Mountains* (see Mk. 11:23).

51. *Words Created The World And Words Create Your World* (read Gen. 1:3-31 and Prov. 18:21).

52. *Words Matter.* Conversation matters. "But I say unto you, That every idle word that men shall speak, they shall give account

thereof in the day of judgment. For by thy words thou shalt be justified, and by thy words thou shalt be condemned" (Matt. 12:36,37).

Be silent about *injustices* to you.

Be silent in discussing the *weaknesses* of others.

Be silent in advertising your own *mistakes*.

Know when *to talk* and when *to listen*.

Know the *power* of your *words* and the *power* of *silence*.

RECOMMENDED BOOKS AND TAPES ON THIS TOPIC

B-24 Seeds of Wisdom on Faith-Talk (Book/$3)

B-91 The Leadership Secrets of Jesus (Book/10)

TS-83 Seeds of Wisdom, Vol. 3 - What I'd Do Differently If I Could Begin My Life Over Again (Six tapes/$30)

Your Rewards In Life
Are Determined
By The Problems
You Are Willing
To Solve For Others.

-MIKE MURDOCK

❧ **52** ❧

WORK

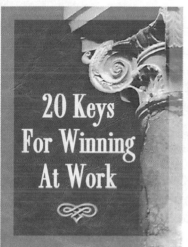

20 Keys For Winning At Work

Happiness Depends On Feeling Good About Yourself.

It is based on your relationships and achievements. When your gifts and abilities are developed and utilized through your life's work, you grow in confidence and strength.

There are *keys* with which you can *unlock* the treasures of accomplishment and confidence in your work.

1. *Accept Work As God's Gift, Not Punishment.* "...to rejoice in his labour; this is the gift of God" (Ecc. 5:19; see Deut. 28:1-14).

2. *Recognize God As Your True Employer.* "With good will doing service, as to the Lord, and not to men:" (Eph. 6:7).

3. *Pursue Work Compatible With Your Abilities And Interests.* "Neglect not the gift that is in thee..." (1 Tim. 4:14). Paul encouraged Timothy (see 2 Tim. 4:5; also see Eph. 4:11). Solomon also recognized skills (see 2 Chr. 2:7-14.)

4. *Learn Everything Possible About Your Job.* "...give attendance to reading," (1 Tim. 4:13). "A wise man will hear, and will increase learning..." (Prov. 1:5).

5. *Do Not Be A Time Thief.* "Redeeming the time, because the days are evil" (Eph. 5:16). "Let him that stole steal no more: but rather let him labour, working with his hands the thing which is good, that he may have to give to him that needeth" (Eph. 4:28).

6. *Keep A Daily Master List Of Priorities And Establish Reasonable Deadlines.* "...this one thing I do..." (Phil. 3:13). "To every thing there is a season..." (Ecc. 3:1).

7. *Ask The Holy Spirit For Wisdom During Decision-Making.* "If any of you lack Wisdom, let him ask of God, that giveth to all men liberally,... and it shall be given him" (James 1:5).

8. *Use Criticism To Your Advantage.* In fact, get on the positive side of it. *Ask* your boss for suggestions and correction: "Poverty and shame shall be to him that refuseth instruction: but he that regardeth reproof shall be honoured" (Prov. 13:18).

9. *Be Honest About Your Mistakes.* "He that covereth his sins shall not prosper: but whoso confesseth and forsaketh them shall have mercy" (Prov. 28:13).

10. *Be Quick To Ask For Help And Information When Needed.* "...a man of knowledge increaseth strength...in multitude of counsellors is safety" (Prov. 24:5,6).

11. *Assist Others In Their Responsibilities When Possible.* "Withhold not good from them to whom it is due, when it is in the power of thine hand to do it" (Prov. 3:27).

12. *Project Jesus In Genuine Love And Enthusiasm.* Resist the "holier-than-thou" attitude: "...the servant of the Lord must not strive; but be gentle unto all men, apt to teach, patient," (2 Tim. 2:24).

13. *Do Not Spread Gossip.* "Speak not evil one of another," (James 4:11). "He that covereth a transgression seeketh love; but he that repeateth a matter separateth very friends" (Prov. 17:9). "The words of a talebearer are as wounds" (Prov. 26:22). "Whoso keepeth his mouth and his tongue keepeth his soul from troubles" (Prov. 21:23).

14. *Project An Attitude Of Forgiveness, Mercy And Favor.* "But the Wisdom that is from above is first pure...full of mercy..." (James 3:17). "Blessed are the merciful: for they shall obtain mercy" (Matt. 5:7).

15. *Do More Than Is Expected Of You.* "And whosoever shall compel thee to go a mile, go with him twain" (Matt. 5:41).

16. *Harness Anger And Control Your Spirit.* "He that hath no rule over his own spirit is like a city that is broken down, and without walls" (Prov. 25:28). "He that is soon angry dealeth foolishly" (Prov. 14:17). "He that is slow to anger is better than the mighty; and he that ruleth his spirit than he that taketh a city" (Prov. 16:32).

17. *Keep Accurate Records.* "Be thou diligent to know the state of thy flocks, and look well to thy herds" (Prov. 27:23).

18. *Avoid Flattery Of Others And Do Not Give Undeserved Praise.* "As he that bindeth a stone in a sling, so he is that giveth honour to a fool...a flattering mouth worketh ruin" (Prov. 26:8,28).

19. *Refuse The Bondage Of Bribery And The Influence Of Intimidation.* "A wicked man taketh a gift out of the bosom to pervert the ways of judgment" (Prov. 17:23). "Be not afraid of their faces: for I am with thee to deliver thee, saith the Lord" (Jer. 1:8).

20. *Make Jesus Your Work Partner.* "Thou wilt keep him in perfect peace, whose mind is stayed on Thee; because he trusteth in Thee" (Isa. 26:3).

The problem you are solving today is scheduling your rewards, promotion and prosperity. Focus on sowing your life with *excellence*...for enduring success.

Your Significance
Is Not In
Your Similarity To Another,
But In
Your Point Of Difference
From Another.

-MIKE MURDOCK

WHY I WROTE THIS BOOK

❖◦⚬◦❖

Wisdom Is The Master Secret Of Life (Read Prov. 4:7).

This Wisdom Commentary includes 52 topics...*for mentoring your* family every Sunday morning of the year.

The Bible refers to Wisdom 479 times. Wisdom is the Master Key to every Miracle and Blessing you will receive during your lifetime. Wisdom enables you to see your circumstances through the eyes of God. It is the door to harmony and happiness in the home. It enables you to see God's purpose in your problems.

▶ *Wisdom Determines Your Wealth.*
▶ *Wisdom Determines Your Favor.*
▶ *Wisdom Determines Your Health.*
▶ *Wisdom Determines Your Success.*
▶ *Wisdom Is The Golden Gate To Greatness.*
▶ *Wisdom Is The Mysterious Magnet For Miracles.*
▶ *Wisdom Is The Unseen Persuader In Negotiations.*
▶ *Wisdom Is The Unstoppable Weapon Of Winning Warriors.*
▶ *Wisdom Is The Secret Of Successful Marriages.*
▶ *Wisdom Is The Only Weapon Needed To Win Any War.*
▶ *Wisdom Is The Bridge From Poverty To Prosperity.*
▶ *Wisdom Is The Golden Key To Recovering From Any Crisis In Life.*

Wisdom Is The Law Of God...Applied Accurately.
Wisdom Is The Scriptural Solution To Any Problem.
I Want To Spend My Life Mending Broken People.
The only cure is..."The Wisdom of God.

That's why I wrote this book.

-MIKE MURDOCK